# The Bushcraft Bible

# The Bushcraft Bible
## The Ultimate Guide to Wilderness Survival

*Edited by* **James Henry**

Skyhorse Publishing

Skyhorse Publishing books may be purchased in bulk at special discounts for sales promotion, corporate gifts, fund-raising, or educational purposes. Special editions can also be created to specifications. For details, contact the Special Sales Department, Skyhorse Publishing, 307 West 36th Street, 11th Floor, New York, NY 10018 or info@skyhorsepublishing.com.

Skyhorse® and Skyhorse Publishing® are registered trademarks of Skyhorse Publishing, Inc.®, a Delaware corporation.

Visit our website at www.skyhorsepublishing.com.

10 9 8 7 6 5 4 3

Library of Congress Cataloging-in-Publication Data is available on file.

Cover design by Rain Saukas

Print ISBN: 978-1-63450-367-9
Ebook ISBN: 978-1-5107-0116-8

Printed in the United States of America

# Contents

# What to Pack

# Personal Equipment

In discussion of the details of equipment, I shall first of all take up in turn each and every item you could possibly need, whether you intend to travel by horse, by canoe, or on your own two feet. Of course you will not carry all of these things on any one trip. What is permissible for horse traveling would be absurd for a walking trip; and some things—such as a waterproof duffle bag—which you would need on a foot tramp, would be useless where you have kyacks and a tarpaulin to protect your belongings. Therefore I shall first enumerate all articles of all three classes of equipment, and then in a final summary segregate them into their proper categories.

## Concerning Hats

Long experience by men practically concerned seems to prove that a rather heavy felt hat is the best for all-around use. Even in hot sun it seems to be the most satisfactory, as, with proper ventilation, it turns the sun's rays better even than light straw. Witness the Arizona cowboy on his desert ranges. You will want a good hat, the best in material that money can buy. A cheap article sags in the brim, tears in the crown, and wets through like blotting paper the first time it rains. I have found the Stetson, of the five- to seven-dollar grade, the most satisfactory. If it is intended for woods travel where you are likely to encounter much brush, get it of medium brim. In those circumstances I find it handy to buy a size smaller than usual, and then to rip out the sweat band. The friction of the felt directly against the forehead and the hair will hold it on in spite of pretty sharp tugs by thorns and wind. In the mountains or on the plains, you can indulge in a wider and

stiffer brim. Two buckskin thongs
sewn on either side and to tie
under the "back hair" will hold it
on, even against a head wind. A
test will show you how this can
be. A leather band and buckle—or
miniature cinch and latigos—
gives added security. I generally
cut ample holes for ventilation.
In case of too many mosquitoes
I stuff my handkerchief in the
crown.

## Kerchiefs

About your neck you will want
to wear a silk kerchief. This is
to keep out dust, and to prevent
your neck from becoming
reddened and chapped. It, too,
should be of the best quality. The
poorer grades go to pieces soon,
and their colors are not fast. Get
it big enough. At night you will
make a cap of it to sleep in; and
if ever you happen to be caught
without extra clothes where it is
very cold, you will find that the
kerchief tied around your middle,
and next to the skin, will help
surprisingly.

## Coats

A coat is useless absolutely. A
sweater is better as far as warmth
goes; a waistcoat beats it for
pockets. You will not wear it
during the day; it wads up too
much to be of much use at night.
Even your trousers rolled up make
a better temporary pillow. Leave it
home; and you will neither regret
it nor miss it.

## Sweaters

For warmth, as I have said, you
will have your sweater. In this
case, too, I would impress the
desirability of purchasing the best
you can buy. And let it be a heavy
one, of gray or a neutral brown.

## Buckskin Shirts

But to my mind the best extra
garment is a good ample buckskin
shirt. It is less bulky than the
sweater, of less weight, and
much warmer, especially in a
wind, while for getting through
brush noiselessly it cannot be

improved upon. I do not know where you can buy one; but in any case get it ample in length and breadth, and without the fringe. The latter used to possess some significance beside ornamentation, for in case of need the wilderness hunter could cut from it thongs and strings as he needed them. Nowadays a man in a fringed buckskin shirt is generally a fake built to deceive tourists. On the other hand a plain woodsmanlike garment, worn loose and belted at the waist, looks always at once comfortable and appropriate. Be sure that the skins of which it is made are smoke tanned. The smoke tanned article will dry soft, while the ordinary skin is hardening to almost the consistency of rawhide. Good buckskins are difficult to get hold of—and it will take five to make you a good shirt—but for this use they last practically forever.

## Overshirts

Of course such a garment is distinctly an extra or outside garment. You would find it too warm for ordinary wear. The outer shirt of your daily habit is best made of rather a light weight of gray flannel. Most new campers indulge in a very thick navy blue shirt, mainly, I believe, because it contrasts picturesquely with a bandana around the neck. Such a shirt almost always crocks, is sure to fade, shows dirt, and is altogether too hot. A lighter weight furnishes all the protection you need to your underclothes and turns sun quite as well. Gray is a neutral color, and seems less often than any other to shame you to the wash soap. A great many wear an ordinary cotton work shirt, relying for warmth on the underclothes. There is no great objection to this, except that flannel is better should you get rained on.

## Underclothes

The true point of comfort is, however, your underwear. It should be of wool. I know that a great deal has been printed against it, and a great many hygienic principles are invoked to prove that linen, cotton, or silk are better. But experience with all of them merely leads back to the starting point. If one were certain never to sweat freely, and never to get wet, the theories might hold. But once you let linen or cotton or silk undergarments get thoroughly moistened, the first chilly little wind is your undoing. You will shiver and shake before the hottest fire, and nothing short of a complete change and a rub-down will do you any good.

Now, of course in the wilderness you expect to undergo extremes of temperature, and occasionally to pass unprotected through a rainstorm or a stream. Then you will discover that wool dries quickly, that even when damp it soon warms comfortably to the body. I have waded all day in early spring freshet water with no positive discomfort except for the cold ring around my legs which marked the surface of the water.

## Wear Woolen Underclothes Always

And if you are wise, you will wear full long-sleeved woolen undershirts even on a summer trip. If it is a real trip, you are going to sweat anyway, no matter how you strip down to the work. And sooner or later the sun will dip behind a cloud or a hill; or a cool breezelet will wander to you resting on the slope; or the inevitable chill of evening will come out from the thickets to greet you—and you will be very glad of your woolen underwear.

A great many people go to the opposite extreme. They seem to think that because they are to live in the open air, they will probably freeze. As a consequence of this delusion, they purchase underclothes an inch thick. This is foolishness, not only because such a weight is unnecessary and unhealthful, but also—even if it were merely a question of warmth—because one suit of thick garments is not nearly so warm as two suits of thin.

Whenever the weather turns very cold on you, just put on the extra undershirt over the one you are wearing, and you will be surprised to discover how much warmth two gauze tissues—with the minute air space between them—can give. Therefore, though you must not fail to get full-length woolen underclothes, you need not buy them of great weight. The thinnest Jaeger is about right.

## The Laundry Problem

Two undershirts and three pairs of drawers are all you ever will need on the most elaborate trip. You perhaps cannot believe that until you have gotten away from the idea that laundry must be done all at once. In the woods it is much handier to do it a little at a time. Soap your outershirt at night; rinse it in the morning; dry it on top of your pack during the first two hours. In the meantime wear your sweater; or, if it is warm enough, appear in your undershirt. When you change your underclothes—which should

be one garment at a time—do the same thing. Thus always you will be possessed of a clean outfit without the necessity of carrying a lot of extras.

## Trousers

The matter of trousers is an important one, for unless you are possessed of abundant means of transportation, those you have on will be all you will take. I used to include an extra pair, but got over it. Even when trout fishing I found that by the time I had finished standing around the fire cooking, or yarning, I might have to change the underdrawers, but the trousers themselves had dried well enough. And patches are not too difficult a maneuver.

## Moleskin and Khaki

The almost universal wear in the West is the copper-riveted blue canvas overall. They are very good in that they wear well. Otherwise they are stiff and noisy in the brush. Kersey is excellent where much wading is to be done or much rainy weather encountered—in fact it is the favorite "driving" trousers with rivermen—but like all woven woolen materials it "picks out" in bad brush. Corduroy I would not have as a gift. It is very noisy, and each raindrop that hits it spreads at once to the size of a silver dollar. I verily believe an able pair of corduroys can, when feeling good, soak up ten pounds of water. Good moleskin dries well, and until it begins to give out is soft and tough. But it is like the one-hoss shay: when it starts to go, it does the job up completely in a few days. The difficulty is to guess when that moment is due to arrive. Anything but the best quality is worthless. Khaki has lately come into popularity. It wears remarkably well, dries quickly, and is excellent in all but one particular: it shows every spot of dirt. A pair of khakis three days along on the trail look as though they had been out a year. The new green khaki is a little better. Buckskin is all right until

you get it wet, then you have—temporarily—enough material to make three pairs and one for the boy.

The best trousers I know of is a combination of the latter two materials. I bought a pair of the ordinary khaki army riding breeches, and had a tailor cover them completely—fore, aft, and sideways—with some good smoke-tanned buckskin I happened to have. It took a skin and a half. These I have worn now for three seasons, in all kinds of country, in all kinds of weather, and they are today as good as when I constructed them. In still hunting they are noiseless; horseback they do not chafe; in cold weather they are warm, and in the hot sun they turn. The khaki holds the stretch of buckskin when wet—as they have been for a week at a time. Up to date the smoke tan has dried them soft. Altogether they are the most satisfactory garment of this kind I have experimented with.

There remains the equally important subject of footwear.

## Socks

Get heavy woolen lumberman's socks, and wear them in and out of season. They are not one whit hotter on the feet than the thinnest you can buy, for the impervious leather of the shoe is really what keeps in the animal heat—the sock has little to do with it. You will find the soft thick wool an excellent cushion for a long tramp; and with proper care to avoid wrinkles, you will never become tender-footed nor chafed. At first it seems ridiculous to draw on such thick and apparently hot socks when the sun peeping over the rim of the desert promises you a scorching day. Nothing but actual experience will convince you; but I am sure that if you will give the matter a fair test, you will come inevitably to my conclusion.

## The Ideal Footwear

If a man were limited to a choice between moccasins and shoes, it would be very difficult to decide wisely which he should take.

Each has its manifest advantages over the other, and neither can entirely take the place of the other.

The ideal footwear should give security, be easy on the feet, wear well, and give absolute protection. These qualities I have named approximately in the order of their importance.

Security of footing depends on the nature of the ground over which you are traveling. Hobnails only will hold you on a slope covered with pine needles, for instance; both leather and buckskin there become as slippery as glass. In case of smooth rocks, however, your hobnails are positively dangerous, as they slide from under you with all the vicious force and suddenness of unaccustomed skates. Clean leather is much better, and buckskin is the best of all. Often in hunting deer along the ledges of the deep box canyons I, with my moccasins, have walked confidently up slants of smooth rock on which my hobnailed companion was actually forced to his hands and knees. Undoubtedly also a man carrying a pack through mixed forest is surer of his footing and less liable to turned ankles in moccasins than in boots. My experience has been that with the single exception mentioned, I have felt securer in the buckskin.

As for ease to the feet, that is of course a matter of opinion. Undoubtedly at first the moccasin novice is literally a tenderfoot. But after astonishingly few days of practice a man no longer notices the lack of a sole. I have always worn moccasins more or less in the woods, and now can walk over pebbles or knife-edge stones without the slightest discomfort. In fact the absence of rolling and slipping in that sort of shifting footing turns the scale quite the other way.

The matter of wear is not so important. It would seem at first glance that the one thin layer of buckskin would wear out before the several thick layers of a shoe's sole. Such is not always the case. A good deal depends on the sort of ground you cover. If you wet moccasins, and then walk down hill with them over granite shale, you can get holes to order. Boots wear rapidly in the same circumstances. On the other hand I have on at this moment a pair of mooseskin moccasins purchased three years ago at a Hudson's Bay Company's post, which have seen two summers' off and on service in the Sierras. Barring extraordinary conditions, I should say that each in its proper use, a pair of boots and a pair of moccasins would last about the same length of time. The moccasin, however, has this advantage: it can be readily patched, and even a half dozen extra pairs take up little room in the pack.

## Waterproofing

Absolute protection must remain a tentative term. No footwear I have succeeded in discovering gives absolute protection. Where there is much work to be done in the water, I think boots are the warmest and most comfortable, though no leather is perfectly waterproof. Moccasins then become slimpsy, stretched, and loathsome. So likewise moccasins are not much good in damp snow, though in dry snow they are unexcelled.

In my own practice I wear boots on a horseback trip, and carry moccasins in my pack for general walking. In the woods I pack four pair of moccasins. In a canoe, moccasins of course.

## About Boots

Do not make the common mistake of getting tremendously heavy boots. They are clumsy to place, burdensome to carry, and stiff and unpliable to the chafing point. The average amateur woodsman seems to think a pair of elephantine brogans is the proper thing—a sort of badge of identification in the craft. If he adds big hobnails to make tracks with, he is sure of himself. A medium weight boot, of medium height, with medium heavy soles armed only with the small Hungarian hobnail is about the proper thing. Get them 8 inches high, supplied with very large eyelets part way, then the heaviest hooks, finishing with two more eyelets at the top. The latter will prevent the belt-lacing you will use as shoestrings from coming unhooked.

You will see many advertisements of waterproof leather boots. No such thing is made. Some with good care will exclude water for a while, if you stay in it but a few minutes at a time, but sooner or later as the fibers become loosened the water will penetrate. In the case of the show window exhibit of the shoe standing in a pan of water, pressure of the foot and ground against the leather is lacking, which of course makes all the difference. This porosity is really desirable. A shoe wholly waterproof would retain and condense the perspiration to such an extent that the feet would be as wet at the end of the day. Such is the case with rubber boots. All you want is a leather that will permit you to splash through a marsh, a pool, or a little stream, and will not seek to emulate blotting paper in its haste to become saturated.

## The Most Durable Boots

Of the boots I have tried, and that means a good many, I think the Putman boot and the river driver's boot, made by A. A. Cutter of Eau Claire, Wis., are made of the most durable material. The Putman boot is the more expensive; and in the case of the three pairs I know of personally, the sewing has been defective. The material, however, wears remarkably well, and remains waterproof somewhat longer than any of the others. On the other hand the Cutter shoe is built primarily for rivermen and timber cruisers of the northern forests, and is at once cheap and durable. It has a brace of sole leather about the heel which keeps the latter upright and prevents it running over. It is an easier shoe on the foot than any of the others,

but does not remain waterproof quite so long as the Putman. Although, undoubtedly, many other makes are as good, you will not go astray in purchasing one of these two.

## Rubber

No shoe is waterproof for even a short time in wet snow. Rubber is then the only solution, usually in the shape of a shoe rubber with canvas tops. Truth to tell, melting snow is generally so very cold that you will be little troubled with interior condensation. Likewise many years' experience in grouse hunting through the thickets and swamps of Michigan drove me finally to light hip rubber boots. The time was always the autumn; the place was always more or less muddy and wet—in spots of course—and there was always the greater or lesser possibility of snow. My native town was a great grouse shooting center, and all hunters, old and young, came to the same conclusion.

But wet snow, such hunting, and of course the duck marsh seem to me the only excuses for rubber. Trout fishing is more comfortable in woolen than in waders. The latter are clumsy and hot. I have known of two instances of drowning because the victims were weighted down by them. And I should much prefer getting wet from without than from within.

You will have your choice of three kinds of moccasin—the oil-tanned shoe pac, the deerhide, and the moosehide.

## Shoe Pacs

The shoe pac is about as waterproof as the average waterproof shoe, and would be the best for all purposes were it not for the fact that its very imperviosity renders it too hot. In addition continuous wear affects the oil in the tanning process to produce rather an evil odor. The shoe pacs are very useful, however, and where I carry but two pairs of moccasins, one is of the oil tan. Shoe pacs can be purchased from any sporting goods dealer.

## Moccasins

The deerhide moccasin, in spite of its thinner texture, wears about as well as the moosehide, is less bulky to carry, but stretches more when wet and is not as easy on the feet. I use either sort as I happen to get hold of them. Genuine buckskin or moose is rather scarce. Commercial moccasins with the porcupine quills and "Souvenir of Mackinaw" on them are made by machinery out of sheepskin. They are absolutely useless, and last about long enough to get out of sight of the shop. A great majority of the moccasins sold as sportsman's supplies are likewise very bogus. My own wear I have always purchased from Hudson's Bay posts. Undoubtedly many reliable firms carry them; but I happen to know by personal experience that the Putman Boot Company of Minneapolis has the real thing.

## Waistcoats

Proceeding to more outer garments, a waistcoat is a handy affair. In warm weather you leave it open and hardly know you have it on; in cold weather you button it up, and it affords excellent protection. Likewise it possesses the advantage of numerous pockets. These you will have your womenfolk extend and deepen for you, until your compass, notebook, pipe, matches, and so forth fit nicely in them. As it is to be used as an outside garment, have the back lined. If you have shot enough deer to get around to waistcoats, nothing could be better by way of material than the ever-useful buckskin.

## Waterproofs

I am no believer in waterproof garments. Once I owned a Pantasote outer coat which I used to assume whenever it rained. Ordinarily when it is warm enough to rain, it is warm enough to cause you to perspire under the exertion of walking in a pantasote coat. This I discovered. Shortly I would get wet, and would be quite unable to decide whether the rain had soaked through from the outside or I had soaked through from the inside. After that I gave the coat away to a man who had not tried it, and was happy. If I must walk in the rain I prefer to put on a sweater— the rough wool of which will turn water for some time and the texture of which allows ventilation. Then the chances are that even if I soak through I do not get a reactionary chill from becoming overheated.

## Ponchos

In camp you will know enough to go in when it rains. When you have to sally forth you will thrust your head through the hole in the middle of your rubber blanket. When thus equipped the rubber blanket is known as a poncho, and is most useful because it can be used for two purposes.

## Slickers

Horseback in a rainy country is, however, a different matter. There, transportation is not on your back, but another's; and sitting a horse is not violent exercise. Some people like a poncho. I have always found its lower edge cold, clumsy, and wet, much inclined to blow about, and apt to soak your knees and the seat of your saddle. The cowboy slicker cannot be improved upon. It is different in build from the ordinary oilskin. Call for a "pommel slicker," and be sure it is apparently about two sizes too large for you. Thus you will cover your legs. Should you be forced to walk, a belt around your waist will always enable you to tuck it up like a comic opera king. It is sure ludicrous to view, but that does not matter.

## Chaparejos

Apropos of protecting your legs, there remains still the question of chaparejos or chaps. Unless you are likely to be called on to ride at some speed through thorny brush, or unless you expect to ride very wet indeed, they are a useless affectation. The cowboy needs them because he does a great deal of riding of the two kinds just mentioned. Probably you will not. I have had perhaps a dozen occasions to put them on. If you must have them, get either oil-tanned or hair chaps. Either of these sheds water like a tin roof. The hair chaps will not last long in a thorny country.

## Gloves

You will need furthermore a pair of gloves of some sort, not for constant wear, nor merely for warmth, but to protect you in the handling of pack ropes, lead ropes, and cooking utensils. A good buckskin gauntlet is serviceable, as the cuffs keep the cold breezes from playing along your forearm to your shoulder, and exclude the dust. When you can get hold of the army gauntlet, as you sometimes can in the military stores, buy them. Lacking genuine buckskin, the lighter grades of "asbestos" yellow tan are the best. They cost about two dollars. To my notion a better rig is an ordinary pair of short gloves, supplemented by the close-fitting leather cuffs of a cowboy's outfit. The latter hold the wrist snugly, exclude absolutely chill and dirt, and in addition save wear and soiling of the shirt cuff. They do not pick up twigs, leaves, and rubbish funnel wise, as a gauntlet cuff is apt to do.

That, I think, completes your wearing apparel. Let us now take up the contents of your pockets, and your other personal belongings.

| SUMMARY | |
|---|---|
| **Minimum for comfort** | **Maximum** |
| Felt hat | Felt hat |
| Silk kerchief | Silk kerchief |
| Waistcoat | Waistcoat |
| Buckskin shirt or sweater | Buckskin shirt and sweater |
| Gray flannel shirt | Gray flannel shirt |
| 2 undershirts and drawers | 2 undershirts, 3 drawers (includes one suit you wear) |
| Trousers—buckskin over khaki | Trousers |
| 3 pairs heavy socks | 4 pairs socks |
| 3 pairs moccasins | 1 pair boots |
| or | Moccasins |
| 1 pair boots | Slicker |
| 1 pair moccasins | Gloves and leather cuffs |
| Gloves and leather cuffs | |

## Matches

Matches, knife, and a compass are the three indispensables. By way of ignition you will take a decided step backward from present-day civilization in that you will pin your faith to the old sulphur "eight-day" matches of your fathers. This for several reasons. In the first place they come in blocks, unseparated, which are easily carried without danger of rubbing one against the other. In the second place, they take up about a third of the room the same number of wooden matches would require. In the third place, they are easier to light in a wind, for they do not flash up and out, but persist. And finally, if wet, they can be spread out and dried in the sun, which is the most important of all. So buy a nickel's worth of sulphur matches.

## Match Safes

The main supply you will pack in some sort of waterproof receptacle. I read a story recently in which a man was recognized as a true woodsman because he carried his matches in a bottle. He must have had good luck. The cardinal principle of packing is never to carry any glassware. Ninety-nine days it may pass safely, but the hundredth will smash it as sure as some people's

shooting. And then you have jam, or chili powder, or syrup, or whiskey, all over the place—or else no matches. Any good screw top can—or better still, two telescoping tubes—is infinitely better.

The day's supply you will put in your pocket. A portion can go in a small waterproof match safe; but as it is a tremendous nuisance to be opening such a contrivance every time you want a smoke, I should advise you to stick a block in your waistcoat pocket, where you can get at them easily. If you are going a-wading, and pockets are precarious, you will find your hat band handy.

The waterproof pocket safe is numerous on the market. A ten-gauge brass shell will just chamber a twelve-gauge. Put your matches in the twelve-gauge, and telescope the ten over it. Abercrombie & Fitch, of New York, makes a screw-top safe of rubber, which has the great advantage of floating if dropped, but it is too bulky and the edges are too sharp. The Marble safe, made by the Marble

Axe Company, is ingenious and certainly waterproof; but if it gets bent in the slightest degree, it jams, and you can no longer screw it shut. Therefore I consider it useless for this reason. A very convenient and cheap emergency contrivance is the flint and steel pocket cigar lighter to be had at most cigar stores. With it as a reserve you are sure of a fire no matter how wet the catastrophe.

## Knives

Your knife should be a medium size two-bladed affair, of the best quality. Do not get it too large and heavy. You can skin and quarter a deer with an ordinary jackknife. Avoid the "kit" knives. They are mighty handy contraptions. I owned one with two blades, a thoroughly practicable can opener, an awl or punch, a combined reamer, nail pull and screwdriver, and a corkscrew. It was a delight for as long as it lasted. The trouble with such knives is that they are too round, so that sooner or later they are absolutely certain to roll out of your pocket and be lost. It makes no difference how your pockets are constructed, nor how careful you are, that result is inevitable. Then you will feel badly—and go back to your old flat two-bladed implement that you simply cannot lose.

## Sheath Knives

A butcher knife of good make is one of the best and cheapest of sheath knives. The common mistake among amateur hunters is that of buying too heavy a knife with too thick a blade. Unless you expect to indulge in hand-to-hand conflicts, or cut brush, such a weapon is excessive. I myself have carried for the last seven years a rather thin and broad blade made by the Marble Axe Company on the butcher knife pattern. This company advertises in its catalogue a knife as used by myself. They are mistaken. The knife I mean is a longer-bladed affair, called a "kitchen or camp knife." It is a most excellent piece of steel, holds an edge well, and is useful alike as a camp and hunting knife. The fact that I have killed some thirty-four wild boars with it shows that it is not to be despised as a weapon.

## Compasses

Your compass should be large enough for accuracy, with a jewel movement. Such an instrument can be purchased for one to two dollars. It is sheer extravagance to go in for anything more expensive unless you are a yachtsman or intend to run survey lines.

## Concerning Guns

I have hesitated much before deciding to say anything whatever of the sporting outfit. The subject has been so thoroughly discussed by men so much more competent than myself; there are so many theories with which I confess myself not at all conversant, and my own experience has been so limited in the variety of weapons

and tackle, that I hardly felt qualified to speak. However, I reflected that this whole series of articles does not pretend to be in any way authoritative, nor does it claim to present the only or the best equipment in any branch of wilderness travel, but only to set forth the results of my own twenty years more or less of pretty steady outdoor life. So likewise it may interest the reader to hear about the contents of my own gunrack, even though he himself would have chosen much more wisely.

## My Rifle

My rifle is a .30-.40 box magazine Winchester, with Lyman sights. This I have heard is not a particularly accurate gun. Also it is stated that after a few hundred shots it becomes still more inaccurate because of a residue which only special process can remove from the rifling. This may be. I only know that my own rifle today, after ten years' service, will still shoot as closely as I know how to hold it, although it has sixty-four notches on its stock and has probably been fired first and last—at big game, small game, and targets—upward of a thousand times. I use the Lyman aperture sight except in the dusk of evening, when a folding bar sight takes its place. At the time I bought this rifle the .33 and .35 had not been issued, and I thought, and still think, the .30-.30 too light for sure work on any animal larger than a deer. I have never used the .35, but like the .33 very much. The old low-power guns I used to shoot a great deal, but have not for some years.

## Pistol a Handy Weapon

The handiest weapon for a woods trip where small game is plentiful is a single-shot pistol. Mine is a Smith & Wesson, blued, 6-inch barrel, shooting the .22 caliber long-rifle cartridge. An 8-inch barrel is commonly offered by the sporting dealers, but the 6-inch is practically as accurate, and less cumbersome to carry. The ammunition is compact and light.

With this little pistol I have killed in plenty ducks, geese, grouse, and squirrels, so that at times I have gone two or three months without the necessity of shooting a larger weapon. Such a pistol takes practice, however, and a certain knack. You must keep at it until you can get four out of five bullets in a 3-inch bull's-eye at twenty yards before you can even hope to accomplish much in the field.

## Revolver Experiences

My six-shooter is a .45 Colt, New Service model. It is fitted with Lyman revolver sights. Originally it was a self-cocker, but I took out the dog and converted it to single action. The trigger pull on the double action is too heavy for me, and when I came to file it down, I found the double action caused a double jerk disconcerting to steady holding. Now it goes off smoothly and almost at a touch—the only conditions under which I can do much with a revolver. It is a very reliable weapon indeed, balances better than the single-action model, and possesses great smashing power. I have killed three deer in their tracks with it, and much smaller game. This summer, however, I had the opportunity of shooting a good deal with two I like better. One is the Officer's Model Colt, chambered to shoot interchangeably either the .38 Colt long or short, or the .38 Smith & Wesson special. In finish it is a beautiful weapon, its grip fits the hand, its action is smooth, and it is wonderfully accurate. The other is the special target .44 Russian. The automatics I do not care for simply because I never learned to shoot with the heavier trigger pull necessary to their action.

## Shotguns

I have two shotguns. One I have shot twenty-one years. It has killed thousands of game birds, is a hard hitter, throws an excellent pattern, and is as strong and good as the day it was bought. I use it today for every sort of shooting except ducks, though often I have had it in the blinds lacking the heavier weapon. It is doubtful if there are in use to-day many guns with longer service, counting not so much the mere years of its performance, as the actual amount of hunting it has done. The time of its construction was before the days of the hammerless. It was made by W. & C. Scott & Sons, is 16 gauge, and cost $125. My other is a heavily choked Parker twelve. It I use for wild fowl, and occasionally at the trap.

The main point with guns, no matter what the kind, is to keep them in good shape. After shooting, clean them, no matter how tired you may be. It is no great labor. In the field a string cleaner will do the business, but at once when you get to permanent camp use a rod and elbow grease. In a damp country, oil them afresh every day, so they will give you good service. The barrels of my 16 are as bright as new. The cleaning rods you can put in your leather fishing-rod case.

## Duffle Bags

Now all these things of which
we have made mention must be
transported. The duffle bag is
the usual receptacle for them. It
should be of some heavy material,
waterproofed, and should not
be too large. A good one is of
pantasote, with double top to tie.
One of these went the length of a
rapids, and was fished out without
having shipped a drop. On a
horseback trip, however, such a
contrivance is at once unnecessary
and difficult to pack. It is too long
and stiff to go easily in the kyacks,
and does not agree well with the
bedding on top.

This is really no great
matter. The heavy kyacks, and
the tarpaulin over everything,
furnish all needed protection
against wet and abrasion. A bag
of some thinner and more pliable
material is quite as good. Brown
denim, unbleached cotton, or
even a clean flour sack are entirely
adequate. You will find it handy
to have them built with puckering
strings. The strings so employed

will not get lost, and can be used
as a loop to hang the outfit from a
branch when in camp.

## Toilet Articles

A similar but smaller bag is useful
to be reserved entirely as a toilet
bag. Tar soap in a square—not
round—celluloid case is the
most cleansing. A heavy rubber
band will hold the square case
together. The tooth brush should
also have its case. Tooth wash
comes in glass, which is taboo;
tooth powder is sure sooner or
later to leak out. I like best any
tooth soap which is sold in handy
flat tin boxes, and cannot spill. If
you are sensible you will not be
tenderfoot enough to go in for
the discomfort of a new beard.
Razors can be kept from rusting
by wrapping them in a square of
surgeon's oiled silk. Have your
towel of brown crash—never of
any white material. The latter is so
closely woven that dirt gets into
the very fiber of it, and cannot be
washed out. Crash, however, is
of looser texture, softens quickly,

and does not show every speck of dust. If you have the room for it, a rough towel, while not absolutely necessary, is nevertheless a great luxury.

## Medicines

By way of medicines, stick to the tablet form. A strong compact medicine case is not expensive. It should contain antiseptics, permanganate for snake bites, a laxative, cholera remedy, quinine, and morphine. In addition antiseptic bandages and rubber or surgeon's plaster should be wrapped in oiled silk and included in the duffle outfit.

The fly problem is serious in some sections of the country and at some times of year. A head net is sometimes useful about camp or riding in the open—never when walking in the woods. The ordinary mosquito bar is too fragile. One of bobbinet that fits ingeniously is very effective. This and gloves will hold you immune—but you cannot smoke, nor spit on the bait.

## Fly Dopes

The two best fly dopes of the many I have tried are a commercial mixture called "lollacapop," and Nessmuk's formula. The lollacapop comes in tin boxes, and so is handy to carry, but does not wear quite as well as the other. Nessmuk's dope is:

| Oil pine tar | 3 parts |
| Castor oil | 2 parts |
| Oil pennyroyal | 1 part |

## Fly Dopes

It is most effective. A dab on each cheek and one behind each ear will repel the fly of average voracity, while a full coating will save you in the worst circumstances. A single dose will last until next wash time. It is best carried in the tiny "one drink" whiskey flasks, holding, I suppose, 2 or 3 ounces. One flask full will last you all summer. At first the pine tar smell will bother you, but in a short time you will get to like it. It will call up to your memory the reaches of trout streams, and the tall still aisles of the forests.

| SUMMARY | |
|---|---|
| **Minimum for comfort** | **Maximum** |
| Matches and safe | Matches and safe |
| Pocket knife (2 blade) | Pocket knife |
| Sheath knife | Sheath knife |
| Compass | Compass |
| 1 bandana | 2 bandanas |
| Sporting outfit | Sporting outfit |
| Duffle bag | Duffle bag |
| Soap and case | Soap and case |
| Crash towel | Crash towel |
| Tooth brush | Bath towel |
| Tooth soap | Tooth brush |
| Shaving set in oiled silk | Tooth soap |
| Medicines and bandages | Shaving set in oiled silk |
| Fly dope (sometimes) | Medicines and bandages |
|  | Fly dope and head net |

# The Woodman's Ax and Its Use

On the ax more than on anything else depends the comfort and success of the northern forest traveler, whatever his calling. He may, to lighten his load, discard all of the articles in his outfit which are not absolutely essential, but never by any chance is the ax among those cast aside, because this tool is the most necessary and the most useful article used by the bushman. Not a day passes that the ax is not put to strenuous use, and on the trap line nearly every hour of the day finds the ax at work, smoothing the rough path of the traveler and providing for his comfort and welfare.

How could the wilderness trapper exist without the aid of this most useful tool? On it he must depend for his night's supply of firewood, and when the weather is cold this means not only comfort, but life itself, for the hardiest trapper could not long survive a temperature of forty below without a good warm fire beside which to spread his bed. With the ax he cuts poles for the framework of his night's camp; he uses it to blaze the trail that he may follow it again when he goes the rounds to glean his harvest from the traps which he has set; he uses it when making the sets themselves, for cutting the drooping, snow-laden branches across his trail, and many minor uses which cannot now be mentioned. When making a hard trip he may leave his gun in camp, and may even travel and camp without blankets, shelter, or cooking utensils, but the ax must go with him on every trip.

We are told that in early days the Indians paid fabulous prices for the most simple and common tools, and it has been said that as much as a hundred dollars in furs has been paid by an Indian hunter for an ax. It seems like wholesale robbery, but the bargain had two sides—two points of view. The Indian simply exchanged what was practically worthless to him for what was of priceless value, and from his point of view he drove as shrewd a bargain as did the trader. When we leave civilization behind us values change, and utilitarian worth counts more than intrinsic value, therefore, the ax becomes more valuable than a whole season's catch of furs.

If any class of people need perfect goods it is the class who must depend on these goods for their existence. The woodsman should have a perfect gun, perfect traps, perfect camp equipment, the best food he can buy, but above all a perfect ax. It should be of the finest material and of the best temper, tough but not hard. When put to a great strain steel will do one of two things—it will bend or it will break. If of good quality, with the proper proportion of carbon, it will stand an unusually severe test before it will do either, but when it does give it should bend rather than break. Of this kind of steel the trapper's ax should be made, and it should have a temper which will enhance these good qualities. If the ax is tempered a little too hard the edge will break when cutting into hard knots or frozen wood, or when the frost has not been drawn from the edge before using. When once the edge becomes dulled it is difficult to sharpen, for the trapper of the great woods has no grindstone, and must depend on file and whetstone to keep his cutting tools in perfect condition. A hard ax cannot be filed, so that puts the taboo on the ax with high temper.

I have emphasized the necessity for perfection in the trapper's ax, and that you may realize the seriousness of this, I will repeat what I said at the beginning of this article, that often the camper's life depends on the ax and its ability to stand the woodsman's test. The northern or western trapper frequently finds it necessary to make long trips in terribly cold weather, camping out night after night. Since the entire camp outfit and food supply must be carried on these journeys, the outfit taken must of necessity be meager. Only a single blanket and a small, light canvas shelter can be taken and to sleep without a fire under such conditions is out of the question. A good hot fire must be kept going and such a fire will consume nearly half a cord of wood during the long northern night. This must be cut into lengths that can be handled and what would become of the camper if his ax were to break before the night's wood was cut, he far from the home camp, darkness at hand, and the temperature far below the zero mark. Freezing to death could be the only possible outcome, unless he could retrace his steps in the dark and travel all the long night. So you see it will pay you to test your ax well before you take it into the woods, and take only one that will stand the most severe trial, even if you break a dozen axes before you get one that is satisfactory.

What I have said of the material of the ax head applies with equal force to the ax handle. It should be of sound, strong, straight-grained, springy wood, for sometimes a broken ax handle is as disastrous as a broken blade. I have never found a better wood for ax handles than good second-growth hickory, but young white oak, the sapwood, is almost as good.

Even if the temper and material of the ax and handle leave nothing to be desired, if the ax is not of the right pattern, weight, and length, it will be unsatisfactory. Perhaps the most useful pattern for the wilderness trapper is that having a long narrow blade, but this should not be carried to the extreme, as a narrow blade is more easily broken. The long blade is very useful when cutting holes into the sides of trees for setting marten traps or in making deadfalls, and for many similar uses about camp where the simplicity of the outfit necessitates making of the ax a general utility tool. If made extremely long and narrow, however, the consequent weakening and the fact that a narrow blade is not so satisfactory for hewing and for chopping in heavy wood more than offset the good qualities of the long blade. The eye of the ax should be large, so that the handle may be large in the eye of the ax and close by the head, and it should be enlarged slightly at both edges. This will make it possible to wedge the handle so that it will hold the head solidly, and it will leave the handle if fitted well, thickest where the greatest strain comes, close to the eye of the ax.

In the shaping of an ax blade there are some rules that must be remembered and adhered to if the maximum of efficiency is desired. These same rules must be known to the user of the tool, for in the grinding, a bad chopping ax may often be made better, while bad grinding makes it worse. One of these rules, and the most important, is to have the blade or bit thinnest on the "inside corner," which is the end of the

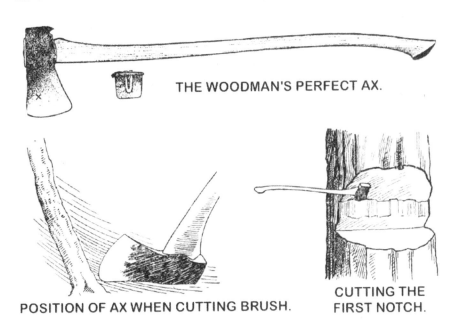

THE WOODMAN'S PERFECT AX.

POSITION OF AX WHEN CUTTING BRUSH.

CUTTING THE FIRST NOTCH.

blade nearest to the user. The hasty conclusion would be that if this corner were thinnest, the opposite side of the blade should be thickest. This is wrong. The thickest part of the blade should be two-thirds of the way across from the inside corner, the place marked X in the drawing of what I call "the woodsman's perfect ax." A blade so shaped will have the maximum chopping power, will sink easily into the tree, will burst the chip well, and will not bind in the wood.

I think it best that the ax head be made of wrought iron, split, and a welded-in steel bit. This gives the maximum strength. The butt of the ax might also be of steel, and would be more convenient for the trapper if it had a claw for drawing trap staples. If the eye of the ax is not tempered, in the least the entire head may be made of steel and will be almost, if not fully, as strong, while the making is simplified.

You may wonder why a trapper need concern himself with the making of the ax if he can buy it ready made, but if there is a trapper's perfect ax made, I do not know of it. I know, however, that many readers of this article have in their locality a blacksmith who is fully capable of making such an ax to order.

For the northern forest and the western mountain district the ax that I would recommend would weigh only about 2 pounds, handle not included in the weight. Some of you may think this entirely too light, but the northern Indians use axes of only one and a half pounds, and find them heavy enough for practical purposes, while light to carry on the trail. To make a light ax effective, however, it must have a long handle. An ax like this should have a handle of from thirty to 34 inches over all, and with such a tool you will be surprised to see what heavy work can be done.

As said before, I do not know of a better wood for ax handles than hickory. It is very strong and springy and it always stays smooth, as cold to the touch as the ax head itself. It is difficult to get ax handle wood when we reach the upper part of the northern tier of states or Canada, for hickory is not found there. Hard maple is used extensively for ax handles in these places; but it does not compare well with hickory. About the only way to get a handle of the proper length for the woodsman's ax is to remove the handle from a large ax and work it over into the proper shape and thickness. The full size single bit axes usually have clubs of handles and there is plenty of wood on which to work.

Did you ever wonder why an ax handle is curved in an S shape? It is made to fit the hands of the user without strain on the arms or wrists, and this curved shape enables him to hold the ax more solidly when striking a blow than could be done with a straight handle. The handle should be quite thick and "hand-fitting" near the end where it is grasped by the left hand (or right, according to whether the user is right or left handed), but the other part should be shaped so the hand can slide easily back and forth while chopping.

The handle should be fastened into the ax with a wedge, which in turn is held in place by a screw. The wedge has a head so that when the screw is removed it is easily pried out, and then if it is necessary to remove the handle the ax can be driven into the top of a stump or into a log, and the handle easily detached. Such wedges may be bought from almost any hardware company.

This is my idea of what a woodsman's ax should be, and such a tool weighing 2 pounds, with a well-shaped handle thirty or 32 inches long from the end to the ax eye, makes an efficient tool of light weight and a great article for use on the trail or trap line. I might say of it, as Davy Crockett said of his knife: "It will jump higher, dive deeper, shave more hogs and stand more bending without breaking than any other made."

As nearly all woodsmen are good axmen, it may seem superfluous to give advice regarding the care of an ax, the way to grind it, and how to use it, but this article is not intended for those who know, but for these who do not, and are desirous to learn. By a reckless, careless blow at a hemlock knot I have seen the entire bit broken off an ax, while other axes of no better temper but properly ground and well handled have gone through an entire season of "bark peeling" without a nick of any consequence. I have seen axes ruined in a half day's work cutting brush close to the ground, and have myself used an ax day after day at the same kind of work without making a nick which could not be whetted out in a few minutes with a small ax stone.

There is also a lot of danger in the careless use of an ax. I have known of at least two men who have cut their heads by splitting wood under a clothes line. The same thing may happen when working under a tree with low, drooping branches. In the woods it will pay double to make it a rule on every occasion to be sure that there is not even the smallest twig in the way to catch the ax before you make a stroke with it. Trim all brush away from around a tree before you commence to cut it, and observe the same precautions when you cut it into lengths or when lopping the branches. When cutting the fallen tree into lengths, the common and most convenient way is to stand on the log and chop it half way through between the feet, then turn and cut the other side in the same way. Use double precaution when doing this, for I have known of an ax being deflected and a nasty cut being the result. It seems that the smallest branch or sprout can turn the ax toward the foot of the chopper.

When chopping down timber the tree can nearly always be thrown either of three ways—the way the tree inclines or to either side, but not the opposite way from its inclination. In addition to the incline of the tree, the influence of the wind and the weight of the branches must be considered, and when all of these forces are brought to bear the timber cutter must be well "onto his job" to know just how to cut the tree to make it fall in the desired direction. A good chopper, however, can throw the tree to any spot designated within the falling zone almost every time. The wind is a great factor and must be considered, especially when the breeze is strong or when the tree appears to stand perfectly straight. A tree on a slope that appears to be perpendicular will, in nearly every case, fall down hill if free to fall as it wills, providing there is no contrary wind. If the tree really stands perfectly upright and there is no wind, it will fall best toward the side that has the most branches, or to the side having the greatest weight. If allowance must be made, however, for both wind and gravity, it is then the judgment of the chopper is put to the test. If he can estimate accurately the power of each of these forces, he can drop his tree exactly where he wants to, but how?

It is very simple. In cutting a tree a notch is cut on the side toward which the tree is to fall.

Remember that this notch should be cut into the center of the tree, and when finished, should be exactly at a right angle to the line on which the tree is to fall. A notch is then cut on the opposite side, just a little higher on the tree, and when this notch is cut in almost to the center the tree will fall. If the tree is notched to fall the way it inclines and there is nothing to prevent it going that way, the second notch should be cut exactly parallel to the first. If, however, the tree leans a little to one side, if there are more branches on that side, or if the wind blows in that direction, the second cut should not be parallel with the first, but should be farther from it on the side from which the wind comes, so that there will be more wood to break on that side. In no case should the notches entirely meet on the other side, for if they do, should the tree be cut entirely off on one side, it will settle farther over to that side. Just how near you dare cut it off on the one side and how much you must hold on the opposite side can be learned only from experience.

There are other little things that have a certain amount of influence. For instance, if there is nothing to interfere, the tree in falling will draw slightly toward the high side of the notch first cut. Then, too, if the notch is not perfectly cut, if it is more acute on one side than on the other, as the tree falls the top and bottom of the notch will meet on one side before they do on the other, and this is certain to swing the tree slightly toward the wide or obtuse side of the notch. A heavy weight of branches, too, on one side may cause the tree to roll slightly in falling.

For your own safety it is always best to get back a safe distance from the tree when it starts to fall, because if it falls over a rock, a log, or a little rise in the ground, the butt of the tree will kick and may lift your head off, which would be decidedly unpleasant. If there are other trees in the way, look out for falling branches.

I have already told how to cut the tree in sections, but the branches must be trimmed off before it can be cut up entirely. In trimming, work from the butt toward the top, as the branches usually grow that way, cut easier, and are not in the way while chopping. Hold the ax rigidly when trimming, as the knots are likely to be hard and an ax that is not held firmly may break or bend. Make it a rule to do no more trimming than necessary on such woods as hemlock and fir, which have very hard knots. Frozen wood is also likely to break the ax.

When splitting wood strike straight and don't try to spring the split open by prying with the ax, for that is the easiest way I know to break an ax handle. Usually it is easier and better to merely start the split with the ax and finish opening it up with wooden wedges, using the ax only to drive the wedges and to cut the contrary fibers. Just how to split a block easiest can be learned only from experience. Sometimes it is best to go right at a knot or the toughest place, and sometimes you must attack the clearest place, depending on circumstances. Ordinarily a piece of wood splits easiest by starting the end of the block with the ax and following up with a pair of wedges, using the ax to cut the binding splints.

Learn to cut close to the ground without striking the stones. It requires care, that is all, but one careless stroke may mean a badly damaged ax and an hour or more of hard work to make it sharp again. Don't strike downward when cutting brush; grasp the shrub, if a small one, with the left hand, and cut it by a single stroke, as illustrated, using the ax with one hand only. If the shrub is a large one, handle the ax with both hands and cut close to the ground, making a strong, slashing blow.

Grinding an ax requires some care, but it is really quite easy and it is surprising how many axmen will not attempt to grind an ax. I have known many good choppers, working in log camps, who could not grind an ax, or at least thought they could not.

As the ax comes from the store it usually has a decided bevel on the edge, and the first grinding means considerable work, for this bevel must be ground entirely away. Start well back on the blade and grind it slightly rounding down to the edge, until the edge is clean and even, then grind the other side in the same way. Some axmen maintain that the ax cuts better, or to use the woodsman's expression, "draws" better if in finishing the grinding the ax is given a wobbling motion. Keep in mind what I said about the shape of the blade, and if it is not already the proper form, try to improve it each time you put it on the grindstone. After grinding, whet the edge thoroughly with a fine whetstone until the scratched effect caused by grinding has given place to a smooth surface and a clean keen edge. If you do not whet it after grinding, the edge will crumble away and the ax will cut "dead."

The first grinding will tell you whether the ax is hard or soft.

You can tell by the sound of it and by its grip on the grindstone. If it is soft it cuts rapidly, grips the stone hard, and gives a dull, dead sound. If hard, it gives a ringing sound and the stone glides smoothly under it, cutting slowly and wearing the steel bright.

The woodsman cannot take a grindstone into the woods and the best substitute is a file. I always choose a flat mill file about 8 inches long. Always push the file from well back on the bit down to the edge, and never from the edge towards the eye of the ax, or you will be almost certain to cut your hands before you have finished. After the filing, whet the ax until you have a smooth, sharp edge.

It will be evident that an ax that must be kept sharp with a file and whetstone must not be too hard, for a file will not cut hard steel. The axes sold by the Hudson's Bay Company to the Indian trappers are very soft, so that they may be filed easily, and the Indian files only on the edge, so that the ax soon has a bevel almost equal to a chisel. The average Indian takes just about as much care of an ax as a woman does of a butcher knife.

As the minister says, "Just one word more," and that is in regard to carrying the ax on the trail. I have tried many ways, but do not find anything more satisfactory than having a leather pouch to slip over the head of the ax and tucking it head down in the pack. When drawing a toboggan it is slipped under the binding cords. If I am carrying my outfit and do not have a gun, I carry the ax in my hand, which is the most satisfactory way on such occasions. The Indian thrusts his ax through his sash, handle to the rear and blade down, but I never fancied that way of carrying an ax.

# Packing a Bug-Out Bag

It's important to understand that packing a bug-out bag is a very personal thing. Some items are going to be absolutely critical to your survival, while others will simply serve to make life a bit more comfortable for you. This book is going to provide some suggestions about what you might choose to include in your personal survival kit, but they are merely suggestions. You, and you alone, will be responsible for making sure that you pack the right types of items that you need to survive. Your first priority when it comes to packing a bug-out bag is survival. With survival in mind, think about the things that you *can't* live without. This doesn't include your laptop or tablet computer, either. We know that water and food are essential to everyone's survival, but your particular situation may be different than another person's situation. For example, you may require a certain type and amount of prescription medication to survive for three days that someone else doesn't need. You may also have certain food allergies that will need to be taken into consideration when preparing a bug-out bag. Let's first review the basic necessities that you'll need to survive. As we've previously discussed, FEMA lists water, food, and clean air at the top of their list of items to include in a seventy-two-hour survival kit. Everyone, regardless of their personal situation, requires these three things to survive. Consequently, it makes sense to talk about these items first.

## Water

As you may remember, in a document written on the subject of emergency preparedness, FEMA says that a normally active person needs a minimum of one half gallon of clean water per day just for drinking. They go on to say that each person should have another half gallon per day to use for sanitation purposes. Keep in mind that when preparing a bug-out bag, someone is going to have to carry it. Young children may not be able to carry this much water themselves, which may mean that as the responsible parent, you may need to carry some of your children's share of water. This doesn't mean that they shouldn't have water in their survival kit. They absolutely

should! You would hope that they never become separated from you, but if something were to cause you to become separated, they will need to have enough water in their bug-out bag to survive. The author of this book prefers to pack commercially bottled water for a couple of reasons. The first is that bottled water is treated to last without spoiling and the second is that once the bottles are used, the empty bottles become convenient containers that can be used for other survival purposes.

***Important Note about Water***: There are stories that survival experts tell about people dying of dehydration when they actually have water with them. What the experts believe is happening is that people are so concerned with conserving their water rations that they don't drink enough and, consequently, they end up dying of dehydration. Because of these stories, many survivalists use a saying that goes, "Water is better in you than on you." This basically means that you should drink your daily water ration instead of trying to conserve it. Having water on you will do nothing at all to fend off dehydration, while having it inside you will definitely help.

## Food

Depending on your size, age, and activity level, your daily food requirements will vary. That being said, you'll need to pack enough food to sustain the person who is carrying the bug-out bag for three days. As you can imagine, this creates the question: What kind of food should you pack? Since you never know when you'll have to grab your bug-out bag and run, whatever you pack should be nonperishable and lightweight. Remember, *you* have to carry what you pack, so if your backpack is stuffed with big cans of beef stew, you're going to be pretty miserable if you have to carry your bug-out bag very far. Perhaps a better solution would be to pack a

product like the ER Emergency Ration 3600 Survival Food Bar found at www.quakekare. com or 1-800-2-PREPARE. The manufacturers of this product advertise on their packaging that it is approved by the United States Coast Guard as well as the U.S. Department of Homeland Security. Each 27 oz. packet contains nine individual 410-calorie food ration bars. This equals a total of 3,690 calories that are all wrapped up in a convenient little package.

You don't need to add water to it and you don't need to cook it. You just open a package and eat it. This product is marketed as a three-day food ration package. Divided over three days, these emergency ration bars will provide 1,230 calories per day. Because of their small size, you can easily pack two emergency ration packages, which will provide extra calories to fend off hunger. Their small size also means that you should have enough room to pack some comfort foods, such as candy.

Having access to these comfort foods will make surviving more tolerable—especially for children. People seem to have a difficult time deciding what foods to pack in a bug-out bag. Products like this emergency ration bar may not be on par with a steak dinner, but they're cheap ($4.09 on Amazon.com), they don't take up much space, they have a five-year shelf life, and they're energy dense. They also come in a vacuum-sealed bag to keep the product neatly packed away and fresh for when you need to eat it. They may not exactly be gourmet, but they will provide you with enough calories to survive. We'll talk about having access to comfort foods, which will make surviving easier, later on in this book.

## Clean Air

Some preppers go all out and carry high-end gas masks to ensure that they will have clean air to breathe after a disaster hits. Whether you choose to go to that extent will be up to you. At the very least, you should probably pack some dust masks, cotton shirts, or bandanas that can be used to help filter the air that you'll be breathing. You may not need to use this item, but you'll be glad that you have it if the air quality is in fact poor and you have to bug-out.

## Medications

A three-day supply of any medications that you need to take should be kept in your bug-out bag, as well. If your medications require refrigeration, you may want to check with your doctor and tell him or her that you are preparing a bug-out bag. He or she may be able to give you some samples of medications that don't require refrigeration to get you through the seventy-two-hour time period. This is something that you'll have to figure out with your doctor's help.

*Warning*: Medication can be dangerous if not taken properly.

You should use your own discretion as to whether or not to pack it in your children's bug-out bags. Only you know whether your children are mature enough to have their medications packed in their own bags. You may prefer to pack it in your bag and dispense it to them at the appropriate time under your direct supervision.

## Infant Supplies

If you'll be caring for an infant that requires infant formula, don't forget to pack enough formula and diapering supplies to last for three days. You'll also need to plan accordingly and make sure that you pack enough extra water to mix the formula for each feeding. Be sure and check to see if the formula you are packing is actually supposed to be mixed with water, as some infant formula is already premixed.

The same holds true if you'll be caring for a toddler that needs to eat canned baby food. You'll

be able to survive just fine on emergency ration bars and candy, but your young toddlers may not do so well on this kind of food. Since toddlers can't be expected to carry their own bug-out bags, you'll be responsible for carrying the supplies that they'll need to survive so be sure and plan accordingly.

## Important Family Documents

You should probably also carry copies of any important family documents that you think might be of use to you. These documents should be stored in a waterproof bag so they don't get ruined if you find yourself having to survive in less than ideal weather conditions.

Some examples of the types of documents that you might want to carry are:

1) Photo identification.
2) Important medical information, such as medical history, medical conditions, allergies,

or the medications that you might take.

3) Copies of insurance policies or medical insurance cards.

4) Important contact information, including phone numbers and addresses of relatives, close friends, and family doctors.

5) Bank account information.

6) Accurate location of your strategically hidden bug-out caches as well as directions to them. This might include GPS coordinates or perhaps even maps with the location of the caches clearly marked on them.

## Protection from the Elements

Depending on where you live, you may find yourself having to deal with cold weather when you bug-out. Hypothermia is a very real risk in cold climates and it's nothing to take lightly. Simply put, if you're not prepared for the cold, it can kill you.

With this in mind, you should pack at least one change of warm clothing, including a coat or jacket, a long sleeve shirt, long pants, warm shoes or boots, gloves, socks, and a hat. Additionally, each person should have a sleeping bag or warm blanket in his or her survival kit. While we're on the subject of blankets, now would be a good time to address survival blankets. More specifically, the tightly folded mylar blankets that look like huge sheets of aluminum foil. These emergency blankets, sometimes referred to as "space blankets," should be packed in addition to—not in place of—a sleeping bag or warm blanket. They can be used for a multitude of things including reflecting body heat back toward a person who is wrapped up in the emergency blanket. They can also be used as a reflective surface that may be useful when signaling for help. Again, you probably shouldn't rely on these blankets as your only means of keeping warm, but they are useful items to have on hand and they won't take up much space in your bug-out bag, either.

**Warning**: This item can be dangerous for small children because it may pose a suffocation hazard. Mylar space blankets are not permeable and, if placed over the mouth and nose of a child, the child may suffocate. You should use your own discretion as to whether you are comfortable packing this item in your children's bug-out bags. Only you know whether your child is mature enough to safely use this item. If you choose to let your children use this item, it should only be under your direct supervision. Spending the night in a warm sleeping bag can make the difference between a restful night's sleep and a miserable one. A good sleeping bag can be purchased for $50 to $100, and these bags usually come with compression sacks that make packing them down to a small and

easy-to-handle size quite simple. One note about buying sleeping bags is to make sure you buy one that is sized appropriately for the person who will be sleeping in it. Contrary to what you might think, sleeping bags are not one-size-fits-all items. If you're 6' 4" tall, you'll be glad that you thought ahead and bought a sleeping bag that was long enough to fit your entire body. On the flip side of this scenario, small children don't need to have a full-sized adult sleeping bag strapped to their bug-out packs either. This will just add to the bulk and weight that they end up having to carry. Chemical hand warming pouches are also very useful when trying to fend off the cold. Once opened, these little packs produce heat for several hours. They do eventually stop producing heat, but having access to them could provide an extra measure of comfort that you'll really appreciate having. Not to mention, being able to hand these little wonders to your cold children will help put your mind at ease and help take the chill off of them. Because they can help you keep warm, they may do wonders for your morale and sense of well-being while you try to survive.

*Warning*: Ingesting the contents of the hand warmer can be dangerous. If you choose to let your child use one of these chemical hand warmers, it should only be under your direct supervision.

A small, lightweight tent is also a good thing to have strapped to your bug-out pack. You can survive without a tent, but sleeping in one will be more comfortable than sleeping under the stars. Since this book is about remaining comfortable when you have to bug-out, the author highly recommends that you pack a tent with your bug-out bag. Not only can a tent provide some shelter from the rain and snow, but it will also keep biting flies and mosquitoes off you. It will even keep you a bit warmer at night!

Depending on the number of people that will be bugging out with you, you may have to pack a few tents. It's much easier to have a few people each carry a small dome tent than it is to pack one large cabin-type tent that could accommodate your entire family.

If, however, you are bugging out by yourself, you might want to pack what is called a "bivy sack" in lieu of a tent. A bivy sack is essentially a very small tent that is just big enough to fit your sleeping bag and a few supplies. It will protect your sleeping bag and supplies from the elements as well as keep the mosquitoes off you while still being so small and lightweight that you'll hardly realize you're packing it with you.

Another very useful item to have with you that can help protect you from the elements is a plastic tarp. You can use this item a variety of ways in survival situations. It can be used as a protective barrier to keep your sleeping bag off the damp ground as well as a cover to protect your supplies from rain and snow. In a pinch, it can even be used as a signaling device.

*Warning*: This item can be dangerous, as it is not permeable and may pose a suffocation hazard if young children get wrapped up in it. If you choose to let your child carry a plastic tarp in their bug-out bag, it should only be under your direct supervision.

## Footwear

Since you might have to hike for some distance when you bug-out, it's important to have the proper type of footwear. For this reason, you might want to consider keeping a good-quality pair of hiking boots next to your bug-out bag. Then, if you ever have to bug-out, you can ditch your flip-flops and put on your hiking boots before you leave your house.

Keeping your hiking boots with your family's bug-out bags has an added benefit. If you have children, you know that they inevitably have a hard time finding both of their shoes when they are looking for them. By storing their hiking boots with

their bug-out bag, you're taking that risk out of the equation. This can and will save you time when you are trying to bug-out in a hurry.

## Personal Sanitation Supplies

Items like moist towelettes, toilet paper, hand sanitizer, feminine hygiene products, personal hygiene products, and garbage bags with plastic ties can come in really handy for taking care of everyday hygiene and sanitation needs. These items are easy to overlook when packing a bug-out bag, but when you find yourself needing them, you'll be kicking yourself for not having packed them. Whatever you do, don't make that mistake.

Keep in mind, however, that luxury items like makeup kits and hand mirrors will only add to the bulk and weight that a person has to carry. Your teenage daughter may think that she can't live without these items for three whole days, but she'll be better off if she doesn't have to carry the added weight on her back. Also, not carrying these items means that there will be more room for actual survival items in the backpack.

*Warning*: Garbage bags should not be included in young children's bug-out bags because they pose a suffocation hazard. Additionally, young children should not be allowed to play with them.

## First Aid Kit

Oftentimes during emergency situations, people will become injured and require emergency medical care of some sort. If you're equipped with the proper supplies and knowledge to dress and treat wounds, your chances of surviving until you can get professional medical care will increase substantially. Notice that the word "knowledge" was included in this last statement. It's important for each bug-out bag to contain a first aid kit, but if you

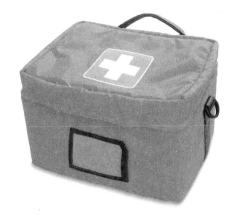

don't know how to use it, it will be of little use to you.

You may want to pack a book on first aid to refer to, but good old knowledge about performing first aid is something that doesn't take up any space at all in your bug-out bag—and it's something that everyone should have. It's highly advisable that you take the time as soon as possible to get some first aid training. Be sure to include your entire family in this training. After all, you never know when the knowledge that your family has may end up saving *your* life.

*Warning*: Some items that are included in first aid kits could potentially be dangerous if handled by young children. You should inspect the first aid kits that you pack in your children's bug-out bags to make sure that there aren't any items in the kit that may harm them.

## Multitool

As we discussed in Section 1, a multitool can be invaluable to have on hand. It can be used as a wrench to help you turn off utilities, as a knife to use for cutting, and much more. You may remember that there are a lot of cheap knockoffs on the market when it comes to multitools. It has been the experience of the author that it's worth spending the money on a high-quality name brand multitool. They're built much better than cheaper versions and the added quality that they bring to the table may be the difference between them saving your bacon and being a

worthless pile of junk. It's also worth pointing out that when you are buying a multitool, you are in fact buying a *tool* that will be used. With this in mind, the cute little keychain-sized multitools should probably be avoided—they aren't equipped to handle the same types of jobs as good-quality, regular-sized multitools.

*Warning*: This item can be dangerous because multitools are usually equipped with a knife blade. You should use your own discretion as to whether to pack it in your children's bug-out bags. Only you know whether your child is mature enough to safely use this tool.

## Survival Knife

Depending on the climate and the time of year that you find yourself bugging out, you may have to build shelter or light a fire. A good-quality survival knife that is substantial enough to be used for the tasks of cutting limbs

or chopping wood can be very useful in this type of a situation. This author likes the Gerber Gator Machete Jr. for this purpose. It's a large, double-edged knife that has a chopping edge as well as a good-quality saw on the back edge. It has a 10.75-inch blade and measures a total of 18.75 inches in length. It's a good hacking and sawing tool that comes with a sheath and will only set you back about $25 or $30.

*Warning*: This tool is potentially dangerous and should not be packed in a child's bug-out bag. Additionally, it should only be used by an adult.

## Fire-Starting Kit

A good-quality fire-starting kit is essential for any adult's bug-out bag. Be sure and include items that will make it easy for you to start a fire. Even if you know how to make a fire with a fire bow, you'll be glad that you thought ahead and packed items like a high-quality magnesium stick, a

new butane lighter, waterproof matches, and dry tinder. Being able to start a fire—and quickly—can save your life during extreme, cold survival situations. It can provide heat, light, protection from biting insects, a way of signaling for help, and even protection from predatory animals. Not to mention, fire is a great comforter when a person is in a survival situation.

Here's a helpful tip! If you pack a new butane lighter in a hard plastic container that is used for holding a travel toothbrush, the lever that releases the gas on the lighter won't accidentally be depressed when you pack it in your bug-out pack. If you don't pack it this way and the lever does accidentally become depressed while the lighter is being jostled around in your pack, all of the gas could escape and the lighter will be of little use to you when you actually need to use it.

**Warning:** Starting a fire can be dangerous, as there is potential of suffering burns or other injuries. You should use your own discretion as to whether to pack fire-starting tools in your children's bug-out bags. Only you know whether your child is mature enough to safely use them.

# Basic Knots

By Samuel A. Moffat, Boy Scouts of America

Every scout knows what rope is. From the earliest moment of his play life he has used it in connection with most of his games. In camp life and on hikes he will be called upon to use it again and again. It is therefore not essential to describe here the formation of rope, its various sizes and strength. The important thing to know is how to use it to the best advantage. To do this an intelligent understanding of the different knots and how to tie them is essential. Every day sailors, explorers, mechanics, and mountain climbers risk their lives on the knots that they tie. Thousands of lives have been sacrificed to ill-made knots. The scout therefore should be prepared in an emergency, or when necessity demands, to tie the right knot in the right way.

There are three qualities to a good knot:

1. Rapidity with which it can be tied.
2. Its ability to hold fast when pulled tight.
3. The readiness with which it can be undone.

The following knots, recommended to scouts, are the most serviceable because they meet the above requirements and will be of great help in scoutcraft. If the tenderfoot will follow closely the various steps indicated in the diagrams, he will have little difficulty in reproducing them at pleasure.

In practicing knot-tying, a short piece of hemp rope may be used. To protect the ends from fraying a scout should know how to "whip" them. The commonest method of "whipping" is as follows:

Lay the end of a piece of twine along the end of the rope. Hold it to the rope with the thumb of your left hand while you wind the standing part around it and the rope until the end of the twine has been covered. Then with the other end of the twine lay a loop back on the end of the rope and continue winding the twine upon this second end until all is taken up. The end is then pulled back tight and cut off close to the rope.

For the sake of clearness a scout must constantly keep in mind these three principal parts of the rope:

1. *The Standing Part*—The long unused portion of the rope on which he works;
2. *The Bight*—The loop formed whenever the rope is turned back upon itself; and,
3. *The End*—The part he uses in leading.

Before proceeding with the tenderfoot requirements, a scout should first learn the two primary knots: the overhand and figure-of-eight knots.

### *The Overhand Knot.*

Start with the position shown in the preceding diagram. Back the end around the standing part and up through the bight and draw tight.

### *The Figure of Eight Knot.*

Make a bight as before. Then lead the end around back of the standing part and down through the bight.

After these preliminary steps, the prospective tenderfoot may proceed to learn the required knots.

### *Square or Reef Knot.*

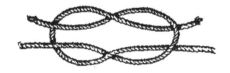

The commonest knot for tying two ropes together. Frequently

used in first aid bandaging. Never slips or jams; easy to untie.

### False Reef or Granny.

If the ends are not crossed correctly when making the reef knot, the false reef or granny is the result. This knot is always bad.

### Sheet Bend or Weaver's Knot.

This knot is used in bending the sheet to the clew of a sail and in tying two rope-ends together.

Make a bight with one rope A, B, then pass end C, of other rope up through and around the entire bight and bend it under its own standing part.

### The Bowline.

A noose that neither jams nor slips. Used in lowering a person from a burning building, etc.

Form a small loop on the standing part leaving the end long enough for the size of the noose required. Pass the end up through the bight around the standing part and down through the bight again. To tighten, hold noose in position and pull standing part.

### Halter, Slip, or Running Knot.

A bight is first formed and an overhand knot made with the end around the standing part.

### Sheepshank.

Used for shortening ropes. Gather up the amount to be shortened, then make a half hitch round each of the bends as shown in the diagram.

### Clove Hitch.

Used to fasten one pole to another in fitting up scaffolding; this knot holds snugly; is not

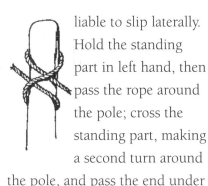

liable to slip laterally. Hold the standing part in left hand, then pass the rope around the pole; cross the standing part, making a second turn around the pole, and pass the end under the last turn.

## The Fisherman's Bend.

Used aboard yachts for bending on the gaff topsail halliards. It consists of two turns around a spar or ring, then a half hitch around the standing part and through the turns on the spar, and another half hitch above it around the standing part.

## Timber Hitch.

Used in hauling timber. Pass the end of the rope around the timber. Then lead it around its standing part and bring it back to make two or more turns on its own part. The strain will hold it securely.

## Two Half Hitches.

Useful because they are easily made and will not slip under any strain. Their formation is sufficiently indicated by the diagram.

## Blackwall Hitch.

Used to secure a rope to a hook. The standing part when hauled tight holds the end firmly.

## Becket Hitch.

For joining a cord to a rope. May be easily made from diagram.

## The Fisherman's Knot.

Used for tying silk-worm gut for fishing purposes. It never slips; is easily unloosed by pulling the two short ends.

The two ropes are laid alongside one another, then with each end an overhand knot is made around the standing part of the other. Pull the standing parts to tighten.

### Carrick Bend.

Used in uniting hawsers for towing. Is easily untied by pushing the loops inwards.

Turn the end of one rope A over its standing part B to form a loop. Pass the end of the other rope across the bight thus formed, back of the standing part B over the end A, then under the bight at C, passing it over its own standing part and under the bight again at D.

# Building a Shelter

# Choosing a Camp Site

From *The Book of Camp-Lore and Woodcraft* by Dan Beard

When choosing a camp site, if possible, choose a forest or grove of young trees. First, because of the shade they give you; secondly, because they protect you from storms; and thirdly, because they protect you from lightning.

Single trees, or small groups of trees in open pastures, are exceedingly dangerous during a thunderstorm; tall trees on the shores of a river or lake are particularly selected as targets for thunder bolts by the storm king. But the safest place in a thunderstorm, next to a house, is a forest. The reason for this is that each wet tree is a lightning rod silently conducting the electric fluid without causing explosions. Do not camp at the foot of a very tall tree, or an old tree with dead branches on it, for a high wind may break off the branches and drop them on your head with disastrous results; the big tree itself may fall even when there is no wind at all.

Once I pitched my camp near an immense tree on the Flathead Indian Reservation. A few days later we returned to our old camp. As we stopped and looked at the site where our tents had been pitched we looked at each other solemnly, but said nothing, for there, prone upon the ground, lay that giant veteran tree!

But young trees do not fall down, and if they did they could not create the havoc caused by the immense bole of the patriarch of the forest when it comes crashing to the earth. A good scout must "Be Prepared," and to do so must remember that safety comes first, and too close neighborhood to a big tree is often unsafe.

Remember to choose the best camp site that can be found; do not travel all day, and as night comes on stop at any old place, but in the afternoon keep your eyes open for likely spots.

Halt early enough to give time to have everything snug and in order before dark.

In selecting camping ground, look for a place where good water and wood are handy. Choose a high spot with a gentle slope if possible; guard your spring or water hole from animals, for if the day is hot your dog will run ahead of the party and jump into the middle of the spring to cool himself, and horses and cattle will befoul the water.

If camping in the Western states on the shores of a shallow stream which lies along the trail, cross the stream before making camp or you may not be able to cross it for days. A chinook wind suddenly melting the snows in the distant mountains, or a cloud-burst miles and miles up stream, may suddenly send down to you a dangerous flood even in the dry season. I have known of parties being detained for days by one of these sudden roaring floods of water, which came unannounced, the great bole of mud, sticks, and logs sweeping by their camp and taking with it everything in its path.

A belt of dense timber between camp and a pond or swamp will act as a protection from mosquitoes. As a rule, keep to windward of mosquito holes; the little insects travel with the wind, not against it. 'Ware ant hills, rotten wood infested with ants, for they make poor bedfellows and are a nuisance where the food is kept.

A bare spot on the earth, where there are no dry leaves, is a wind-swept spot; where the dust-covered leaves lie in heaps the wind does not blow. A windy place is generally free from mosquitoes, but it is a poor place to build a fire; a small bank is a great protection from high wind and twisters. During one tornado I had a camp under the lee of a small elevation; we only lost the fly of one tent out of a camp of fifty or more, while in more exposed places nearby great trees were uprooted and houses unroofed.

It must not be supposed that the camping season is past because the summer vacation is over. The real camping season begins in the Wild Rice Moon, that is, September. Even if school or business takes all our time during the week, we still have weekends in which to camp. Saturday has always been a boys' day. Camping is an American institution, because America affords the greatest camping ground in the world.

The author is seated in his own log house, built by himself, on the shores of Big Tink Pond. Back of him there is pitched a camp of six rows of tents, which are filled with a joyful, noisy crowd of youngsters.

It is here in the mountains of Pike County, Pennsylvania, where the bluestone is stratified in horizontal layers, that one may study the camp from its very birth to the latest and finished product of this century.

Everywhere in these mountains there are outcroppings of the bluestone, and wherever the face of a ridge of this stone is exposed to the elements, the rains or melting snows cause the water to drip from the earth on top of the stone and trickle down over the face of the cliff. Then, when a cold snap turns the moisture into ice in every little crack in the rock, the expansion of the ice forces the sides of the cracks apart at the seams in the rock until loose pieces from the undersides slide off, leaving small spaces over which the rock projects. The little caves thus made make retreats for white-footed mice and other small mammals, chipmunks, and cave rats. When these become deeper they may become dens in which snakes sleep through the winter.

The openings never grow smaller, and in course of time are large enough for the coon, then the fox, and in olden times they made dens for wolves and panthers, or a place where the bear would "hole" up for the winter.

Time is not considered by Dame Nature; she has no trains to catch, and as years and centuries roll by the little openings in the bluestone become big enough to form a shelter for a crouching man, and the crouching man used them as a place in which to camp when the Norsemen in their dragon ships were braving the unknown ocean. When Columbus, with his toy boats, was blundering around the West Indies, the crouching man was camping under the bluestone ledges of old Pike County, Pennsylvania. There he built his campfires and cooked his beaver and bear and deer and elk, using dishes of pottery of his own make and ornamented with crude designs traced in the clay before the dishes were baked.

We know all this to be true history, because within a short walk of the author's log house there are overhanging ledges of bluestone, and underneath these ledges we, ourselves, have crouched and camped, and with sharp sticks have dug up the ground from the layer of earth covering the floor rock. And in this ground we have found bits of pottery, the split bones of different wild animals—split so that the savage camper might secure the rich marrow from the inside of the bones—arrowheads, bone awls and needles, tomahawks, the skulls of beaver and spearheads; all these things have been found under the overhanging bluestone.

Wherever such a bluestone ledge exists, one may make a good camp by closing up the front of the cave with sticks against the overhanging cliff and thatching the sticks with browse or balsam boughs, thus making the simplest form of a lean-to. The Indians used such shelters before the advent of the white man; Daniel Boone used them when he first visited Kentucky, and, in spite of the great improvement in tents, the overhanging ledge is still used in Pennsylvania by fishermen and hunters for overnight camps.

But if one uses such a site for his overnight camp or his weekend camp, one should not desecrate the ancient abode by introducing under its venerable roof, modern up-to-date cooking and camp material, but should exercise ingenuity and manufacture, as far as possible, the conveniences and furniture necessary for the camp.

Since the author is writing this in a camp in the woods, he will tell the practical things that confront him, even though he must mention a white man's shop broom.

In the first place, the most noticeable defect in the tenderfoot's work is the manner in which he handles his broom and wears the broom out of shape. A broom may be worn to a stub when properly used, but the lopsided broom is no use at all because the chump who handled it always used it one way until the broom became a useless, distorted, lopsided affair, with a permanent list to starboard or port, as the case may be.

To sweep properly is an art, and every all-around outdoor boy and man should learn to sweep and to handle the broom as skillfully as he does his gun or ax. In the first place, turn the broom every time you notice a tendency of the latter to become one-sided, then the broom will wear to a stub and still be of use. In the next place, do not swing the broom up in the air with each sweep and throw the dust up in the clouds, but so sweep that the end of the stroke keeps the broom near the floor or ground.

Now a word about making beds. In all books on woodcraft you are directed to secure balsam boughs from which to make your beds, and there is no better forest bedding than the fragrant balsam boughs, but unfortunately the mountain goose, as the hunters call it, from which you pluck the feathers to make your camp bed, is not to be found in all localities.

A bag filled with dry leaves, dry grass, hay, or straw will make a very comfortable mattress; but we are not always in the hay and straw belt and dry leaves are sometimes difficult to secure; a scout, however, must learn to make a bed wherever he happens to be. If there happens to be a swale nearby where brakes and ferns grow luxuriantly, one can gather an armful of these, and with them make a mattress. The Interrupted fern, the Cinnamon, the Royal fern, the Lady fern, the Marsh fern and all the larger ferns are useful as material.

A camping party should have their work so divided that each one can immediately start at his own particular job the moment a halt is made. One chops up the firewood and sees that a plentiful supply of firewood is always on hand; usually he carries the water. One makes camp, puts up the tents, clears away the rubbish, fixes the beds, etc., while a third attends strictly to kitchen work, preparing the meals, and washing up the dishes.

With the labor divided in this manner, things run like clock work and camp is always neat and tidy. Roughing it is making the best of it; only a slob and a chump goes dirty and has a sloppy-looking camp. The real

old-time veteran and sourdough is a model of neatness and order. But a clean, orderly camp is much more important than a clean-faced camper. Some men think so much of themselves and their own personal cleanliness that they forget their duty to the others. One's duty is about in this proportion: first to the animals if any, secondly to the men, and lastly to oneself.

Before pitching your tent, clear out a space for it to occupy; pick up the stones, rubbish and sticks, rake off the ground with a forked stick. But do not be rude to your brother, the ground pine; apologize for disturbing it; be gentle with the fronds of the fern; do not tear the trailing arbutus vine up by its roots, or the plant of the almond scented twin flowers; ask pardon of the thallus of the lichen which you are trampling under your feet. Why? O! well— because they had first right to the place, and because such little civilities to the natural objects around you put your own mind in accord with nature, and make camping a much more enjoyable affair.

When you feel you are sleeping on the breast of *your mother*, the earth, while *your father*, the sky, with his millions of eyes is watching over you, and that you are surrounded by your brother, the plants, the wilderness is no longer lonesome even to the solitary traveler.

Another reason for taking this point of view is that it has a humanizing effect and tends to prevent one from becoming a wilderness Hun and vandal. It also not only makes one hesitate to hack the trees unnecessarily, but encourages the camper to take pride in leaving a clean trail. As my good friend, John Muir, said to me: "The camping trip need not be the longest and most dangerous excursion up to the highest mountain, through the deepest woods or across the wildest torrents, glaciers or deserts, in order to be a happy one; but however short or long, rough or smooth, calm or stormy, it should be one in which the

able, fearless camper sees the most, learns the most, loves the most and leaves the cleanest track; whose camp grounds are never marred by anything unsightly, scarred trees or blood spots or bones of animals."

It is not the object of this book to advertise, or even advise the use of any particular type of outfitting apparatus other than the plain, everyday affairs with which all are familiar. What we want to do is to start the reader right, then he may make his own choice, selecting an outfit to suit his own taste. There are no two men, for instance, who will sing the praise of the same sort of a tent, but there is perhaps no camper who has not used, and been very comfortable in, the old-style wall tent. It has its disadvantages, and so has a house, a shack, or a shanty. As a rule, the old wall tent is too heavy to carry with comfort and very difficult for one man to pitch alone—unless one knows how.

# Pitching a Tent

## Tent Pegs

Are necessary for almost any kind of a tent; you can buy them at the outfitter's and lose them on the way to camp; they even have iron and steel tent pegs to help make camping expensive, and to scatter through the woods. But if you are a real sourdough you will cut your own tent pegs, shaped according to circumstances and individual taste. Fig. 286 shows the two principal kinds: the fork and the notched tent pegs. For the wall tents one will need a ridge pole (Fig. 288), and two forked sticks, or rods, to support the ridge pole; the forks on these should be snubbed off close so that they will not thrust themselves up against the canvas on the top of the tent and endanger the fabric; these poles should be of a proper height; otherwise if the poles are too long, the tent will not touch the

ground at all, or if the poles are too short, the tent will wrinkle all over the ground like a fellow's trousers when his suspenders break.

See that the ground is comparatively level, but with a slant in one direction or another so that water will drain off in case of rain. Never, for instance, pitch your tent in a hollow or basin of ground, unless you want to wake up some night slopping around in a pool of water. Do not pitch your tent near a standing dead tree; it is liable to fall over and crush you in the night. Avoid camping under green trees with heavy dead branches on them. Remember the real camper always has an eye to safety first, not because he is a coward, but because the real camper is as brave a person as you will find anywhere, and no real brave person believes in the carelessness which produces accidents. Do not pitch your tent over protruding stones which will make stumbling-blocks for you on which to stub your toes at night, or torture you when you spread your blankets over them to sleep. Use common sense, use gumption. Of course, we all know that *it hurts one's head to think*, but we must all try it, nevertheless, if we are going to live in the big outdoors.

At a famous military academy the splendid cavalrymen gave a brilliant exhibition of putting up wall tents; it required four men to put up each tent. Immediately following this some of the scouts took the same tents, with one scout to each tent, and in less time than the cavalrymen took for the same job, the twelve-year-old boys, single-handed, put up the same tents.

## How to Pitch and Ditch Single-Handed

Spread out your tent all ready to erect, put your ridge pole and your two uprights in place, and then drive some tent stakes, using the flat of your ax with which to drive them, so that you will not split the tops of the stakes (Fig. 287); drive the two end stakes A and B (Fig. 289) at an angle to the ends of the tent. After the tent stakes are arranged in a row, like the ones in Fig. 289, adjust the forks of the uprights 2 inches from the ends of the ridge pole (Fig. 288), then make fast the two extreme end guy ropes A and B to the tent pegs; the others are unimportant for the present, after that is done, raise one tent pole part of the way up (Fig. 290), then push the other part of the way up (Fig. 291); gradually adjust these things until the strain is even upon your guy ropes. You will now find that your tent will stand alone, because the weight is pulling against your guy ropes (Fig. 292). This will hold your tent steady until you can make fast the guy ropes to the pegs upon the other side, not too tightly, because you need slack to straighten up your tent poles.

Next see that the back guy pole is perpendicular, after which it is a very easy matter to straighten up the front pole and adjust the guy rope so that it will stand stiff as in Fig. 293.

Remember, when you are cutting the ridge poles and the uprights, to select fairly straight sticks, and they should be as free as possible from rough projections, which might injure the canvas; also the poles should be as stiff as possible so as not to sag or cause the roof to belly.

## Ditching

Just as soon as your tent is erected and you feel like resting, get busy on ditching; no matter how dry the weather may be at the time, put a ditch around the tent that will drain the water away from your living place. There is no positive rule for digging this ditch;

it varies according to surface of ground, but the gutter should be so made that the water will run away from the tents and not to it, or stand around it (Fig.294). Fig.295 shows how to make a tent by folding a floor cloth or piece of tarpaulin; of course it must have a tent pole to support the top, and the floor pieces may be drawn together in the center. Make one out of a piece of writing paper and you will learn how to do it, because although the paper is small, the folds would be just the same as if it was as large as a church.

In sandy or soft ground it often taxes one's ingenuity to supply anchors for one's tent; an anchor is a weight of some sort to which the guy ropes may be

attached. Fig. 296 shows a tent anchored by billets of wood; these are all supposed to be buried in the ground as in Fig. 308, and the ground trampled down over and above them to keep them safe in their graves. Fig. 297 shows the first throw in the anchor hitch, Fig. 298 the second throw, and Fig. 299 the complete hitch for the anchor. Fig. 303 shows the knot by which the anchor rope is tied to the main line. Figs. 300, 301, and 302 show the detail of tying this knot, which is simplicity itself, when you know how, like most knots. Fig. 303 shows the anchor hitch complete.

Stones, bundles of fagots, or bags of sand all make useful anchors; Fig. 304 is a stone, Fig. 305 are half billets of wood, Fig. 306 shows fagots of wood, Fig. 307 a bag of sand. All may be used to anchor your tent in the sands or loose ground.

# Different Types of Tents

In many sections of the country you will need a tent, even when traveling afoot. Formerly a man had to make a choice between canvas, which is heavy but fairly waterproof, and drill, which is light but flimsy. A seven by seven duck tent weighs fully twenty-five pounds when dry, and a great many more when wet. It will shed rain as long as you do not hit against it. A touch on the inside, however, will often start a trickle at the point of contact. Altogether it is unsatisfactory, and one does not wonder that many men prefer to knock together bark shelters.

## Tent Material

Nowadays, however, another and better material is to be had. It is the stuff balloons are made of, and is called balloon silk. I believe, for shelter purposes, it undergoes a further waterproofing process, but of this I am not certain. A tent

"A" Tent Pitched as Shelter.

of the size mentioned, instead of weighing twenty-five pounds, pulls the scales down at about eight. Furthermore, it does not absorb moisture, and is no heavier when wet than when dry. One can touch the inside all he wishes without rendering it pervious. The material is tough and enduring.

I have one which I have used hard for five years, not only as a tent, but as a canoe lining, a sod cloth, a tarpaulin, and a pack canvas. Today it is as serviceable as ever, and excepting for inevitable soiling, two small patches represents its entire wear and tear.

"A" Tent Pitched Between Two Trees.

## Don't Use a Tent Curtain

Abercrombie & Fitch, who make this tent, will try to persuade you, if you demand protection against mosquitoes, to let them sew on a sod-cloth of bobbinet and a loose long curtain of the same material to cover the entrance. Do not allow it. The rig is all right as long as there are plenty of flies. But suppose you want to use the tent in a flyless land? There still blocks your way that confounded curtain of bobbinet, fitting tightly enough so that you have almost to crawl when you enter, and so arranged that it is impossible to hang it up out of the way. The tent itself is all right, but its fly rigging is all wrong.

## Best Tent Protection from Flies

I have found that a second tent built of cheesecloth, and without any opening whatever, is the best scheme. Tapes are sewn along its ridge. These you tie to the ridge pole or rope of the tent—on the inside of course. The cheesecloth structure thus hangs straight down. When not in use it is thrust to one side or the other. If flies get thick, you simply go inside and spread it out. It should be made somewhat larger in the wall than the tent so that you can weight its lower edge with fishing rods, rifles, boots, sticks, or rocks. Nothing can touch you.

"A" Tent Pitched on Treeless Ground.

## Shape of Tent

The proper shape for a tent is a matter of some discussion. Undoubtedly the lean-to is the ideal shelter so far as warmth goes. You build your fire in front, the slanting wall reflects the heat down and you sleep warm even in winter weather. In practice, however, the lean-to is not always an undiluted joy. Flies can get in for one thing, and a heavy rainstorm can suck around the corner for another. In these circumstances four walls are highly desirable.

On the other hand a cold snap makes a wall tent into a cold storage vault. Tent stoves are little devils. They are either red hot or stone cold, and even when doing their best, there is always a northwest corner that declines to be thawed out. A man feels the need of a camp fire, properly constructed.

## "A" Tent the Best

For three seasons I have come gradually to thinking that an A or wedge tent is about the proper thing. In event of that rainstorm or those flies its advantages are obvious. When a cold snap comes along, you simply pull up the stakes along one side, tie the loops of that wall to the same stakes that hold down the other wall—and there is your lean-to all ready for the fire.

When you get your tent made, have them insert grommets in each peak. Through these you will run a light line. By tying each end of the line to a tree or sapling, staking out the four corners of your tent, and then tightening the line by wedging under it (and outside the tent, of course) a forked pole, your tent is up in a jiffy. Where you cannot

Method of Tightening Rope.

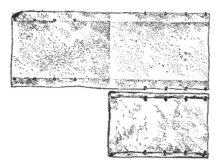

Tarpaulin, Open and Folded.

find two trees handily placed, poles crossed make good supports front and rear. The line passes over them and to a stake in the ground. These are quick pitches for a brief stop. By such methods an "A" tent is erected as quickly as a "pyramid," a miner's, or any of the others. In permanent camp, you will cut poles and do a shipshape job.

## Uses of the Tarpaulin

Often, however, you will not need to burden yourself with even as light a tent as I have described. This is especially true on horseback trips in the mountains. There you will carry a tarpaulin. This is a strip of canvas or Pantasote 6 x 16 or 17 feet.

During the daytime it is folded and used to protect the top packs from dust, wet, and abrasion. At night you spread it, make your bed on one half of it, and fold the other half over the outside. This arrangement will fend quite a shower. In case of continued or heavy rain, you stretch a pack rope between two trees or crossed poles, and suspend the tarp over it tent wise, tying down the corners by means of lead ropes. Two tarps make a commodious tent. If you happen to be alone, a saddle blanket will supplement the tarp to give some sort of protection to your feet, and, provided it is stretched tightly, will shed quite a downpour.

The tarp, as I have said, should measure 6 x 16. If of canvas, do not get it too heavy, as then it will be stiff and hard to handle. About a 10-ounce duck is the proper thing. After you have bought it, lay it out on the floor folded once, as it will be when you have made your bed in it. To the lower half and on both edges, as it lies there, sew a half dozen snap hooks. To the upper canvas, but about 6 inches in from the edge, sew corresponding rings for the snap hooks. Thus on a cold night you can bundle yourself in without leaving cracks along the edges to admit the chilly air.

## Rubber Blankets

In the woods you will want furthermore a rubber blanket. This is unnecessary when the tarpaulin is used. Buy a good poncho. Poor quality sticks badly should it chance to become overheated by the sun.

## Blankets

A six- or seven-pound blanket of the best quality is heavy enough. The gray army blanket, to be purchased sometimes at the military stores, is good, as is also the "three-point" blanket issued by the Hudson's Bay Company. The cost is from $6 to $8. One is enough. You will find that another suit of underwear is as warm as an

extra blanket, and much easier to carry. Sleeping bags I do not care for. They cannot be drawn closely to the body, and the resulting air space is difficult to warm up. A blanket you can hug close to you, thus retaining all the animal heat. Beside which a sleeping bag is heavier and more of a bother to keep well aired. If you like the thing occasionally, a few horse blanket pins will make one of your blanket.

## To Sleep Warm

It is the purpose of this book to deal with equipments rather than with methods. There are a great many very competent treatises telling you how to build your fire, pitch your tent, and all the rest of it. I have never seen described the woodsmen's method of using a blanket, however. Lie flat on your back. Spread the blanket over you. Now raise your legs rigid from the hip, the blanket of course draping over them. In two swift motions tuck first one edge under your legs from right to left, then the second edge under from left to right, and over the first edge. Lower your legs, wrap up your shoulders, and go to sleep. If you roll over, one edge will unwind but the other will tighten.

## Quilts

In the forest your rubber and woolen blankets will comprise your bed. You will soften it with pine needles or balsam. On a horseback trip, however, it is desirable to carry also an ordinary comforter, or quilt, or

Collapsible Canvas Bucket and Wash Basin.

"sogun." You use it under you. Folded once, so as to afford two thicknesses, it goes far toward softening granite country. By way of a gentle hint, if you will spread your saddle blankets *beneath* your tarp, they will help a lot, and you will get none of the horsey aroma.

## Pillows

A pillow can be made out of a little bag of muslin or cotton or denim. In it you stuff an extra shirt, or your sweater, or some such matter. A very small "goose hair" pillow may be thrust between the folds of your blanket when you have a pack horse. It will not be large enough all by itself, but with a sweater or a pair of trousers beneath it will be soft and easy to a tired head. Have its cover of brown denim.

## Pails

On a pack trip a pail is a necessity which is not recognized in the forest, where you can dip your cup or kettle direct into the stream. Most packers carry a galvanized affair, which they turn upside down on top of the pack. There it rattles and bangs against every overhead obstruction on the trail, and ends by being battered to leakiness. A bucket made of heavy brown duck, with a wire hoop hemmed in by way of rim, and a light rope for handle carries just as much water, holds it as well, and has the great advantage of collapsing flat.

## Wash Basins and Wash Tubs

A wash basin built on the same principle is often a veritable godsend, and a man can even carry a similar contrivance big enough for a washtub without adding appreciably to the bulk or weight of his animal's pack. Crushed flat all three take up in thickness about the space of one layer of blanket, and the weight of the lot is just a pound and a half.

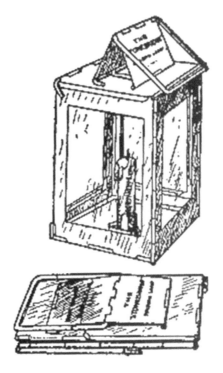

Folding Lantern.

## Lanterns

The Stonebridge folding candle lantern is the best I know of. It folds quite flat, has four mica windows, and is easily put together. The measurements, folded, are only 6 x 4 inches by 1–2 inches thick, and its weight but 13 ounces. The manufacturers make the same lantern in aluminum, but I found it too easily bent to stand the rough handling incidental to a horse trip. The steel lantern costs one dollar.

## Hatchets

If you carry an ax at all, do not try to compromise on a light one. I never use such an implement in the woods. A light hatchet is every bit as good for the purpose of firewood, and better when it is a question of tent poles or pegs. Read Nessmuk's *Woodcraft* on this subject. The Marble Safety Axe is the best, both because of the excellent steel used in its manufacture, and because of the ease of its transportation. I generally carry mine in my hip pocket. Get the metal handle and heaviest weight. I have traveled a considerable part of the Canadian forests with no other implement of the sort.

## Axes

On a horseback trip in the mountains, however, this will not suffice. Often you will be called on to clear trail, to cut timber for trail construction, or to make a footing over some ultra-tempestuous

streamlet. You might peck away until further orders with your little hatchet without much luck. Then you need an ax—not a "half ax," nor a "three-quarter ax"—but a full five-pound weapon with an edge you could shave with. And you should know how to use it. "Chewing a log in two" is a slow and unsatisfactory business.

To keep this edge you will carry a file and a water whetstone. Use your hatchet as much as possible, take care of how and what you chop, and do not wait until the ax gets really dull before having recourse to your file and stone. It is a long distance to a grindstone. Wes Thompson expressed the situation well. He watched the Kid's efforts for a moment in silence.

"Kid," said he sorrowfully at last, "you'll have to make your choice. Either you do *all the chopping or none of it.*"

## Repairs

Needle, thread, a waxed end, and a piece of buckskin for strings and patches completes the ordinary camp outfit. Your repair kit needs additions when applied to mountain trips, but that question will come up under another heading.

| SUMMARY | |
|---|---|
| **Minimum for comfort** | **Maximum** |
| Silk tent (sometimes) | Tarpaulin |
| Rubber blanket | Blanket |
| Blanket | Comforter |
| Pillow case of denim | Small pillow |
| Pocket ax | Canvas bucket |
| File and whetstone | Canvas wash basin |
| Needle and thread | Canvas wash tub |
| Waxed end | Candle lantern and candles |
| Piece of buckskin | Pocket ax |
| | 5-pound ax |
| | File and whetstone |
| | Needle and thread |
| | Waxed end |
| | Piece of buckskin |

# Hiking and Building a Lean-To

## By H. W. Gibson, Boys' Work Secretary, Young Men's Christian Association Massachusetts and Rhode Island

Several things should be remembered when going on a hike: First, avoid long distances. A foot-weary, muscle-tired and temper-tried, hungry group of boys is surely not desirable. There are a lot of false notions about courage and bravery and grit that read well in print, but fail miserably in practice, and long hikes for boys is one of the most glaring of these notions. Second, have a leader who will set a good easy pace, say two or three miles an hour, prevent the boys from excessive water drinking, and assign the duties of pitching camp, etc. Third, observe these two rules given by an old woodsman: (1) Never walk over anything you can walk around; (2) never step on anything that you can step over. Every time you step on anything you lift the weight of your body. Why lift extra weight when tramping? Fourth, carry with you only the things absolutely needed, rolled in blankets, poncho army style.

Before starting on a hike, study carefully the road maps, and take them with you on the walk for frequent reference. The best maps are those of the United States Geological Survey, costing five cents each. The map is published in atlas sheets, each sheet representing a small, quadrangular district. Send to the superintendent of documents at Washington, DC, for a list.

For tramping the boy needs the right kind of a shoe, or the

trip will be a miserable failure. A light-soled or a light-built shoe is not suited for mountain work or even for an ordinary hike. The feet will blister and become "road weary." The shoe must be neither too big, too small, nor too heavy, and be amply broad to give the toes plenty of room. The shoe should be water-tight. A medium weight, high-topped lace shoe is about right. Bathing the feet at the springs and streams along the road will be refreshing, if not indulged in too frequently. See chapter on "Health and Endurance" for care of the feet and proper way of walking.

It is well to carry a spare shirt hanging down the back with the sleeves tied around the neck. Change when the shirt you are wearing becomes too wet with perspiration.

The most practical and inexpensive pack is the one made for the Boy Scouts of America. (Price 60 cents.) It is about 14 x 20 inches square, and 6 inches thick, made of water-proof canvas with shoulder-straps, and will easily hold everything needed for a tramping trip.

A few simple remedies for bruises, cuts, etc., should be taken along by the leader. You may not need them and some may poke fun at them, but, as the old lady said, "You can't always sometimes tell." The amount and kind of provisions must be determined by the locality and habitation.

## The Lean-to

Fig. 1. Frame of lean-to.

Reach the place where you are going to spend the night in plenty of time to build your lean-to, and make your bed for the night. Select your camping spot with reference to water, wood, drainage, and material for your lean-to. Choose a dry, level place, the ground just sloping enough to insure the water running away from your lean-to in case of rain. In building your lean-to look for a couple of good trees standing from 8 to 10 feet apart with branches from 6 to 8 feet above the ground. By studying the illustration (Fig. 1) you will be able to build a very serviceable shack, affording protection from the dews and rain. While two or more boys are building the shack, another should be gathering firewood and preparing the meal, while another should be cutting and bringing in as many soft, thick tips of trees as possible, for the roof of the shack and the beds.

How to thatch the lean-to is shown in illustration Fig. 2. If the camp site is to be used for several days, two lean-tos may be built facing each other, about 6 feet apart. This will make a very comfortable camp, as a small fire can be built between the two thus giving warmth and light.

Fig. 2. Method of thatching.

## The Bed

On the floor of your lean-to lay a thick layer of the fans or branches of a balsam or hemlock, with the convex side up, and the butts of the stems toward the foot of the bed. Now thatch this over with more fans by thrusting the butt ends through the first layer at a slight angle toward the head of the bed, so that the soft tips will curve toward the foot of the bed, and be sure to make the head of your bed away from the opening of the lean-to and the foot toward the opening. Over this bed spread your rubber blankets or ponchos with rubber side down, your sleeping blanket on top, and you will be surprised how soft, springy, and fragrant a bed you have upon which to rest your "weary frame" and sing with the poet:

"Then the pine boughs croon me a lullaby,  And trickle the white moonbeams/ To my face on the balsam where I lie/ While the owl hoots at my dreams."

—*J. George Frederick.*

## Hot-Stone Wrinkle

If the night bids fair to be cold, place a number of stones about 6 or 8 inches in diameter near the fire, so that they will get hot. These can then be placed at the feet, back, etc., as needed, and will be found good "bed warmers." When a stone loses its heat, it is replaced near the fire and a hot one taken. If too hot, wrap the stone in a shirt or sweater or wait for it to cool off.

Boys desire adventure. This desire may be gratified by the establishment of night watchers in relays of two boys each, every two hours. Their imaginations will be stirred by the resistless attraction of the campfire and the sound of the creatures that creep at night.

# The Navajo Hogan, Hornaday Dugout, and Sod House

If the reader has ever built little log-cabin traps he knows just how to build a Navajo hogan or at least the particular Navajo hogan shown by Figs. 148 and 150. This one is six-sided and may be improved by notching the logs (Figs. 162, 164, 165) and building them up one on top of the other, dome-shaped, to the required height. After laying some rafters for the roof and leaving a hole for the chimney, the frame is complete. In hot countries no chimney hole is left in the roof, because the people there do not build fires inside the house; they go indoors to keep cool and not to get warm; but the Navajo hogan also makes a good cold-country house in places where people really need a fire. Make the doorway by leaving an opening

(Fig. 150) and chinking the logs along the opening to hold them in place until the door-jamb is nailed or pegged to them, and then build a shed entranceway (Fig. 153), which is necessary because the slanting sides of the house with an unroofed doorway have no protection against the free entrance of dust and rain or snow, and every section of this country is subject to visits from one of these elements. The house is covered with brush, browse, or sod.

## Log Dugout

Fig. 152 shows how to make a log dugout by building the walls of the log cabin in a level place dug for it in the bank. Among the log cabins proper (Figs. 162 and 166)

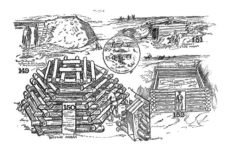

Fig. 149. Fig. 150. Fig. 151. Fig. 152. Fig. 153. Fig. 154.

we tell how to notch the logs for this purpose.

## Forms of Dugouts and Mound Shacks

Fig. 151 shows one of these log dugouts which I have named the Hornaday from the fact that Doctor William Hornaday happens to be sitting in front of the one represented in the sketch. Fig. 154 shows a dugout with walls made of sod which is piled up like stones in a stone wall. The roofs of all these are very flat and made of logs (Figs. 54, 55, and 56), often with a log pegged to the rafters above the eaves to hold the sod. All such houses are good in dry countries, cold countries, and countries frequented by tornadoes or by winds severe enough to blow down ordinary camps.

The Navajo hogan is an easy sort of a house for boys to build because the lads may use small poles in place of logs with which to build the camp and thus make the labor light enough to suit their undeveloped muscles, but the next illustration shows how to build an American boy's hogan of milled lumber such as one can procure in thickly settled parts of the country.

# How to Build an American Boy's Hogan

The first time any working plans of an underground house for boys were published was when an article by the present writer on the subject appeared in the *Ladies' Home Journal*. Afterward it was published with a lot of similar material in "The Jack of All Trades." Since then other writers have not hesitated to use the author's sketches with very little alteration; imitation is the sincerest compliment, although it is not always fair, but it does, however, show the popularity of the underground-house idea.

The American boy's hogan may be built like the preceding shacks of the material found in the woods or it may be constructed of old boards and waste material to be found in village back yards or on the farm, or, if the boys have the price or if they can interest their fathers or uncles in their scheme, it may be built of milled lumber procured at the lumber-yard.

## Frame

Procure some good, sound planks and some pieces of two by four with which to build your frame. The hogan should be large enough to allow room for a table made of a packing-case, some benches, stools, or chairs, and the ceilings should be high enough for the tallest boy to stand erect without bumping his head.

## Furniture

One funny thing about this house is that it must be furnished before it is built, because the doorway and passageway will be too small to admit any furniture larger than a stool. Select or make your furniture and have it ready, then decide upon the location of your hogan, which should be, like the Western dugouts, on the edge of some bank (Fig. 158). In this diagram the dotted line shows how the bank originally sloped.

The original American boy's hogan or underground house.

## Foundation

The real hard work connected with this is the digging of the foundation; one Y. M. C. A. man started to build one of these hogans, but he "weakened" before he had the foundation dug. He wrote the author a long letter complaining of the hard work; at the same time the author was receiving letters from *boys* telling how much fun they had in building and finishing their underground houses.

## Caves

Ever since *Robinson Crusoe* and *Swiss Family Robinson* were written, cave houses have been particularly attractive to boys; no doubt they were just as attractive before these books were written, and that may be the reason the books themselves are so popular; at any rate, when the author was a small boy he was always searching for natural caves, or trying to dig them for himself, and so were all of his companions. One of the most charming features of the "Tom Sawyer" and "Huckleberry Finn" stories is that part connected with the cave.

## Dangerous Caves

The trouble is that with caves, which the boys dig for themselves, there is always serious danger of the roof falling in and smothering the young troglodytes, but a properly built underground hogan is perfectly safe from such accidents.

## Framing

After you have levelled off the foundation, erect the rear posts of 2-by-4s A, B and C, D (Fig. 156). These posts should be of the same height and tall enough to allow the roof to slant toward the front as in Fig. 155. The front posts E, F and G, H, although shorter than the back posts, should be tall enough to allow headroom. One, two, or three more posts may be erected between the post A, B and the post C, D if additional strength is required. The same is true of the sides, and in place of having only one post in the middle of each side (M, N and O, P, Fig. 156), there may be two or three posts, all according to the size of the house you are building; the main point is to make *a compact and strong box* of your framework so that in the wet weather the banks surrounding it will not be tempted to push in the sides and spoil your house.

## Decaying Wood

Locust, chestnut, and cedar will last longer than other varieties of wood when exposed to contact with damp earth, but common wood, which rots easily, may be protected by preservatives, one of which is boiled linseed-oil with pulverized charcoal stirred into it until a black paint is produced. Some people say that a coat of charcoal paint will preserve even a basswood fence post for a lifetime, and if that is true a hogan protected by a coating upon the outside of paint made by stirring fine charcoal into boiled linseed-oil until it is as thick as paint will last longer than any of my readers will have occasion to use the hogan for a playhouse. Erect the frame (Fig. 156) by having some boys hold the uprights in place until they can be secured with temporary braces like those shown running diagonally across from B to E and A to F. You may then proceed to board up the sides from the outside of the frame by slipping the planks between the frame and the bank and then nailing from the inside wherever you lack room upon the outside to swing your hammer. The door-jambs *I*, *J* and *K*, *L* will help support the roof.

## The Roof

The roof may be made of lumber, as shown by Fig. 160, or it may be made of poles like those shown on the Wyoming Olebo (Fig. 236), or it may be made of planks and covered with tar paper (Figs. 296, 297, 298, and 299), or it may be shingled, using barrel staves for shingles, or covered with bits of old tin roofing tacked over the planking—or anything, in fact, which will keep out the water. As for looks, that will not count because the roof is to be afterward covered with sod.

## Cliff-House Roof

If you wish to make the roof as the cliff-dwellers made theirs, put your biggest logs crosswise from *A*, *M*, *E* to *C*, *O*, *G* of your house

for rafters, and across the larger logs lay a lot of small poles as close together as may be, running from the back to the front of the house. Fill in the cracks between with moss or calk them with dry grass; on them place a layer of brush, browse, or small sticks and over this a thick coating of clay, hard-pan, or ordinary mud and pack it down hard by tramping it with your feet until it becomes a smooth and tightly packed crust; over this you can put your sod and weeds to conceal your secret passageway.

To make the frame for the underground hall or passageway (Fig. 156), first nail *Q*, *S* across the door-jambs to form the top to the doorway, after which put in the supports *Q*, *R* and *S*, *T*. Next build the frame *U*, *V*, *X*, *W* and join it to *Q*, *S* by the two pieces *Q*, *U* and *S*, *V* and put in the middle frame support marked ZZZZ.

The passageway should be about 6 feet long and the front doorway (*U*, *V*, *X*, *W*, Figs. 156 and 157) of sufficient size to enable you to creep through with comfort. The bottom piece W, X can be nailed to a couple of sticks driven in the ground for that purpose. The next thing in order is the floor, and to make this firm you must lay a number of 2-by-4s parallel to B, D and F, H and see that they are level. You will need a number of shorter pieces of the same material to run parallel to F, H and W, X for the hall floor, as may be seen in Fig. 157. Across these nail your floor securely as shown in Fig. 155.

There are no windows shown in the diagram, but if the builders wish one it can be placed immediately over the entrance or hallway in the frame marked I, K, Q, S (Fig. 156), in which case the top covering of dirt must be shovelled away from it to admit the light in the same manner that it is in the dugout shown in Fig. 142 and also in the small sketch (Fig. 154). The ventilator shown in Fig. 155 may be replaced, if thought desirable, by a chimney for an open fire. On account of the need of ventilation a stove would not be the proper thing for an underground house, but an open fire would help the ventilation. In the diagram the ventilator is set over a square hole in the roof; it may be made of a barrel or barrels, with the heads knocked out, placed over the hole in the roof, or kegs, according to the size of the roof. When your house is complete fill in the dirt around the edges, pack it down good and hard by the use of a piece of scantling two-by-four or four-by-four as a rammer, then cover the roof with small sticks and fine brush and sod it with growing weeds or grass.

## The Door

You should have a good, stout front door (Fig. 157) and a padlock with which to secure it from trespassers.

## Aures Hinge

A rustic hinge may be made by splitting a forked branch (Fig. 157 C) and using the two pieces nailed to the sides of the door-jambs (Fig. 157 A) to hold the round ends of the rod (Fig. 157 B) run through them. The middle of the B stick is flattened to fit on the surface of the door to which it is nailed. This hinge was invented by Scout Victor Aures of stockade 41144 of Boy Pioneers of America and a description with neat diagrams sent by the inventor to his chief. When all is completed you can conceal the ventilator with dry brush or by planting weeds or shrubs around it, which will not interfere with the ventilation but will conceal the suspicious-looking pipe protruding from the ground. The top of the ventilator should be protected by slats, as in Fig. 161, or by wire netting with about 1/4-inch mesh in order to keep small animals from jumping or hopping down into your clubhouse. Of course, a few toads and frogs, field mice and chipmunks, or even some lizards and harmless snakes would not frighten any real boy, but at the same time they do not want any such creatures living in the same house with them.

## Trapdoor

In place of a ventilator or chimney a trapdoor may be placed in the roof and used as a secret entrance, access to inside being had by a ladder. A description of an appropriate ladder follows (Figs. 169 and 170).

Fig. 159 shows a rude way to make a chandelier, and as long as your candles burn brightly you may know that the air in your little hogan is pure and fresh. When such a chandelier is used pieces of tin should be nailed above the candles to prevent the heat from burning holes through the roof.

# Where to Find Mountain Goose. How to Pick and Use Its Feathers.

I t may be necessary for me to remind the boys that they must use the material at hand in building their shacks, shelters, sheds, and shanties, and that they are very fortunate if their camp is located in a country where the mountain goose is to be found.

## The Mountain Goose

From Labrador down to the northwestern borders of New England and New York and from thence to southwestern Virginia, North Carolina, and Tennessee, the woodsman and camper may make their beds from the feathers of the "mountain goose." The mountain goose is also found inhabiting the frozen soil of Alaska and following the Pacific and the Rocky Mountains the Abies make

their dwelling-place as far south as Guatemala. Consequently, the Abies, or mountain goose, should be a familiar friend of all the scouts who live in the mountainous country, north, south, east, and west.

## Sapin—Cho-kho-tung

I forgot to say that the mountain goose (Figs. 1 and 2) is not a bird but a tree. It is humorously called a goose by the woodsmen because they all make their beds of its "feathers." It is the *sapin* of the French-Canadians, the *cho-kho-tung* of the New York Indians, the balsam of the tenderfoot, the Christmas tree of the little folk, and that particular Coniferæ known by the dry-as-dust botanist as Abies. There is nothing in nature which has a wilder, more sylvan and charming perfume than the balsam, and the scout who has not slept in the woods on a balsam bed has a pleasure in store for him.

## Balsam

The leaves of the balsam are blunt or rounded at the ends and some of them are even dented or notched in place of being sharp-pointed. Each spine or leaf is a scant 1 inch in length and very flat; the upper part is grooved and of a dark bluish-green color. The under-side is much lighter, often almost silvery white. The balsam blossoms in April or May, and the fruit or cones stand upright on the branches. These vary from 2 to 4 inches in length. The balsam-trees are seldom large, not many of them being over 60 feet high with trunks from 1 to less than 3 feet through. The bark on the trunks is gray in color and marked with horizontal rows of blisters. Each of these contains a small, sticky, sap-like glycerine.

Fig. 1. Fig. 2. Fig. 3. Fig. 4. Fig. 5. Fig. 6. Fig. 7.

Fig. 1 shows the cone and leaves of one of the Southern balsams known as the she-balsam, and Fig. 2 shows the celebrated balsam-fir tree of the north country, cone and branch.

## Balsam Beds

The balsam bed is made of the small twigs of balsam trees. In gathering these, collect twigs 18 inches long (to be used as the foundation of the bed) to 10 or 12 inches long (for the top layer). If you want to rest well, do not economize on the amount you gather; many a time I have had my bones ache as a result of being too tired to make my bed properly and attempting to sleep on a thin layer of boughs.

If you attempt to chop off the boughs of balsam they will resent your effort by springing back and slapping you in the face. You can cut them with your knife, but it is slow work and will blister your hands. Take twig by twig with the thumb and fingers (the thumb on top, pointing toward the tip of the bough, and the two forefingers underneath); press down with the thumb, and with a twist of the wrist you can snap the twigs like pipe-stems. Fig. 3 shows two views of the hands in a proper position to snap off twigs easily and clean. The one at the left shows the hand as it would appear looking down upon it; the one at the right shows the view as you look at it from the side.

## Packing Boughs

After collecting a handful of boughs, string them on a stick which you have previously prepared (Fig. 4). This stick should be of strong, green hardwood, 4 or 5 feet long with a fork about 6 inches long left on it at the butt end to keep the boughs from sliding off, and sharpened at the upper end so that it can be easily poked through a handful of boughs. String the boughs on this stick as you would string fish, but do it one handful at a time, allowing the butts to point in different directions. It is astonishing to see the amount of boughs you can carry when strung on a stick in this manner and thrown over your shoulder as in Fig. 5. If you have a lash rope, place the boughs on a loop of the rope, as in Fig. 6, then bring the two ends of the rope up through the loop and sling the bundle on your back.

## Clean Your Hands

When you have finished gathering the material for your bed your hands will be covered with a sticky sap, and, although they will be a sorry sight, a little lard or baking grease will soften the pitchy substance so that it may be washed off with soap and water.

## How to Make Beds

To make your bed, spread a layer of the larger boughs on the ground; commence at the head and shingle them down to the foot so that the tips point toward the head of the bed, overlapping the butts (Fig. 7). Continue this until your mattress is thick enough to make a soft couch upon which you can sleep as comfortably as you do at home. Cover the couch with one blanket and use the bag containing your coat, extra clothes, and sweater for a pillow. Then if you do not sleep well, you must blame the cook.

## Other Bedding

If you should happen to be camping in a country destitute of balsam, hemlock, or pine, you can make a good spring mattress by collecting small green branches of any sort of tree which is springy and elastic. Build the mattress as already described. On top of this put a thick layer of hay, straw, or dry leaves or even green material, provided you have a rubber blanket or poncho to cover the latter. In Kentucky I have made a mattress of this description and covered the branches with a thick layer of the purple blossoms of ironweed; over this I spread a rubber army blanket to keep out the moisture from the green stuff and on top of this made my bed with my other blankets. It was as comfortable a couch as I have ever slept on; in fact, it was literally a bed of flowers.

## The Half-Cave Shelter

The first object of a roof of any kind is protection against the weather; no shelter is necessary in fair weather unless the sun in the day or the dampness or coolness of the night cause discomfort. In parts of the West there is so little rain that a tent is often an unnecessary burden, but in the East and the other parts of the country some sort of shelter is necessary for health and comfort.

The original American was always quick to see the advantages offered by an overhanging cliff for a camp site (Figs. 9, 10). His simple camps all through the arid Southwest had gradually turned into carefully built houses long before we came here. The overhanging cliffs protected the buildings from the rain and weather, and the site was easily defended from enemies. But while these cliff-dwellings had reached the dignity of castles in the Southwest, in the Eastern States—Pennsylvania, for instance—the Iroquois Indians were making primitive camps and using every available overhanging cliff for that purpose.

Today any one may use a pointed stick on the floor of one of these half caves and unearth, as I have done, numerous potsherds, mussel shells, bone awls, flint arrow-heads, split bones of large game animals, and the burnt wood of centuries of campfires which tell the tale of the first lean-to shelter used by camping man in America.

## Half Caves

The projecting ledges of bluestone that have horizontal seams form half caves from the falling apart of the lower layers of the cliff caused by rain and ice and often aided by the fine roots of the black birch, rock oak, and other plants, until nature has worked long enough as a quarry-man and produced half caves large enough to shelter a stooping man (Figs. 8, 9, and 10).

Although not always necessary, it is sometimes best to make a shelter for the open face of such a cave, even if we only need it for a temporary camp (Fig. 10); this may be done by resting poles slanting against the face of the cliff and over these making a covering of balsam, pine, hemlock, palmetto, palm branches, or any available material for thatch to shed the rain and prevent it driving under the cliff to wet our bedding.

## Walls

It is not always necessary to thatch the wall; a number of green boughs with leaves adhering may be rested against the cliffs and will answer for that purpose. Set the boughs upside down so that they will shed the rain and not hold it so as to drip into camp. Use your common sense and gumption, which will teach you that all the boughs should point downward and not upward as most of them naturally grow. I am careful to call your attention to this because I lately saw some men teaching Boy Scouts how to make camps and they were placing the boughs for the lads around the shelter with their branches pointing upward in such a manner that they could not shed the rain. These instructors were city men and apparently thought that the boughs were for no other purpose than to give privacy to the occupants of the shelter, forgetting that in the wilds the wilderness itself furnishes privacy.

The half cave was probably the first lean-to or shelter in this country, but overhanging cliffs are not always found where we wish to make our camp and we must resort to other forms of shelter and the use of other material in such localities.

The half-cave shelter.

# How to Make the Fallen-Tree Shelter and the Scout-Master

Now that you know how to make a bed in a half cave, we will take up the most simple and primitive manufactured shelters.

## Fallen-Tree Shelter

For a one-man one-night stand, select a thick-foliaged fir-tree and cut it partly through the trunk so that it will fall as shown in Fig. 11; then trim off the branches on the under-side so as to leave room to make your bed beneath the branches; next trim the branches off the top or roof of the trunk and with them thatch the roof. Do this by setting the branches with their butts up as shown in the right-hand shelter of Fig. 13, and then thatch with smaller browse as described in making the bed.

This will make a cozy one-night shelter.

## The Scout-Master

Or take three forked sticks (*A*, *B*, and *C*, Fig. 12), and interlock the forked ends so that they will stand as shown in Fig. 12. Over this framework rest branches with the butt ends up as shown in the right-hand shelter (Fig. 13), or lay a number of poles as shown in the left-hand figure (Fig. 12) and thatch this with browse as illustrated by the left-hand shelter in Fig. 13, or take elm, spruce, or birch bark and shingle as in Fig. 14. These shelters may be built for one boy or they may be made large enough for several men. They may be thatched with balsam, spruce, pine, or hemlock boughs, or with cat-tails, rushes (see Figs. 66 and 69), or any kind of long-stemmed weeds or palmetto leaves.

## To Peel Bark

In the first place, I trust that the reader has enough common sense and sufficient love of the woods to prevent him from killing or marring and disfiguring trees where trees are not plenty, and this restriction includes all settled or partially settled parts of the country. But in the real forests and wilderness, miles and miles away from human habitation, there are few campers and consequently there will be fewer trees injured, and these few will not be missed.

## Selecting Bark

To get the birch bark, select a tree with a smooth trunk devoid of branches and, placing skids for the trunk to fall upon (Fig. 38), fell the tree (see Figs. 112, 113, 114, 115, 116, 117, and 118), and then cut a circle around the

trunk at the two ends of the log and a slit from one circle clean up to the other circle (Fig. 38); next, with a sharp stick shaped like a blunt-edged chisel, pry off the bark carefully until you take the piece off in one whole section. If it is spruce bark or any other bark you seek, hunt through the woods for a comparatively smooth trunk and proceed in the same manner as with the birch. To take it off a standing tree, cut one circle down at the butt and another as high as you can reach (Fig. 118) and slit it along a perpendicular line connecting the two cuts as in Fig. 38. This will doubtless in time kill the tree, but far from human habitations the few trees killed in this manner may do the forest good by giving more room

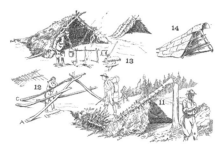

One-night shelter. The fallen tree and the scout-master.

for others to grow. Near town or where the forests are small use the bark from the old dead trees.

## Using Bark

To shingle with bark, cut the bark in convenient sections, commence at the bottom, place one piece of bark set on edge flat against the wall of your shelter, place a piece of bark next to it in the same manner, allowing the one edge to overlap the first piece a few inches, and so on all the way around your shack; then place a layer of bark above this in the same manner as the first one, the end edges overlapping, the bottom edges also overlapping the first row 3 or 4 inches or even more. Hold these pieces of bark in place by stakes driven in the ground against them or poles laid over them, according to the shape or form of your shelter. Continue thus to the comb of the roof, then over the part where the bark of the sides meets on the top lay another layer of bark covering the crown, ridge, comb, or apex and protecting it from the rain. In the wigwam-shaped shelters, or rather I should say those of teepee form, the point of the cone or pyramid is left open to serve as chimney for smoke to escape.

# How to Make the Adirondack, the Wick-Up, the Bark Teepee, the Pioneer, and the Scout

## The Adirondack

The next shelter is what is generally known as the Adirondack shelter, which is a lean-to open in the front like a "Baker" or a "Dan Beard" tent. Although it is popularly called the Adirondack camp, it antedates the time when the Adirondacks were first used as a fashionable resort. Daniel Boone was wont to make such a camp in the forests of Kentucky. The lean-to or Adirondack camp is easily made and very popular. Sometimes two of them are built facing each other with an open space between for the campfire. But the usual manner is to set up two uprights as in Fig. 15, then lay a crosspiece through the crotches and rest poles against this crosspiece (Fig. 16). Over these poles other poles are laid horizontally and the roof thatched with browse by the method shown by Fig. 6, but here the tips of the browse must point down and be held in place by other poles (Fig. 10) on top of it. Sometimes a log is put at the bottom of the slanting poles and sometimes more logs are placed as shown in Figs. 15 and 16 and the space between them floored with balsam or browse.

## The Scout

Where birch bark is obtainable it is shingled with slabs of this bark as already described, and as shown in Fig. 17, the bark being held in place on the roof by poles laid over it and on the side by stakes being driven in the ground outside of the bark to hold it in place as in Fig. 17.

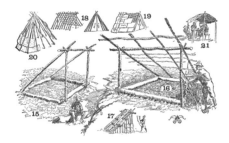

The Adirondack. The scout, the pioneer, and the bark teepee.

## The Pioneer

Fig. 18 shows the Pioneer, a tent form of shack, and Fig. 19 shows how the bark is placed like shingles overlapping each other so as to shed the rain. The doorway of the tent shack is made by leaning poles against forked sticks, their butts forming a semicircle in front, or rather the arc of a circle, and by bracing them against the forked stick fore and aft they add stability to the structure.

## Bark Teepee

Or you may, if you choose, lash three sticks together at the top ends, spread them in the form of a tripod, then lay other sticks against them, their butts forming a circle in the form of a teepee (Fig. 20).

Commence at the bottom as you do in shingling a roof and place sections of birch bark around, others above them overlapping them, and hold them in place by resting poles against them. If your camp is to be occupied for a week or so, it may be convenient to build a wick-up shelter as a dining-room like the one shown in Fig. 21. This is made with six uprights, two to hold the ridge-pole and two to hold the eaves, and may be shingled over with browse or birch, elm, spruce, or other bark; shingle with the browse in the same manner as that described for the bark, beginning at the eaves and allowing each row of browse to overlap the butts of the one below it.

## How to Make Beaver Mats Without Injury to the Trees

### Material

In building a shelter use every and any thing handy for the purpose;

ofttimes an uprooted tree will furnish a well-made adobe wall, where the spreading roots have torn off the surface soil as the tree fell and what was the under-side is now an exposed wall of clay, against which you may rest the poles for the roof of a lean-to. Or the side of the cliff (Fig. 23) may offer you the same opportunity. Maybe two or three trees will be found willing to act as uprights (Fig. 24). Where you use a wall of any kind, rock, roots, or bank, it will, of course, be necessary to have your doorway at one side of the shack as in Fig. 23. The upright poles may be on stony ground where their butts cannot well be planted in the earth, and there it will be necessary to brace them with slanting poles (Fig. 25). Each camp will offer problems of its own, problems which add much to the interest and pleasure of camp making.

## Beaver Mat

The beaver-mat camp is a new one and, under favorable conditions,

a good one. Cut your poles the length required for the framework of the sides, lash them together with the green rootlets of the tamarack or strips of bark of the papaw, elm, cedar, or the inside bark of the chestnut (A, Fig. 22); then make a bed of browse of any kind handy, but make it in the manner described for making balsam beds (Fig. 7). You will, of course, thatch so that when the side is erected it is shingled like a house, the upper rows overlapping the lower ones. Then lash a duplicate frame over the browse-padded frame and the side is complete (B, Fig. 22). Make the other side or sides and the roof (C, Fig. 22) in the same manner, after which it is a simple matter to erect your shack (Fig. 22, and E, Fig. 22).

Shelters adapted to conditions.

The great advantage of this sort of shelter is that it is much easier to do your thatching on the ground than on standing walls, and also, when done, it is so compact as to be practically water-proof.

## Roofs

After the walls are erected, a beaver-mat roof may be placed upon them or a roof made on a frame such as shown in Fig. 28 and thatched with small sticks over which a thatch of straw, hay, rushes (Figs. 66 and 69), or browse may be used to shed the rain.

One great advantage which recommends the beaver-mat and fagot camp to lovers of nature and students of forestry lies in the fact that it is unnecessary to cut down or destroy a single large or valuable young tree in order to procure the material necessary to make the camp. Both of these camps can be made in forest lands by using the lower branches of the trees, which, when properly cut close to the trunk (Fig. 121), do not injure the standing timber. The fagot hut may be made into a permanent camp by plastering the outside with soft mud or clay and treating the inside walls in the same manner, thus transforming it into an adobe shack.

# Birch Bark or Tar Paper Shack

A description of the Pontiac was first published in my *Field and Forest Handy Book*, a book which contains several shelters similar to the ones here given, most of which were originally made for Caspar Whitney while he was editor of *Outing*.

## The Pontiac

The Pontiac, as here given, is my own design and invention (Fig. 36). It is supposed to be shingled with birch bark, but, as is the case with all these camps, other bark may be substituted for the birch, and, if no bark is within reach and you are near enough to civilization, tar paper makes an excellent substitute. Fig. 37 shows the framework of a Pontiac with a ridge-pole, but the ridge-pole is not necessary and the shack may be built without it, as shown in Figs. 36 and 39, where the rafter poles rest upon the two side-plates over which they project to form the apex of the roof. In Fig. 39, although the side-plates are drawn, the rafter or roof poles are not because the diagram is supposed to be a sort of X-ray affair to show the internal construction. The opening for smoke need not be more than half as large as it is in Fig. 39 and it may be covered up in inclement weather with a piece of bark so as to keep out the rain.

## Cutting Bark

Fig. 38 shows a tree felled in order to procure bark. You will note that the bark is cut round at the bottom and at the top and a slit is made connecting the two cuts as already described so that the bark may be peeled off by running a blunt instrument or a stick, whittled to the shape of a paper-cutter or dull chisel, under the edge of the bark and carefully peeling it back. If it is necessary to "tote" the bark any distance over the trail, Fig. 38 shows how to roll it up and how to bind the roll with cord or rope so that it may be slung on the back as the man is "toting" it in Fig. 36.

## Building the Pontiac

To build a Pontiac, first erect the uprights *E* and *E*, Fig. 37, then the other two similar uprights at the rear and lay the side-plates *G* in the forks of the uprights; next erect the upright *H* and one in the rear to correspond, and across this lay the ridge-pole. Next take a couple of logs and put them at the foot of the *E* poles, or, if you want more room, farther back toward where the roof poles *F* will come. Place one of these logs on top of the other as shown in Figs. 36 and 39. Keep them in place by driving sticks on each side of them. Put two more logs upon the other side of the Pontiac and then lay your roof poles or rafters up against the side-plates and over

the logs as shown in diagrams 36, 37, and 39. Fig. 36 shows the roof partially shingled and the sides partially covered, so that you may better understand how it is done.

## Shingling with Bark

Commence at the bottom and lay the first row with the edges overlapping for walls; for the roof you may lay one row of shingles from the bottom up to the ridge and hold them in place by resting a pole on them; then lay the next row of shingles alongside by slipping the edges under the first. When you have the two sides covered, put bark over the ridge as shown in Fig. 36. This will make a beautiful and comfortable little camp.

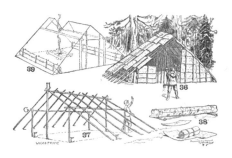

Shelters adapted to conditions.

# The Pontiac of Birch Bark

### To Keep Out Cold

Built as here described, the cold wind might come through in the winter-time, but if you can gather a lot of Sphagnum moss from the nearest swamp and cover your roof with it and then shingle that over with another layer of birch bark, the cold wind will not come through your roof. If you treat your side walls in the same manner and heap dirt up around the edges of them, you will have a comfortable winter camp.

In the winter-time you will find it very difficult to peel the birch bark or any other kind of bark, but when the sap is flowing it is not so difficult to secure bark slabs from many varieties of trees.

# More Information on the Simple Adirondack Shelter

I have a good friend who has a nice one-room cabin located at the end of a twisting dirt road in the mountains of Virginia. I was visiting him one weekend, and as I walked around admiring his new cabin, we talked about trout fishing on a remote creek that was higher in the mountains. "How would you like to hike up to the creek tomorrow for a little fishing and stay in my secret cabin?" he asked. I couldn't say yes fast enough, not so much for the fishing, but to see a cabin I had never heard about. The next afternoon, after a long hike, we reached the headwaters of the creek. It was in a gorge and looked as if no one had ever been there before. I wondered as we walked upstream how he ever got the materials in here to build a cabin. We rounded a bend in the creek, and on a knoll above the creek, I saw his secret cabin. It was an Adirondack lean-to made of logs. In front of the shelter was a well-made reflector fire pit made of rocks. It was one of the most inviting camps I think I have ever seen. We spent the cool night there as comfortably as if we were in a house. We were warm, had plenty of fresh air, and could enjoy the blaze of the fire. I wanted to stay a few more days.

The Adirondack shelter, sometimes referred to as a three-sided cabin, Appalachian Trail lean-to, or Adirondack lean-to, was born out of necessity when the American frontier was Vermont and New York. These shelters were probably first built by Native Americans of the area, but it didn't take long for the early explorers and settlers of the region to realize their value. Records show that many settlers used this type of shelter as their first home, and expanded it into a larger cabin as time permitted. I have read that a family would build a large Adirondack for the first winter on a homestead, and during the next summer build a second one facing the first, with the fire in the middle. The third year they would roof the opening between the two and wall-in the sides. It became a much larger cabin. Adirondacks have been in use ever since those early days and with good reason. When properly built and situated on a site, they make a comfortable shelter. They are inexpensive to build and last for years. Back in the mid 1930s, eleven log Adirondack shelters were built along the Appalachian Trail in Maine. Today six of those shelters are still in use. All along the Appalachian Trail, from Maine to Georgia, there are dozens of these shelters that get hard use year after year and are still very comfortable. Today the Adirondack shelter has found its way throughout North America. I visited with a Cree Indian couple in the Cassier Mountains of British Columbia and stayed in the Adirondack shelter that served as their summer home. One of the most comfortable elk camps I have ever enjoyed had Adirondack shelters for its base camp, and two of the guides lived year round in the shelters.

I felt that the Adirondack shelter belonged in a book about backcountry cabins. It is an ideal shelter for remote locations where use and/or materials may not justify a full-blown cabin. The Adirondack would be an economical starter cabin for someone on a tight budget. I am building one on a creek near our Cross Creek Hollow cabin for use during hot summer nights and as a base camp to teach my grandchildren outdoor skills. The Adirondack gives you the comfort of a cabin but requires the use of camping skills and knowledge, offering more of an outdoor experience. In short, the Adirondack is an outstanding shelter that is a lot of fun to build and to live in. With a shelter that is open on one side, orientation is especially important. To have an Adirondack shelter that is comfortable year-round, you'll need to locate the open side of the shelter opposite to the direction of the prevailing winds and storms. In other words, you want the shelter built with its back to the wind.

A second trick is to build a fire pit off the open side of the shelter so that a reflector fire can be built during cold weather. When a reflector fire is built in front of the Adirondack, it becomes an oven of sorts. The sloping roof catches the heat and throws it downward into the shelter. I have stayed in Adirondacks in sub-freezing weather and been very comfortable as long as the fire was tended. If you don't know how to build a fire, check out a camping book and learn before you build your Adirondack. It's simple to master.

Many Adirondack shelters are built in remote locations inaccessible to trucks, so by necessity are usually built from logs cut on the site. When clearing trees for an Adirondack site, it is best to try to take as many logs as you can. People are usually surprised at how many logs it takes to build an Adirondack shelter. To build an average-sized Adirondack shelter 12 feet across the front and 8 feet deep, a size that can sleep up to six people comfortably, can take up to 60 logs averaging 8 inches in diameter. Even with the logs cut on site, you will still need to pack in tools, hardware, and other building materials, such as roofing. The logs should be cut between July and August so that they peel easily. Trimming and peeling should be done when the trees are cut. Then the logs should be allowed to dry for six weeks before the shelter is built. I could spend the next dozen or so pages telling you how to build an Adirondack shelter out of logs, but that would take away from the planning theme of the book. An excellent 64-page how-to booklet can be purchased from the Maine Appalachian Trail Club (P.O. Box 283, Augusta, ME 04330) or the

Appalachian Trail Conference (P.O. Box 807, Harpers Ferry, WV 25425).

My good friend Chris Drew, Chief Ranger at Baxter State Park in Maine, builds an Adirondack shelter out of log siding that is most comfortable and easy to construct. It is simply framed in and then the log siding is nailed on. The roof can be composition roofing or metal roofing. The raised floor of the shelter serves as a sleeping platform that puts the users off the ground and closer to heat during cold-weather use. A family could construct one of these shelters during a long weekend. It will give years of service with a little periodic maintenance.

While the Adirondack is not a true cabin, it is a great temporary cabin, especially in remote areas, and would make a good shelter to build on your cabin site to stay in while you build the main cabin. It makes a great woodshed, overflow guest quarters, tool shed, or equipment building when the cabin is complete.

## Advantages of the Adirondack Shelter:

- It is an ideal shelter for remote locations where full-sized cabins are not feasible.
- It is very quick and easy to build, with little help necessary.
- Often it can be built from logs cut on the site, and can be used for other purposes later.
- It offers the basic comfort of a small cabin, yet allows the use of camping skills.
- It is the most affordable permanent shelter, and requires little maintenance.

# Set Up Your Camp

# Water

Even with global warming and the droughts we've experienced over the past decade, water in North America is plentiful, and as long as you don't waste it, there's plenty for any off-gridder in the form of groundwater and precipitation.

Some folks are fortunate enough to have direct access to lakes and streams, and they can take water easily by gravity, siphon systems, or pumps. Others of us aren't that lucky, and we'll use the next dozen pages or so to describe what we can do to get our share. In my primary home, with three residents, I average about five gallons per day for cooking and drinking. Maybe twice that for bathing and laundry, and twice again for keeping the garden growing and my xeric landscape looking healthy. My neighbor, on the other hand, waters her enormous lawn and timbered landscape full-throttle for as long as twenty hours a day. With the drought still burning southeast Utah into bits of crispy dust, it seems unusually sinful. Her response to my complaints: "It's well water, so I can do what I want. God will provide."

Here's what the U.S. Geological Survey says about well-users wasting water: "If you own a water-table well and you pump excessive amounts of water from your well, there is a danger of your well going dry as consumption continues and groundwater levels fall. Since aquifers can be quite extensive, the usage of your well can influence other people miles away. Groundwater that supplies your well also feeds streams during periods of low flow, so pumping from your well may also cause the water levels in streams to be lower." If you'd like to read more, go to: http://md.water.usgs.gov/faq/drought.html#GW05.

It's time to stop being greedy with water. The earth has to take care of a huge, expanding population. Your access to well water does not entitle you to unlimited wastefulness.

## Conserving Water

In the chapter on conservation I mentioned several ways to conserve water. Let's emphasize a few points here:

- Fewer flushes.
- Repair leaking toilets and faucets immediately.
- Wash only full loads of laundry.
- Use filtered or treated gray water for gardens and landscapes.
- Don't overwater.

## Wells

Since we're on the subject, let's talk about wells. A well is a hole dug to the water table or an aquifer (see the glossary for definitions), and a pump or other system to draw the water out. Like anything else, wells are highly regulated by the offices of local and state government, especially the health department. A badly done well can leak some nasty contaminants into the local water system. Also, wells are generally not cheap to sink, and you'll probably be wanting a deep well, since the deeper the well, the more likely you are to get truly clean water. Even then, you'll probably end up filtering the water to make sure. So, bottom line: Use a licensed well-driller and get it done right. And when deciding how and where to do your well, get some insight from the farmers and older residents nearby.

If you're lucky enough to have access to the perfect well-drilling site—for instance, a water table 20 feet down, in deep loam or sandy clay with few rocks and no nearby contamination potential—it's quite possible to hand-drive the well. Here's how it's done: To limit the pumping that will have to be done between the well and the house, find a site as close to the house as possible. The site must be at least 100 feet away from and uphill of any source of contamination, such as an outhouse, animal stables, or septic systems. Use a 1.25-inch to 2-inch well point (drive point). A well point is a pipe, usually 18 to 60 inches long, with openings large enough to allow water to enter. The size of the openings depends on the sediment matrix holding the water. The finer the sediment, the smaller the holes will need to be. Holes should let finer particles in but keep large particles out.

Pound the well head down into the soil with a maul. When you need more length, remove the hammering cap, clean the threads, and screw on a new riser pipe (5 to 6 feet in length, with a 6-inch nipple) using some monkey wrenches and with a little joint or pipe thread compound in the threads. Start pounding again and repeat the process. Special drive couplings may be needed during this process to keep the impact off the threads.

There are abundant websites with suggestions for determining whether your well point has entered waterbearing ground. If you reach an artesian source with some pressure, you might get water gushing up through the pipe. Otherwise, you'll have to attach a suction pump to bring up the water.

Boring a well in rock-free soil is possible with a hand-turned auger, but the process is immensely labor-intensive. Posthole augers can be driven by a power head and pressurized with water to soften and clear out the hole.

Keep in mind that you can use the hand-drawing method to bring up water from a well if it's deeper than 200 feet. A suction pump, on the other hand, will not work with water more than 20 feet down. For deeper wells you'll probably use a submerged push-type electric pump (possibly solar- or wind-powered), or a windmill.

Hand-digging a wide shaft and finishing it with a windlass was the traditional way of creating a well years ago. This method is not practical or safe, especially if the shaft is deeper than the diggers are tall and the soil is unconsolidated. Shaft collapse is a common hazard. Get advice and experienced help.

## Springs

A spring is an upwelling of water at the ground's surface. That includes shallow seepages from nearby collectors, natural or unnatural (including lakes, streams, aquifers, saturated sediment, waste dumps). If you intend to use stream water, you absolutely must have it comprehensively tested at a laboratory. The good news is that natural sediments and soil organisms do an excellent job of keeping water clean, but they can become overloaded with heavy or repeated contamination. Pollutants in your test results may mean you need to change sources and go deeper for cleaner water. You may find pesticides from the farm next door, and E. coli or increased phosphates indicate contamination with sewage.

Finding a spring is often easier than it sounds. A good time to look is during the early spring months, in periods of high snowmelt or heavy rain. Watch for small runnels emptying into roadside ditches or otherwise dry canyons or arroyos, and follow them to their sources. Check back monthly and watch the progression of the local vegetation. If it remains green, or the ground remains wet year-round, there's a spring there. Many springs are little more than seeps.

If you live in a wooded area, look for wide, indented lines in the ground. This indicates a channel of some kind, either above or below ground. Seeps will produce a muddy basin or a small pond. The presence of marsh plants growing there in dark soil means a spring is present. It's okay if the marsh stinks a bit; you're going to have the water tested anyway, and smell isn't necessarily an indicator of serious contamination. Once the spring has been located, it needs to be cleaned out and prepared. It's easier to wait until the surrounding area is at its driest before digging out the stagnant sediment (which, again, may have an unpleasant smell). The water that feeds the spring comes from subsurface saturation or from subsurface flows in the deeper sediment or cracks in the bedrock.

The object is to dig out enough to locate this clean source. Then gravel and perforated pipe are put down to collect the water, and a dam of compacted soil, plastic sheeting, or concrete is built downstream of the source, to force the water into the pipe. The pipe is run to a spring box to collect, settle out dirt and sand, and protect the water from contamination. Read about building spring boxes at http:// www.cee.mtu.edu/peacecorps/ documents_july03/springbox_ FINAL.pdf. Here are some simple

- Keep livestock and other potential pollutants and polluters away from the spring.
- Divert surface water, which can contain contaminating sediments, away from the box by digging diversion channels well uphill from it.
- Clean the settling basin out twice each year, or at least once each spring.
- Fix leaks in the pipes or spring box.
- Do not allow the overflow pipe to clog.

instructions to help you maintain the spring:

Once you've got a spring, how do you tap it? By bucket is the easiest way, but for most of us, that's a bit harsh. If the spring is located upslope from the house, the water can be moved through a gravity-flow system to a font, a cistern, or a water tank at the house. The font, cistern, or tank drain should be configured to allow overages of clean water to drain back into the streambed. Bales of hay or straw (or dirt), placed over the box, will help prevent freezing; also, allowing some water to run from the box will retard freezing.

## Harvesting Precipitation: Catchment Systems

A water catchment system (aka, surface-water containment system, rain-harvesting storage system, runoff catchment system) is an attractive alternative where groundwater is contaminated, wells can't be dug, springs can't be found, or where rainwater is low. These types of systems have been in use for thousands of years in countries with poor groundwater resources. Even in the desert, a short rain can deliver enough water to keep the household going until the next storm. The most common form of storm harvesting is a simple rain barrel, fed by the downspout of the rain gutters or eaves of the building. There's a huge inventory of

commercial rain barrels to choose from, some with their own roof-cleaner diverters (they divert the roof water until the roof has been rinsed off). By the way, metal or clay-tile roofs seem to be cleaner than shingled roofs. If you have a shingled roof, you'll want a roof cleaner diverter and perhaps a pre-filter in the system before the water enters the storage device. The water from a barrel is not pressurized, but can be used to water a garden via a hose from the barrel drain. Elevating the barrel (commonly on cinder blocks) a bit increases the pressure, but it won't support a plumbing system of any kind without a pump. Storm harvesting systems that are intended to provide water for drinking, cooking, and bathing will need pumping, filtration, and disinfection systems. The harvesting system may also drain into larger above-ground tanks, into below-ground cisterns, or into dammed reservoirs, some commercial versions of which also have roof cleaners. Aside from roofs, melt- and rain-water can be captured from gullies and washes, but the obvious problem is sediment (mud) buildup and the control of raging floodwaters. Large systems like this can become hazards to anything downstream. A cistern is basically just a tank, made of concrete, steel, fiberglass, or plastic, that sits above or below ground. If your cistern or water tank is above ground and higher than your building's internal plumbing, you can use the weight of the water in the cistern for water pressure. Otherwise, a pump is needed to send water from the catchment to the house. Again, filtering and disinfection will be needed before using the water for drinking, cooking, or bathing. If you're using a rain barrel or any other aboveground storage device, remember to take steps to keep it from freezing.

A 33-gallon garbage-can collector runs 50 to 75 feet of down-slope soaker hose for almost three hours. The gutter drain is placed in the hole in the top of the lid to catch runoff. The screen beneath the lid keeps mosquitoes from breeding. The valve at the bottom allows the hose to be turned on and off. Cost: $18, not including hose.

## Testing Your Water

Test any off-grid water before you drink it. If you can't test it first, you can use a combination of methods to treat and purify it: water treatment tablets from the local sporting goods store, or household bleach (sodium hypochlorite, 3 to 6 percent) at a ratio of 1 teaspoon to 5 gallons of water.

Lab samples for testing for microorganisms, including Giardia cysts, and chemicals need to be fresh (less than twenty-four hours old). Use an independent testing service to do the tests. Comprehensive testing will cost a couple of hundred dollars. The local health department will be able to have the testing done for less, but getting the HD involved may be a mistake. If they shut you down, it could be nearly impossible to get them "uninvolved."

## Water-Source Hygiene

Pay attention to what's happening around your water source and its watershed. Watch for dead animals, contamination by human sewage, and chemical contamination.

Filter your water. Consider putting a filter/chlorinator system at the well head and installing purifiers on or before the faucets that will be used for drinking and cooking water. When it comes to filters, you generally get what you pay for. Expect to fork out some dollars for a good system and be aware that high-tech filtering systems require periodic filter replacement and water testing.

## Water Heating Devices

Storage or tank-type water heaters are the most common in the American home. They are usually 20- to 80-gallon capacity, and fueled by electricity, propane, oil, or natural gas. These units heat up water in an insulated tank and provide a large amount of water

for a short period of time. The disadvantage of these units is that they use energy even when not in operation. The life expectancy of a tank is ten to fifteen years, but can be increased by replacing the tank's internal anode rod.

### Heat Pump Heaters

These units use a heater/compressor and refrigerant fluid to transfer heat from one place to another. They are fueled by electricity, but the heat source is warm air in the vicinity of the heat pump. For this reason heat pumps work best in warm climates. They use less electricity because it takes less energy to move heat than to create it. They are available with built-in water tanks called *integral units*, or as add-ons to existing water heaters. They are expensive and complicated to install, so it's best to hire a contractor for this job.

## Leaving the Grid: Water

### Indirect Water Heaters

Indirect water heaters use the home heating system's

boiler. Hot water is stored in a separate insulated tank. Heat is transferred from the boiler via a small circulation pump and heat exchanger.

Disadvantages include the fact that it's an integral part of the home heating system and that it's usually easiest to install during new building construction by a contractor.

### On-Demand or Tankless Heaters

These heaters only go to work when the water is turned on and reaches a minimum flow rate. A gas flame or heater element switches on, heating water as it passes through a radiator-like heat exchanger. These heaters do not store hot water. Tankless water heaters may include many safety features; for example, a certain flow rate may be required in order for the device to turn on; temperature and pressure-relief valves; and additional heat sensors on the heat exchanger, to mention a few. The flow rate itself is limited by the heating capacity of the device. It allows hot water to flow at limited gallons per minute, and increased flow decreases the temperature of the water. At a moderate rate, hot water runs out only when the gas or the water runs out. Most models are fueled by natural gas or propane. ElectricOff the Grid models are available but use excessive amounts of electricity. This type of water heater is a good choice for small homes.

# Food Storage

## Hunger is the best pickle.

—*Benjamin Franklin*

*Note: The following is a general guide—use your own estimates based on these figures and consider the eating habits of your own family.*

| Food Type | Amount for Adult Per Year | Amount for Child (1–5 years) Per Year |
|---|---|---|
| Baking powder | 1 pound | 1 pound |
| Baking soda | 1 pound | 1 pound |
| Brown sugar | 3 pounds | 3 pounds |
| Canned fruits | 5 #10 cans (more if possible) | 3 #10 cans (more if possible) |
| Cooking oil | 2 gallons | 1 gallon |
| Cornmeal | 30 pounds | 12 pounds |
| Dry beans | 45 pounds | 15 pounds |
| Dry lentils | 5 pounds | 2 pounds |
| Dry lima beans | 5 pounds | 2 pounds |
| Dry pasta | 40 pounds | 22 pounds |
| Dry potatoes | 5 #10 cans (65 cups) | 3 #10 cans (39 cups) |
| Dry soup mix | 7 pounds | 5 pounds |
| Dry soy beans | 40 pounds | 20 pounds |
| Dry split peas | 5 pounds | 2 pounds |
| Dry yeast | ½ pound | ½ pound |
| Enriched white flour | 25 pounds | 12 pounds |
| Enriched white rice | 80 pounds | 30 pounds |
| Evaporated milk | 12 12-ounce cans (2 pounds) | 6 12-ounce cans |
| Honey | 3 pounds | 1 pound |
| Jam | 5 pounds | 2 pounds |

| | | |
|---|---|---|
| Jell-O | 1 pound | 1 pound |
| Mayonnaise | 2 quarts | 1 quart |
| Molasses | 1 pound | 1 pound |
| Peanut butter | 4 pounds | 2 pounds |
| Pearled barley | 80 pounds | 5 pounds |
| Powdered eggs | 3 #10 cans (39 cups) | 2 #10 cans (26 cups) |
| Powdered fruit drink | 6 pounds | 3 pounds |
| Powdered milk | 60 pounds | 30 pounds |
| Rolled oats | 50 pounds | 12 pounds |
| Salad dressing | 1 quart | 1 quart |
| Salt | 10 pounds | 5 pounds |
| Shortening | 4 pounds | 2 pounds |
| Sugar | 40 pounds | 20 pounds |
| Tomatoes | 5 #10 cans sauce or slices | 3 #10 cans sauce or slices |
| Tuna or canned meat | 10 cans or more | 5 cans or more |
| Vinegar | ½ gallon | ½ gallon |
| Wheat | 200 pounds | 75 pounds |

## What other supplies should I store?

Supply of spices: garlic powder, onion powder, basil, oregano, pepper, chili powder, and cinnamon.

Packages of dried fruit and raisins

Beef and chicken bouillon

Baking cocoa

Ketchup and mustard

Salsa

Vanilla

Seeds for sprouting alfalfa, mung, radish, peas, lentil sprouts

Pancake mix

Pickles

Boxes of cereal

Crackers, graham crackers, and babycrackers

Cans of nuts

Ground, vacuum-sealed coffee

Tea

Children's and adult's vitamins

Baby cereal and formula

Meals in a box (such as macaroni and cheese)

# How do I build a food storage?

The simplest, cheapest, and easiest way to build up a food storage is to buy bulk at a price club or when the grocery store is having a sale. If you grow your own, slowly grow more and can and store the increase. There are suppliers who will get you all you need in easy-to-store containers for a price. If you really need to live off your food storage and all you have is the basics you will very quickly get tired of beans and rice and mayonnaise. The extra supplies such as pickles and cocoa at the bottom of the list may be the most important because they will alleviate the drudgery of the same meals all the time—and you should also buy a variety of pasta,

Home-canned food storage.

beans, soups, etc. It is also good to keep some things on hand in the freezer.

# How do I care for a food storage?

Keep the storage in a cool (70°F or less), dry, dark place in containers that are rodent-proof. It is important to rotate the food if it is stored for a long period of time. Don't leave the food in sacks and bags—always store in airtight containers made especially for food, or in plastic buckets lined with food-packaging plastic liners. Moisture and rodents are the biggest enemies of food storage so it is important that you follow the rules and make sure the food is extremely dry before sealing the container.

# How often should I rotate the food?

1–2 years: instant potatoes
2–3 years: powdered milk
3–4 years: hot cocoa, rice
Home-canned food storage

4–5 years: rolled oats, vanilla pudding, white flour, and soup mix

6–8 years: dry pinto beans, dry pink beans, dry white beans, apple slices, spaghetti, macaroni, chopped dry onions

8–10 years: carrots, fruit drink mix

20 years: wheat, sugar

## What kinds of containers are appropriate for food storage?

#10 aluminum cans

Foil pouches

Glass canning jars

PETE (polyethylene terephthalate) plastic bottles

Plastic buckets with food liners

## How much water should I store?

Each person should have 14 gallons for a two-week supply. The purpose of a water storage is to keep some on hand if there isn't any water available, anywhere. It is obviously very cumbersome. If you live in an area with lots of water, investing in a very good water purifier can save space.

# Primitive Heat and Light

**Firelight will not let you read fine stories but it's warm and you won't see the dust on the floor.**

*—Irish Proverb*

## How do I prepare to make a fire?

If you are outside, make a ring with rocks, and clear all the burnable material around the ring for at least 10 feet. Find some water and bring it nearby, or build the fire near water. Make the fire in the center of the circle. Before you start, gather tinder (small pieces of dry stuff) and place it nearby. If you are using a fireplace, it can be helpful to clean out some of the old ashes.

## How do I start a fire using flint?

Use a piece of flint and strike it with a stone over a spongy piece of dry wood until the spark lights the wood.

## How do I make a fire if all I have is a pocketknife?

1. Take a rectangular piece of bark, big enough to put your knee on with plenty of room left over, and cut a triangular notch in the edge of it.
2. Find a 1-to 2-inch stick, about a foot long, and sharpen one end to a point.
3. Take a sturdy stick, and tie a cord of twisted grass, or rope or yarn or whatever is handy, to each end, making a bow with a loose string.
4. Take a flat stone, preferably with a hollow in the middle of it.
5. Find a piece of smaller bark, square.
6. Place the big piece of bark on top of the smaller one with

Long ago, the hearth was the center of the home.

the notch in the middle of the small piece.

7. Kneel down on one knee, placing that knee on the end of the big bark.

8. Stand the pointy stick straight up on the big bark right next to the tip of the notch.

9. Twist the cord of the bow halfway around, making a loop, put the loop around the pointy stick, and put the stone on top, making a primitive drill.

10. Place your left hand on the stone, pressing down firmly. Hold the bow in your right.

11. The drill should work by doing a sawing motion horizontally with the bow, while holding the stick steady with the stone, so that the pointy stick twists back and forth, drilling into the bark.

12. Keep working the drill quickly and smoothly until a black powder forms in your notch, and it starts to smoke.

13. When you see a red coal in the black powder, quickly add the tinder, and stop drilling.

14. Keep adding bigger and bigger sticks as your fire gets as big as you need. You don't need a very big fire to cook on or keep warm.

## How do I find out how hot my fire is?

Hold your hand 3 inches above the spot you want to cook over. Count the seconds until you feel like you have to take your hand away because it is too hot. If you have to move your hand before one second (one-thousand-one), it is between 450–500°. Two to three seconds and it is 400–450°. Six or more is too cool to cook over.

## How do I use a pan over a fire?

You can support a pan or pot with three large stones around the fire

A luxurious campfire kitchen.

and set the pan on them. Or hang a pot from a stick poked into the ground and supported by a rock. Or suspend a stick crosswise Fire drill between two forked sticks stuck straight up in the ground, making a rack for a pot. Or use a Dutch oven.

## Dutch oven size and capacity:

5 inches = 1 pint
8 inches = 2 quarts
10 inches = 4 quarts

12 inches = 6 quarts
12 inches deep = 8 quarts
14 inches = 8 quarts
14 inches deep = 10 quarts
16 inches = 12 quarts

## Seasoning:

When you buy a new Dutch oven, you have to season it. Wash it in hot water and dry it to get off the factory coating. Spread olive or vegetable oil or vegetable shortening (like Crisco) over the inside and outside of it, legs

included (don't use a spray). Put the lid on and turn it upside down in the oven, with aluminum foil on the rack below to catch drips. Turn on the oven to 350°F and bake 1 hour. It will smoke and stink so open the windows. Let it cool in the oven.

## Using a Dutch oven:

Get a good fire going 30–45 minutes before and burn it down to form hot coals. Arrange the hot coals evenly under and on top of the oven. When you're done with it, scrape out the uneaten food and turn on the hot water (never use cold water on a hot oven!). Scrub with a plastic scrubby or brush (don't use soap!). Dry, then coat with light coating of olive or vegetable oil. Never keep the lid on tight when storing the Dutch oven. Stick something between the lid and so the air can circulate.

### Soup:

For soup for twenty or more: Dig a hole twice as big as the kettle, make a fire in it, and let it burn down to red-hot coals. Make a hole in the coals, set the Dutch oven in it, and cover it all with dirt. In 4–8 hours the soup should be done.

### Bread:

Grease and preheat the oven, then set a loaf in it that is already risen and ready, or pour in batter for cornbread (don't need to preheat) or cake. Set the oven in a hole, as for soup, and make sure it's level. Cover with coals and dirt and cook for three hours.

*Biscuits and pie:*

Grease and preheat the oven. For biscuits, put chunks of firm dough in the bottom while the pan is sitting on the coals. Turn them over when they're brown and then put the lid on. Put coals on the lid, and cook ten minutes. Cook pies by putting a pie pan right inside the oven.

## How do I put out a fire?

1. Get water and sprinkle it on the top. Then stir it around with a stick, sprinkle again, and stir again.
2. Keep putting water in the fire until you don't feel any more heat, even underneath, and all the sticks are completely out. If you have no water, get sandy dirt and stir it into the fire. Every last spark should be killed. Scatter it all so that no one would know you were there.

## Features of woodstoves:

*Catalytic combustion:* Burns up the gas given off by burning

A properly installed woodstove.

wood. This gets rid of creosote and uses less fuel. These kinds of woodstoves are for heating. To work well, the chimney must remain hot, the bypass to the honeycomb has to be engaged when the stove has been 550° for at least fifteen minutes, and it has to be cleaned twice a year.

*Non-catalytic stove:* Preheats the combustion air and puts it in the firebox where it mixes with flammable gases. This is clean and efficient, but is a newer design and thus more expensive.

## How do I install a woodstove?

1. The stove should be put in a central location, but not where it can block traffic or an exit—a basement is a good choice. It also must have enough room to store some wood and load up the stove. In very cold climates some people put the stove on the north side of the house so that the coldest side of the house stays warmer.

2. Some houses need the floor braced for the extra weight, so test the strength of your floor (especially if it is wood). Again, a basement with a concrete floor is a good choice.

3. If the legs are less than 6 inches tall, and it is on a wood floor, you should lay stone, brick, or concrete at least 8 inches thick under it. On a concrete floor, if the legs are shorter than 6 inches, place a layer 4 inches tall. Even if the legs are longer

than 6 inches, and the floor is concrete, put down a layer 2–4 inches thick.

4. If you need to place it near the wall, put it at least 36 inches away, unless you put heat-resistant material on the wall, in which case it only needs to be 18 inches away.

5. The indoor stovepipe should be at least 24-gauge blued steel (not galvanized) with no more than 1 elbow and as short as possible. Join the pipe A properly installed woodstove sections with the crimped end closer to the stove.

6. The outdoor pipe must be 3 feet above the roof and 2 feet above any part of the cabin within 10 feet. If it is too short there won't be enough draft for the fire and too much smoke— too long and it pulls the fire up the chimney.

## What other things do I need for my woodstove?

You will need a fire extinguisher, a container for kindling, an ash bucket, a poker, and small broom and stove attachments. If you can't get an extinguisher, keep a full container of water nearby.

## Cleaning a chimney (or stack):

1. Creosote is the gunk that gradually builds up in your chimney. If you can scrape off an inch or more of it out of the stack, or if it's hard and difficult to scrape out, it's time to clean it. You should also clean it if the stove is burning less efficiently, and in spring and fall.
2. Cover the floor to protect it. You will need to cover your face with a dust mask or cloth, and wear gloves. You will also need a wire brush specially designed for cleaning chimneys.
3. Climb up on the roof to the top of the chimney and use the brush to clean out the pipe as far as you can. If it doesn't reach all the way down, tie a rope to it and lower it farther.

Use a flashlight to check your progress.

4. Some debris may get stuck halfway down or the buildup may be particularly hard near the bottom. Go back inside and use a chisel or hammer to chip deposits loose.
5. Clean out your stove and pick up all the debris. If you got more than 2 gallons of gunk then you need to clean more often than once a year.

## How a woodcook stove works:

On one end is the firebox with vents and dials. The dials regulate the amount of air that goes through the vents and into the firebox, and the more open the vents are the hotter your fire will be. The ash door can be used for a surge of air but that is for more experienced people. At the back of the firebox is a sliding mechanism (called a slide unit) that directs the smoke around the oven box before going up the chimney so the oven is heated more consistently.

## To heat the cookstove:

It takes about 15 minutes to heat the oven to 350°. First the slide mechanism needs to be directed to the chimney (each stove is different on which direction this is), or else there will be no draft to pull the smoke out and it will go into the room. After starting the fire it must be watched for temperature drops. At first, use quickburning wood with a lot of heat. After it heats to 350°, use a slower-burning piece of wood.

## To bake with the cookstove:

If the stove gets too hot, open the door briefly, but not very long or you will lose too much heat. Some stoves have hot spots that need to be watched. If bread bakes badly, there is soot buildup around the sides, so just scrape it off. Woodstoves need to be watched in order to maintain a steady temperature and good results.

## Cooking on the wood range:

The circles on the top are not burners. The whole stove surface is hot, and is divided into temperature zones. The hottest is directly over the firebox (either on the right or the left), the medium temperature is in the middle, and the coolest is on the front opposite the firebox. Remember to watch your stove for temperature changes.

## Grilling:

Remove one of the circles over the firebox and place a heat-resistant grate directly over the flame. The fire needs to be hotter than during normal grilling because usually a barbecue is a bit closer to the fire.

## Cleaning and care of a cookstove:

Clean only when the stove is cool. Use wet soapy water to clean decorative trim, metal backsplash, and warming oven. Use a nonabrasive cleaner or a razor blade to remove baked-on food residue. Avoid spilling or splashing since you won't be able to clean it right away. Don't put a wet pot on the stove—cast iron rusts and left too long pits will form. Use a metal sanding pad to remove bad spots, and only work in one direction or it will look scratched.

After buffing with metal use a *very* thin layer of cooking oil over the whole thing to season it.

Periodically clean out the small opening under the decorative nameplate right under the oven. Clean out the sides of the ash compartment periodically. Scrape off ash that collects on the top of the oven box (see below) monthly in summer and weekly in winter. Inspect the gasket around the top of the stove every year and replace if worn.

## Cleaning the oven box:

Remove the panels that make up the cooking surface (set on newspaper), then scrape the ash that is collected on the top of the oven box into the ash pan slowly (too fast and it will go in your face). Use a long-handled scraper and scrape the sides of the box. The soot will fall to the bottom use the little door (disguised as a nameplate) to remove where you can it.

## Fire safety:

Don't store the bucket or extinguisher behind the stove.

Don't burn corrugated boxes, plastic, paper, or treated wood from power poles or railroad ties. Don't use kindling as a major fuel—put in heavy wood. Never use kerosene, charcoal lighter fluid, or lantern fuel to start the fire. Don't throw an icy log into the stove or it can explode.

Know the signs of a chimney fire: air sucking noises, a loud roar, and the stovepipe shaking.

Have a fire drill and figure out where you would escape from areas of the house during a fire.

Don't use anything in the oven that you wouldn't put in a regular oven.

Don't position handles over the stove that you couldn't put over a gas burner.

Don't ever put a plastic bowl on the stove even if you think it's safe.

## How do I start a fire in a woodstove?

1. Make 4–5 balls of paper and put them in the firebox near the air supply.
2. Put sticks about the width of a finger on top of the paper, and then put 3–4 pieces of wood the width of your wrist on top of that. Curvy sticks work best because they won't roll.
3. Put slightly bigger sticks across the previous sticks, so that they form a tic-tac-toe pattern.
4. Light the fire and open the air intake holes, or leave the door open.
5. After 3–4 minutes rearrange the wood and add two bigger sticks and close the door.
6. In 15 minutes when the two big sticks are in the fire, add your seasoned firewood.

## What do I do if there is a chimney fire?

Get everyone out of the house and call a fire department (if possible). If you want to try to put it out yourself, close the dampers then open the stove and spray it with the extinguisher so that the chemical will be sucked up the chimney.

## How do I know if I have enough wood to warm my house?

A family goes through seven cords of wood a year for heating. A cord is a pile of logs 8 feet long, stacked 4 feet high and 4 feet wide. A stack, or face cord, is 1/3 of a cord. A typical family uses 5–8 cords per winter for heating exclusively with wood. When buying a cord of wood, make sure that it really equals a cord, and is not just a pile of wood in a pickup truck. You need to have access to that much wood, as well as the skills to cut it and chop it and the equipment to haul it in. If your

house is not energy-efficient, you could be using double the amount of wood you would otherwise.
If you are heating with your cookstove, then you will use more wood. Softwood burns faster and hotter, and dry wood is slower and has a steadier temperature. You may want to use softwood in the heat stove during the day, and hardwood at night and in your cookstove.

## How do I make firewood?

Cut through the top of the log in a series of firewood lengths—typically about 1 to 1 1/2 feet long. Then roll the log over and cut through the other side of each cut. Don't saw into the ground because that dulls the blade. Use an ax to split each round chunk of wood into smaller pieces.

## How do I prepare firewood?

If the wood is 8 inches or more in diameter, it needs to be split. Even smaller wood can be split if you want it to dry faster. A good woodshed is simply a ventilated shelter with a raised floor and some kind of walls to hold the wood in a stack. When the wood is dry enough for burning it will start to crack on the ends.

# Furnishing the Home Camp

A single day's work will do wonders towards making a cabin comfortable. Sometimes through press of more important work, such as getting out a line of traps while the season is yet young, the trapper may well neglect these touches of comfort, and the simplest of camp furnishings will answer until a stormy day keeps him indoors, when he can make good use of his time in making camp furniture. A bed and a stove or fireplace are the only absolutely necessary furnishings to start with, if other work demands immediate attention.

But in our own case such neglect is not at all necessary. The preceding chapter saw our cabin completed, that is the walls, roof, and floor, all that can really be called cabin, but much more work will be required before it is really comfortable and ready for occupancy. Providing the camp with suitable furniture and adding conveniences and comfort is the next step, so while we have time and there is nothing to hinder the work we will push it along.

Most important of all camp furnishings is the stove. Nothing else adds so much to the cheerfulness and home-like aspect of a camp as a properly enclosed, well-behaved fire, which warms up the room, enables us to cook our food indoors, and dispenses the gloom of night by driving the darkness into the farthest corners. If the weather is cold nothing in the camp is so indispensable.

For the lodge which we built in the preceding chapter we will make a stove of sheet iron. I have made a number of camp stoves by riveting together four sections of new, unbent stovepipe into a square sheet, bending this into proper shape, fitting ends, and cutting holes for cooking utensils and for the pipe. But for this camp we have secured from a hardware store a pipe of sheet iron 3 feet wide by 4 feet long. We now place this on the floor of the cabin and measure off from each end 17 inches, then on each edge at the 17-inch mark we make a 3-inch cut. This we do by holding the sheet metal on a block or flat topped stump, placing the corner of the ax on the metal at the proper place, and striking on the head with a billet of wood. Then we place a straight-edged strip of wood across the end on the 17-inch mark, and standing on this wood we pull the end of the metal upward, bending it to a right angle. The other end is treated the same way and this leaves the metal in the form of a box, 3 feet long, 17 inches high, and 14 inches wide, open on top and at both ends. Now we turn this upside down and in the top we cut two 7-inch holes, as round as we can make them. These are to hold the cooking utensils. Near one end we cut a small hole, not more than 3.5 inches in diameter.

The edge of this hole we cut at intervals all the way around, making straight, 1/2-inch cuts. Then we turn these edges up, and we have a stovepipe hole, with a collar to hold the pipe in place. We now close the rear end of the stove by bending 3 inches of the sides into a right angle, the same amount of the top being bent down. This is the purpose of the 3-inch cuts we made when we first commenced the work. Now we rivet a piece of sheet-iron into this end, using for rivets the head ends of wire nails. They must be cut short and riveted on the head of an ax. Beneath the top of the stove, between the cooking holes we rivet a folded strip of metal; this is to stiffen the top. Then we turn in 3 inches of the front of the stove and rivet the corners where they lap. This leaves an 8-inch opening in front over which we will hinge a door. This door must have some kind of fastening, and a simple little twist of wire working in a punch hole is easily arranged and convenient. We can make a very crude stove of this if we like, but we do not want that kind, so we take plenty of time and turn out a satisfactory article.

Our stove is now completed except for the covers which are easily made. We set it up in the box-shaped opening left in the floor and fill around it with sand to a height of 6 inches, also fill the inside to that height. While doing this we must see that the stove stands perfectly level, and that the pipe hole is directly beneath the hole in the roof. This makes a fireproof stove and the bed of sand holds it rigidly in place. A draft is made beneath the door by

scraping away a little sand. The pipe is 5-inch size and we fit it with a damper for that is the way to regulate the draft and keep the heat from going up the pipe.

Our stove completed and in working order we next turn our attention to the bed, since it ranks second in importance. We set an upright post 4 inches thick and 3 feet long against the sidewall about 5 feet from the end of the room and nail it firmly in position. Then at a height of about 2 feet from the floor we fasten to the wall another 4-inch piece, this extending in a horizontal position from the post to the end wall. Then we set up a corner post at the foot of the bed, placing it 5 feet from the end wall and nailing the top securely to the roof binding pole. In line with this against the end wall we set up another three-foot post and spike it solidly to the logs of the wall. Then we cut notches in these two latter posts 2 feet above the floor and into this we fit and nail fast a 4-inch cross strip. We now have the foundation for our

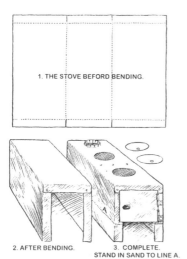

1. THE STOVE BEFORD BENDING.

2. AFTER BENDING.    3. COMPLETE. STAND IN SAND TO LINE A.

bed and we make the bottom of straight, smooth poles, nailed fast to the horizontal ends. These poles must all be of about the same thickness to make a satisfactory bed, otherwise some of them will bend or spring while the stiff ones will not. If it were summer now we would line this bunk with bark to keep the balsam needles from falling through, but since we cannot get bark at this time of year we cannot do this. We make the side and end of the bed by nailing poles against the posts. Then we fill the bed with balsam boughs. These are the ends of the branches and the heaviest stems are less than a 1/4-inch thick. We commence at the head and stand the boughs on end at an angle, stems down. When entirely filled we have a soft and fairly comfortable bed, of course not equal to the spring bed we have at home, but then we are not expecting home comforts in the big woods, and we are always tired enough to rest well in a bough bed. For pillows we use grain bags in which we place our extra clothing.

This bed is at its best when freshly filled. Each night's use reduces its softness, and the comfort decreases at a like rate. The only way to keep a bough bed in good condition is to replace the bough filling occasionally with fresh evergreens. When we kill some big game animal, a deer or caribou, we will dry the skin and place it on our bed, hair side up, for this will make the bed warmer and softer.

The table is next in order. Many trappers think a table too much of a luxury and accordingly dispense with it, but a home camp is far from complete without it and it is an easy piece of furniture to make. It should be placed on the south side of the cabin before the window, so that we can get the advantage of the light. We will stand up two posts of the proper height about 2 feet from the wall and 6 feet apart. These we secure in place by nailing them to the floor. From the tops of these posts to the wall we place flattened pieces of wood and secure them by nailing to the wall and to the posts. This is the foundation or framework for our table. The top we will make of three straight 8-inch logs hewn on one side to the center, and flattened on the other side at the ends. When placed on the supports, flat side up, and fastened by nailing at the ends, we have the table completed. It is rough, but it answers our purpose as well as a more finished one.

In front of the table we will place a bench. This we will make from a hewn log, half round, and in the round side near each end we bore holes for the legs. These are bored at such an angle

CAMP FURNITURE. TABLE, BENCH and LAMP SHELF.

that the legs will stand about 20 inches apart at the base. The legs are made of 2-inch sticks whittled to fit the holes and driven in, the lower ends being cut off afterwards at the proper length to make the bench stand firmly, and at the right height. We will also make another shorter bench which we will place by the side of the stove. Perhaps when a stormy day comes we will make a couple of chairs, but for the present at least these two benches will serve very well.

We cannot be long in the woods until we realize the need of some means of securing our food where it will be inaccessible to woods mice. These little creatures are a serious pest and can soon ruin a bag of flour or a side of bacon if they are able to get at it. In an effort to place my flour where they could not reach it I suspended it from the ridgepole with a piece of codfish line, but the nimble mice went up and down that cord like monkeys. Then I made a platform and suspended it from the roof with four pieces of hay baling wire. On this I placed my food; but even here I found it was not safe, for the mice dropped onto the platform from the roof poles. The only way I found that was perfectly satisfactory was to make a tight box with a well-fitted cover in which to keep the food supply. As a result I made a food box for each camp.

We have now found that it is necessary to have some means of preserving our food from the ravages of mice, and profiting by experience we do not waste our time on theories, but set to work to make a tight wooden box. If it were a time of the year when bark would peel we would make a frame of poles and cover it with bark. But this is impossible now, so we split boards from balsam and cedar and hew them flat and smooth. For the ends we make these boards 2 feet long and fasten them together by nailing strips across the ends of the boards after they have been placed side by side with the edges fitting one against another. The boards for the bottom and sides are made 3 feet long and these we nail to the ends. The cover is fitted to the top, but is not fastened.

Luxuries become necessities through use. The furnishings which we have so far brought into our cabin may be considered as coming properly under the heading of necessities. But there are many little extra pieces that may be added which may be called luxuries at first, but through use they become almost indispensable. On the walls we will build shelves and we find them very useful places for storing odds and ends. A small shelf is placed on the wall near the stove to hold the lamp, and another similar shelf for the same purpose is placed above the left end of the table. Then there are two or three longer shelves placed in convenient locations. These shelves are all made of hewn boards supported by stout pins driven into auger holes.

If we are not by this time too tired of making boards with an ax, we will make a wooden tub in which to wash our clothes. Since we have a saw this is not as difficult as it first appears. It is made square with sloping sides. The boards must be carefully fitted and securely nailed. Then, after we have made it as tight as possible by nailing we will gather a small quantity of spruce gum and run it into the cracks from the inside by means of a hot iron, in much the same way that we would solder tin plate. A wash basin can be made in the same way, but we have a tin basin in our outfit so we'll not need to make one.

Behind the stove we nail a slender pole, horizontally, onto wooden pins driven into auger holes, so that the pole is parallel with the wall and about 6 or 8 inches from it. On this pole we place our socks and mitts to dry when we come in from the day's tramp. We hang our coats on nails driven into the wall. Our snowshoes we suspend from the roof with snare wire in the coolest part of the camp, so that the mice cannot eat the filling or the heat make it brittle.

Perhaps you would be interested in our camp outfit, for it is adapted to use in a camp of this kind. We have come into the woods for the fall and winter, and while we will go out occasionally for supplies of food, our outfit is supposed to be complete, and in it are all the articles needed for an entire winter's stay in the wilds. The following are the articles which we have brought with us as camp outfit: two rabbit skin blankets, two large all-wool blankets, one large and one medium enameled kettle, two tea pails, one water pail, one large frying pan and two small ones, with sockets for handles, three enameled plates, two enameled cups, two table knives, two forks, two table spoons, two tea spoons, one reflecting baker, one wash basin, one small mirror, four towels, one alarm clock, one small oil lamp (bottom portion of a railroad lantern), three small axes with long handles, one cross-cut saw, one hand saw, two flat files, two sharpening stones (pocket size), one auger, one hammer, assorted nails, a dozen small bags for holding food, a small box of medicines, and a repair kit, consisting of needles, thread, wax, scissors, awl, and small pliers.

The above is the actual camp outfit and does not include personal belongings, such as guns, traps, toilet articles, compasses clothing, snowshoes, etc., things which are used more on the trail than in camp, and while necessary in our business cannot rightfully be considered a part of the camp equipment. Even some of the articles mentioned, for instance the two small frying pans, are more for use on the trail than in the home cabin.

This, and the preceding chapter, describe what to my mind is an ideal camp for two persons and a perfect equipment for same. The camp site described could not be improved upon, and it is seldom that we find all of the requirements in any one place, yet the description is that of one of my own camp sites, and except for the size of camp and a few details of furnishings and outfit, also describes one of my cabins, one which I constructed and used while trapping in Canada.

# The World's Best Outhouse

The remote cabin may not have running water, and if not that rules out the modern bathroom. Usually the next best option is an outhouse, or privy, as some prefer to call the little house out back. During the thirty-plus years of my outdoor career, I have had firsthand experience with outhouses throughout much of the world, and most of it has not been very pleasant. I have seen very few outhouses I liked. When I decided to build my Cross Creek Hollow cabin, I decided that I would build an outhouse that would always be clean, bright, insect-free, odorless, and roomy enough for the visit to be pleasant, even for the visitor who had never seen such a restroom.

As I was researching the perfect outhouse plan, I read in a newspaper that the U.S. Forest Service had a new plan for odor-free privies, and that they were going to rework all of their outhouses. It occurred to me that they should know, as they were at that time the manager of twelve thousand outhouses in our national forest, and they build about three hundred new ones each year. The development of the odor-free outhouse was done at the Forest Service research lab in California. I got in contact with them and used their research for designing, building, and managing my outhouse. I also obtained some useful outhouse design tips from several missionary groups who were helping remote villages in Central America build outhouses that are more sanitary.

## Building Cross Creek Hollow's Outhouse

My first step in building the outhouse was to check with my county health department to see that it was permissible. It was, so long as it was well away from any water supply such as a well or spring, and it didn't require a permit. The site I selected for the outhouse was 100 feet from the cabin and downwind from the prevailing wind. There was no water source anywhere near the privy, and the water table was known to be many feet lower than the bottom of the pit. It would be convenient to the cabin, and I positioned the front door so there would be a good view from the inside looking out with the door open. The 57-by-60-inch building was staked out, and I was ready to start to work.

First, I dug a 48-by-48-inch square pit, 5 feet deep. To shore up the pit, I built a boxlike structure from pressure-treated lumber, just a simple box of 1-by-8-by-48-inch boards spaced 2 inches apart, screwed into a 2-by-4 in each corner. There is no bottom or top. The box was pushed down into the pit with the top level with the floor of the outhouse. Its role is to keep the sides of the pit from caving in over time. On top of this, I

framed-in the outhouse floor using pressure-treated framing and 3/4-inch marine plywood. Since I was using a purchased seat assembly for the actual "throne," I had to make sure the floor joists were spaced to allow for the opening in the floor. Also, before installing it was important to mark the opening needed for the seat assembly and cutout the floor with a saber saw. I cut the opening in the floor for the vent pipe at the same time. Cutting these holes after the walls went up would be difficult.

With the floor in place, the framing went up quickly. I finished the walls with log siding to match the cabin. At the top of each sidewall, I cut a vent opening and installed hardware cloth to keep insects from coming in through the vents. For roofing, I used translucent fiberglass so the outhouse would be bright during the day. I cut a hole in the roof and pushed a 6-inch PVC sewer drainpipe down from the roof into the floor to serve as a pit vent pipe, leaving it higher than the roof to ensure good ventilation. The pipe, held in place with pipe strapping, was painted black above the roof so it would collect solar heat and pull air from the pit.

Following this, I installed the floor covering, a light-colored linoleum that would be easy to clean and give the floor a tight seal. After cutting a hole in the floor covering, I installed the stainless steel seat assembly. Finally, I built a homemade door from 1-by-6-inch boards, and painted a quarter moon on the finished door to keep with tradition.

I painted the inside walls with an off-white enamel to brighten the interior, and mounted a battery-operated light on the wall, a toilet paper dispenser, within easy reach. A container of builder's lime sits next to the seat. As a finishing touch, I added some pictures to the walls.

## Maintaining the Outhouse

It is a requirement that a cup of builder's lime be thrown in the pit after each use of the toilet. This is our method of flushing. Also, I ask that the seat lid be kept shut so that the gases will go out the vent pipe and not into the building, and it keeps any insects from getting into the building. Twice each year I pour a solution of one package of yeast in one quart of warm water into the pit. The fermentation breaks down the deposits. I have a strict rule that no other waste, such as garbage, is thrown into the pit. I have seen many outhouses be ruined when they were used as a garbage dump. Use it for only what it was designed for. Some outhouse owners I know take one can of common household lye and shake it down in the pit once a month to eat away the waste. I have never tried this, as the method I use works great. In fact, my outhouse has been used for over ten years without any problems or getting too full.

Hanging inside the outhouse is a broom for cleaning. On a shelf is extra toilet tissue and air freshener. On the outside of the outhouse next to the steps is a solar-powered light that shows the way to the building from the cabin at night.

My outhouse is not insulated, as we do not need it in the South, but in colder climates, it would be easy to insulate the building. We do have a Styrofoam seat cover for cold mornings.

For really cold days, I put a Coleman BlackCat catalytic heater in the outhouse. This heater is designed for use in enclosed areas and uses a 16.4-ounce propane cylinder as a fuel source. It features flameless platinum catalytic technology and has an 8-inch heating head. It is rated for 3,000 BTU output. It will take the chill out of a cold outhouse in just a few minutes. I have also posted the rules for using the outhouse and the cabin on the door at eye level when sitting on the seat. It just reminds us all of how the property is to be taken care of.

- Always keep the door closed unless you are enjoying the view during the visit.
- Keep the toilet lid closed when not in use.

- Use a cup of lime after depositing waste in the pit.
- Pour in a quart of yeast/warm water once monthly.
- Do not put anything but human waste and toilet paper in the pit. Toilet paper rolls, sanitary napkins, paper towels, cigarette butts, and garbage of any kind goes into the cabin trash.
- Clean out the vent pipe twice annually. Spider webs will cause it not to function.
- Clean off the roof twice annually, as leaves will cut out the light.
- Sweep out the outhouse daily.
- Clean the interior walls, toilet seat, and floor every three months with a disinfectant cleaner.
- Spray for insects each May and August.
- Wash your hands in the washbasin on the cabin porch before entering the cabin.

I have found that these rules prevent problems. Many of my guests have never spent time in a self-sufficient cabin before, and you can't expect them to know all these things. I don't think the rules have ever made anyone mad, and our outhouse has been consistently odor-free, clean, bright, and insect-free for years.

## Waterless Composting Toilets

If you want a toilet inside the self-sufficient cabin, or you want to have a state-of-the-art outhouse, then you should consider one of the waterless, self-contained composting toilets. These units require no water, no septic system, no chemicals and they do not smell or pollute. The system is really simple, and uses nature to solve our sewage problem. The unit uses the continuous action of aerobic microbes to reduce waste into reusable compost. Waste material enters the toilet; about 90 percent of it is water. The toilet evaporates most of the water, and the vapors are carried up through the vent pipe and dispersed into the air, odorlessly. Heat, oxygen, and organic material break down the remaining waste into compost.

I have seen these units in remote lodges, family-size cabins, oil exploration camps, mines, and native villages throughout the world and when properly used they work great. There are two units that I have experience with, the Envirolet Basic Plus and the #NE unit sold by Lehman's. Both are non-electric. I will discuss these two units here.

There are several things to like about these units. First, they are self contained. They are easy to install and come with a vent kit. The Envirolet Basic Plus, made by Sancor, measures 25 inches wide by 33 inches long by 25 inches high (19.75 inches height to toilet seat). It weighs 74 pounds. The Lehman's #NE measures 31 inches high by 22.5 inches wide by 33 inches long. (The seat height is 17 inches.) This unit weighs 95 pounds. The Envirolet unit cost $1,175 and the Lehman's $879 at this writing. These units are designed to be used in cabins accommodating three to six people. Use of the toilet is simple. A small amount of peat moss is added to the toilet when it is used. Every few days the toilet is agitated and mixed with a built-in mixer, in an odorless process. The compost drops down into a bottom drawer for removal. This is only required every few weeks or less, depending upon use.

One of the real pluses of these units is that they may be used or left unattended in the winter without worrying about freezing up. They work regardless of temperature. These units are made from durable material and are easy to clean.

Both companies offer a variety of models; some larger units work well where electricity is available. These toilets are the closest you can get to a modern toilet in the backcountry where electricity and running water are not possible. They can give you the comfort and convenience of an indoor toilet.

## Burning Human Waste

Here is a more expensive method of human waste disposal, but a good one. The propane Storburn toilet, sold by Lehman's, is designed for remote locations. It does not need electricity or running water, so it can be installed about anywhere, even in the coldest regions. It has the capacity to handle eight full-time users or ten part-time users. It works like an incinerator, treating human waste by burning it, reducing the waste to minerals and water vapor. The burner is fired by propane and is approved by both Canadian and American Gas Associations. It is sanitary, safe (harmful bacteria is destroyed by heat), and non-polluting. Since there are no moving parts or electrical systems, maintenance is simple, just sweep out the ashes.

Operating the burning cycle is easy. Starting the burner is about as easy as lighting a gas grill: add a packet of anti-foam, close the unit, and press a button to light the burner. There is no chance of burning yourself as the unit must be closed and locked before it will burn. Start the cycle before going to bed, and when you wake up the toilet chamber is clean and empty. This toilet, which is known for having no foul odors, sells for $2,650 at this writing, a little expensive, but it is a great way to handle human waste in remote locations.

## Options

There are other means of handling human waste in self-sufficient cabins. Some people use portable chemical toilets, but I find these messy to handle and I don't think I have seen one that was used over a long weekend, especially in the summer, that didn't have bad breath. Also, there are some toilets that are simply holding tanks that leave a lot to be desired. I would hate to face a trip home Sunday afternoon from my cabin with a container of human waste in the car.

The modern bathroom is hard to beat, but if you want a self-sufficient cabin in the backcountry, the well-designed outhouse or waterless composting toilet can be almost as good.

# First Aid

# Basic First Aid

It's impossible to predict when an accident will occur, but the more you educate yourself ahead of time, the better you'll be able to help should the need arise. The first step in an emergency situation should always be to call for help, but there are many things you can do to help the victim while you're waiting for assistance to arrive. The most important procedures are described in this section.

## Drowning

1. As soon as the patient is in a safe place, loosen the clothing, if any.
2. Empty the lungs of water by laying the body breastdown and lifting it by the middle, with the head hanging down. Hold for a few seconds until the water drains out.
3. Turn the patient on his breast, face downward.
4. Give artificial respiration: Press the lower ribs down and forward toward the head, then release. Repeat about twelve times to the minute.
5. Apply warmth and friction to extremities, rubbing toward the heart.
6. Don't give up! Persons have been saved after hours of

Keep a buoy nearby whenever spending time in or near the water.

steady effort, and after being underwater for more than twenty minutes.

7. When natural breathing is reestablished, put the patient into a warm bed, with hot-water bottles, warm drinks, fresh air, and quiet.

## Sunstroke

1. Move the patient to a cool place, or set up a structure around the patient to produce shade.
2. Loosen or remove any clothing around the neck and upper body.
3. Apply cold water or ice to the head and body, or wrap the patient in cold, damp cloths.
4. Encourage the patient to drink lots of water.

## Burns and Scalds

1. Cover the burn with a thin paste of baking soda, starch, flour, petroleum jelly, olive oil, linseed oil, castor oil, cream, or cold cream.

2. Cover the burn first with the paste, then with a soft rag soaked in the paste.
3. Shock always accompanies severe burns, and must be treated.

## Shock or Nervous Collapse

A person suffering from shock has a pale face, cold skin, feeble breathing, and a rapid, feeble pulse, and will appear listless.

1. Place the patient on his back with head low.
2. Give stimulants, such as hot tea or coffee.
3. Cover the patient with blankets.
4. Rub the limbs and place hot-water bottles around the body.

## Fainting

Fainting is caused by a lack of blood supply to the brain and

A simple hand bandage can be made from any square cloth or handkerchief.

is cured by getting the heart to correct the lack.

1. Have the person lie down with the head lower than the body.
2. Loosen the clothing. Give fresh air. Rub the limbs. Use smelling salts.
3. Do not let the person get up until fully recovered.

## Snake Bite

1. Put a tight cord or bandage around the limb between the wound and the heart. This should be loose enough to slip a finger under it.
2. Keep the wound lower than the heart. Try to keep the patient calm, as the faster the heart beats, the faster the venom will spread.

## Cuts and Wounds

1. After making sure that no dirt or foreign substance is in the wound, apply a tight bandage to stop the bleeding.
2. Raise the wound above the heart to slow the bleeding.

### How to Make a Tourniquet

The tourniquet is an appliance used to check severe bleeding. It consists of a bandage twisted more or less lightly around the affected part. The bandage—a cloth, strap, belt, necktie, neckerchief or towel—should be long enough to go around the arm or leg affected. It can then be twisted by inserting the hand, and the blood stopped.

1. If a stick is used, there is danger of twisting too tightly.
2. The tourniquet should not be used if bleeding can be stopped without it. When used it should be carefully loosened every 15 to 20 minutes to avoid permanent damage to tissues.
3. If you cannot get to a doctor quickly, suck the wound many times with your mouth or use a poison suction kit, if available.

3. If the blood comes out in spurts, it means an artery has been cut. For this, apply a tourniquet: Make a big knot in a handkerchief, tie it around the limb, with the knot just above the wound, and twist it until the flow is stopped.

## Hemorrhage or Internal Bleeding

Internal bleeding usually comes from the lungs or stomach. If from the lungs, the blood is bright red and frothy, and is coughed up; if from the stomach, it is dark, and is vomited.

1. Help the patient to lie down, with head lower than body.
2. Encourage the patient to swallow small pieces of ice, and apply ice bags, snow, or cold water to the place where the bleeding is coming from.
3. Hot applications may be applied to the hands, arms, feet, and legs, but avoid stimulants, unless the patient is very weak.

## Insect Stings

1. Wash with oil, weak ammonia, or very salty water, or paint with iodine.
2. A paste of baking soda and water also soothes stings.

## Poison

1. First, get the victim away from the poison. If the poison is in solid form, such as pills, remove it from the victim's mouth using a clean cloth wrapped around your finger. Don't try this with infants because it could force the poison further down their throat.
2. If the poison is corrosive to the skin, remove the clothing from the affected area and flush with water for 30 minutes.
3. If the poison is in contact with the eyes, flush the victim's eyes for a minimum of 15 minutes with clean water.

## How to Put Out Burning Clothing

1. If your clothing should catch fire, do not run for help, as this will fan the flames.

2. Lie down and roll up as tightly as possible in an overcoat, blanket, rug, or any woolen article—or lie down and roll over slowly, at the same time beating the fire with your hands. Smother the fire with a coat, blanket, or rug. Remember that woolen material is much less flammable than cotton.

## Ice Rescue

1. Always have a rope nearby if you're working or playing on ice. This way, if someone falls through, you can tie one end to yourself and one to a tree or other secure anchor onshore before you attempt to rescue the person.
2. You could also throw one end to the victim if his head is above water.
3. Do not attempt to walk out to the victim. Push out to him or crawl out on a long board or rail or tree trunk.
4. The person in the water should never try to crawl up on the

For elbow, arm, or wrist injuries, a simple sling can be made out of a piece of cloth or clothing.

broken ice, but should try merely to support himself and wait for help, if it is at hand.

## Broken Bone

A simple fracture is one in which the bone is broken but does not break the skin. In a compound fracture, the bone is broken and the skin and tissue are punctured or torn. A simple fracture may be converted into a compound fracture by careless handling, as a broken bone usually has sharp, saw-tooth edges, and just a little

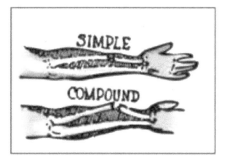

A compound fracture is one that breaks through the flesh.

twist may push it through the skin.

1. Do not move the patient without supporting broken member by splints.
2. In a compound fracture, bleeding must be checked— by bandage over compress, if possible, or by tourniquet in extreme cases. Then splints may be applied.
3. Where skin is broken, infection is the great danger, so exercise care that compress or dressing is sterile and clean.

## Dislocation

A dislocation is an injury where the head of a bone has slipped out of its socket at a joint.

1. Do not attempt to replace the joint. Even thumb and finger dislocations are more serious than usually realized.

Grip to form basket seat

Two-handed chair carry

Chair carry

"Three bearers' position for lift"

"Three bearers' lift"

Arm carry

Horseback carry

There are many ways to carry someone with an injury. If neck or spine injury is suspected, do not attempt to move the victim if you can get help to come to the victim instead. If the victim must be moved, the head and neck must first be carefully stabilized.

2. Cover the joint with cloths wrung out in very hot or very cold water. For the shoulder— apply padding and make a sling for the arm.

3. Seek medical assistance.

## First Aid Checklist

To administer effective first aid, it is important to maintain adequate supplies in each first aid kit. A firs-aid kit should include:

- **Adhesive bandages**: These are available in a large range of sizes for minor cuts, abrasions, and puncture wounds.
- **Butterfly closures**: These hold wound edges firmly together.
- **Rolled gauze**: These allow freedom of movement and are recommended for securing a

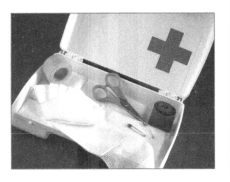

### Nature's First Aid

*Antiseptic or wound-wash:* A handful of salt in a quart of hot water.

*Balm for wounds:* Balsam fir. The gum can be used as healing salve, usually spread on a piece of linen and laid over the wound for a dressing.

*Cough remedy:* Slippery elm or black cherry inner bark boiled, a pound to the gallon, boiled down to a pint, and given a teaspoonful every hour. Linseed can be used the same way; add honey if desired. Or boil down the sap of the sweet birch tree and drink it on its own or mixed with the other remedies.

*Diuretic:* A decoction of the inner bark of elder is a powerful diuretic.

*Inflammation of the eyes or skin:* Wash with a strong tea

made of the bark of witch hazel. *Lung balm:* Infusion of black cherry bark and root is a powerful tonic for lungs and bowels. Good also as a skin wash for sores.

*Poison ivy:* Wash every hour or two with hot soapy water, then with hot salt water.

wound dressing and/or pads. These are especially good for hard-to-bandage wounds.

- **Nonstick sterile pads:** These are soft, superabsorbent pads that provide a good environment for wound healing. These are recommended for bleeding and draining wounds, burns, or infections.
- **First aid tapes:** Various types of tapes should be included in each kit. These include adhesive, which is waterproof and extra strong for times when rigid strapping is needed; clear, which stretches with the body's movement and is good for visible wounds; cloth, recommended for most first aid taping needs, including taping heavy dressings (less irritating than adhesive); and paper, which is recommended for sensitive skin and is used for light and frequently changed dressings.
- Items that can also be included in each kit are tweezers, first aid cream, thermometer, an analgesic or equivalent, and an ice pack.

Witch hazel bark can be brewed and used to soothe irritated skin or eyes.

# Excerpt from the U.S. Air Force Survival Handbook

## 7-1. Introduction:

a. Foremost, among the many things that can compromise a survivor's ability to return, are medical problems encountered during ejection, parachute descent, and(or) parachute landing. In the Southeast Asian conflict, some 30 percent of approximately 1,000 U.S. Air Force survivors, including 322 returned PWs, were injured by the time they disentangled themselves from their parachutes. The most frequently reported injuries were fractures, strains, sprains, and dislocations, as well as burns and other types of wounds.

b. Injuries and illnesses peculiar to certain environments can reduce survival expectancy. In cold climates, and often in an open sea survival situation, exposure to extreme cold can produce serious tissue trauma, such as frostbite, or death from hypothermia. Exposure to heat in warm climates, and in certain areas on the open seas, can produce heat cramps, heat exhaustion, or life threatening heatstroke.

c. Illnesses contracted during evasion or in a captivity environment can interfere with successful survival. Among these are gastrointestinal disorders, respiratory diseases, skin infections and infestations, malaria, typhus, cholera, etc.

d. A review of the survival experiences from World War II, Korea, and Southeast Asia indicates that, while U.S. military personnel generally knew how to administer first aid to others, there was a marked inability to administer self-aid. Further, only the most basic medical care had been taught to most military people. Lastly, it was repeatedly emphasized that even minor injuries or ailments, when ignored, became major problems in a survival situation. Thus, prompt attention to the most minor medical problem is essential in a survival episode. Applying principles of survival medicine should enable military members to maintain health and well-being in a hostile or nonhostile environment until rescued and returned to friendly control.

e. Information in this chapter is a basic reference to self-aid techniques used by PWs in captivity and techniques found in folk medicine. The information describes procedures which can maintain health in medically austere situations. It includes items used to prevent and treat injuries and illnesses. Because there is no "typical" survival situation, the approach to self-

aid must be flexible, placing emphasis on using what is available to treat the injury or illness. Further, survivors recognize that medical treatment offered by people of other cultures may be far different from our own. For example, in the rural areas of Vietnam, a poultice of python meat was and is used to treat internal lower back pain. Such treatment may be repugnant to some U.S. military personnel; however, medical aid offered to survivors in non-U.S. cultures may be the best available in the given circumstance.

f. The procedures in this chapter and must be viewed in the reality of a true survival situation. The results of treatment may be substandard compared with present medical standards. However, these procedures will not compromise professional medical care which becomes available following rescue. Moreover, in the context of a survival situation, they may represent the best available treatment to extend the individual's survival expectancy.

## 7-2. Procedures and Expedients.

Survival medicine encompasses procedures and expedients that are:

a. Required and available for the preservation of health and the prevention, improvement, or treatment of injuries and illnesses encountered during survival.
b. Suitable for application by nonmedical personnel to themselves or comrades in the circumstances of the survival situation.
(1)Survival medicine is more than first aid in the conventional sense. It approaches final definitive treatment in that it is not dependent upon the availability of technical medical assistance within a reasonable period of time.

(2)To avoid duplication of information generally available, the basic principles of first aid will not be repeated, nor will the psychological factors affecting survival.

## 7-3. Hygiene.

In a survival situation, cleanliness is essential to prevent infection. Adequate personal cleanliness will not only protect against disease germs that are present in the individual's surroundings, but will also protect the group by reducing the spread of these germs.

a. Washing, particularly the face, hands, and feet, reduces the chances of infection from small scratches and abrasions. A daily bath or shower with hot water and soap is ideal. If no tub or shower is available, the body should be cleaned with a cloth and soapy water, paying particular attention to the body creases (armpits, groin, etc.), face, ears, hands, and feet. After this type of "bath," the body should be rinsed thoroughly with clear water to remove all traces of soap which could cause irritation.

b. Soap, although an aid, is not essential to keeping clean. Ashes, sand, loamy soil, and other expedients may be used to clean the body and cooking utensils.

c. When water is in short supply, the survivor should take an "air bath." All clothing should be removed and the body simply exposed to the air. Exposure to sunshine is ideal, but even on an overcast day or indoors, a 2-hour exposure of the naked body to the air will refresh the body. Care should be taken to avoid sunburn when bathing in this manner. Exposure in the shade, shelter, sleeping bag, etc., will help if the weather conditions do not permit direct exposure.

d. Hair should be kept trimmed, preferably 2 inches or less in length, and the face should be clean-shaven. Hair provides a surface for the attachment of parasites and the growth of bacteria. Keeping the hair short and the face clean-shaven will provide less habitat for these organisms. At least once a week, the hair should be washed with soap and water. When water is in short supply, the hair should be combed or brushed thoroughly and covered to keep it clean. It should be inspected weekly for fleas, lice, and other parasites. When parasites are discovered, they should be removed.

e. The principal means of infecting food and open wounds is contact with unclean hands. Hands should be washed with soap and water, if available, after handling any material which is likely to carry germs. This is especially important after each visit to the latrine, when caring for the sick and injured, and before handling food, food utensils, or drinking water. The fingers should be kept out of the mouth and the fingernails kept closely trimmed and clean. A scratch from a long fingernail could develop into a serious infection.

## 7-4. Care of the Mouth and Teeth.

Application of the following fundamentals of oral hygiene will prevent tooth decay and gum disease:

a. The mouth and teeth should be cleansed thoroughly with a toothbrush and dentifrice at least once each day. When a toothbrush is not available, a "chewing stick" can be fashioned from a twig. The twig is washed, then chewed on one end until it is frayed and brushlike. The teeth can then be brushed very thoroughly with the stick, taking care to clean all tooth surfaces. If necessary, a clean strip of cloth can be wrapped around the finger and rubbed on the teeth to wipe away food particles which have collected on them. When neither toothpaste nor toothpowder are available, salt, soap, or baking soda can be used as substitute dentifrices. Parachute inner core can be used by separating the filaments of the inner core and using this as a dental floss. Gargling with willow bark tea will help protect the teeth.

b. Food debris which has accumulated between the teeth should be removed by using dental floss or toothpicks. The latter can be fashioned from small twigs.

c. Gum tissues should be stimulated by rubbing them vigorously with a clean finger each day.

d. Use as much care cleaning dentures and other dental appliances, removable or fixed, as when cleaning natural teeth. Dentures and removable bridges should be removed and cleaned with a denture brush or "chew stick" at least once each day. The tissue under the dentures should be brushed or rubbed regularly for proper stimulation. Removable dental applicances should be removed at night or for a 2- to 3-hour period during the day.

## 7-5. Care of the Feet.

Proper care of the feet is of utmost importance in a survival situation, especially if the survivor has to travel. Serious foot trouble can be prevented by observing the following simple rules:

a. The feet should be washed, dried thoroughly, and massaged each day. If water is in short supply, the feet should be "air cleaned" along with the rest of the body (Figure 7-3).

b. Toenails should be trimmed straight across to prevent the development of ingrown toenails.

c. Boots should be broken in before wearing them on any mission. They should fit properly, neither so tight that they bind and cause pressure spots nor so loose that they permit the foot to slide forward and backward when walking. Insoles should be improvised to reduce any friction spots inside the shoes.

d. Socks should be large enough to allow the toes to move freely but not so loose that they wrinkle. Wool socks should be at least one size larger than cotton socks to allow for shrinkage. Socks with holes should be properly darned before they are worn. Wearing socks with holes or socks that are poorly repaired may cause blisters. Clots of wool on the inside and outside should be removed from wool socks because they may cause blisters. Socks should be changed and washed thoroughly with soap and water each day. Woolen socks should be washed in cool water to lessen shrinkage. In camp, freshly laundered socks should be stretched to facilitate drying by hanging in the sun or in an air current. While traveling, a damp pair of socks can be dried by placing them inside layers of clothing or hanging them on the outside of the pack. If socks become damp, they should be exchanged for dry ones at the first opportunity.

e. When traveling, the feet should be examined regularly to see if there are any red spots or blisters. If detected in the early stages of development, tender areas should be covered with adhesive tape to prevent blister formation.

and socks should be changed daily. If water is in short supply, clothing should be "air cleaned." For air cleaning, the clothing is shaken out of doors, then aired and sunned for 2 hours. Clothing cleaned in this manner should be worn in rotation. Sleeping bags should be turned inside out, fluffed, and aired after each use. Bed linen should be changed at least once a week, and the blankets, pillows, and mattresses should be aired and sunned.

## 7-6. Clothing and Bedding.

Clothing and bedding become contaminated with any disease germs which may be present on the skin, in the stool, in the urine, or in secretions of the nose and throat. Therefore, keeping clothing and bedding as clean as possible will decrease the chances of skin infection and decrease the possibility of parasite infestation. Outer clothing should be washed with soap and water when it becomes soiled. Under clothing

## 7-7. Rest.

Rest is necessary for the survivor because it not only restores physical and mental vigor, but also promotes healing during an illness or after an injury.

a. In the initial stage of the survival episode, rest is particularly important. After those tasks requiring immediate attention are done, the survivor should inventory available resources, decide upon a plan of action, and even have a meal.

This "planning session" will provide a rest period without the survivor having a feeling of "doing nothing."

b. If possible, regular rest periods should be planned in each day's activities. The amount of time allotted for rest will depend on a number of factors, including the survivor's physical condition, the presence of hostile forces, etc., but usually, 10 minutes each hour is sufficient. During these rest periods, the survivor should change either from physical activity to complete rest or from mental activity to physical activity as the case may be. The survivor must learn to become comfortable and to rest under less than ideal conditions.

## 7-8. Rules for Avoiding Illness.

In a survival situation, whether short-term or long-term, the dangers of disease are multiplied. Application of the following simple guidelines regarding personal hygiene will enable the survivor to safeguard personal health and the health of others:

a. ALL water obtained from natural sources should be purified before consumption.

b. The ground in the camp area should not be soiled with urine or feces. Latrines should be used, if available. When no latrines are available, individuals should dig "cat holes" and cover their waste.

c. Fingers and other contaminated objects should never be put into the mouth. Hands should be washed before handling any food or drinking water, before using the fingers in the care of the mouth and teeth, before and after caring for the sick and injured, and after handling any material likely to carry disease germs.

d. After each meal, all eating utensils should be cleaned and disinfected in boiling water.

e. The mouth and teeth should be cleansed thoroughly at least once each day. Most dental problems associated with long-term survival episodes can be prevented by using a toothbrush and toothpaste to remove accumulated food debris. If necessary, devices for cleaning the teeth should be improvised.

f.  Bites and insects can be avoided by keeping the body clean, by wearing proper protective clothing, and by using head nets, improvised bed nets, and insect repellants.

g.  Wet clothing should be exchanged for dry clothing as soon as possible to avoid unnecessary body heat loss.

h.  Personal items such as canteens, pipes, towels, toothbrushes, handkerchiefs, and shaving items should not be shared with others.

i.  All food scraps, cans, and refuse should be removed from the camp area and buried.

j.  If possible, a survivor should get 7 or 8 hours of sleep each night.

k.  Aircrew members should keep all immunization "shots" current.

# 7-9. General Management of Injuries:

**a. Bleeding.**
Control of bleeding is most important in survival situations where replacement transfusions are not possible. Immediate steps should be taken to stop the flow of blood, regardless of its source. The method used should be commensurate with the type and degree of bleeding. The tourniquet, when required and properly used, will save life. If improperly used, it may cost the life of the survivor. The basic characteristics of a tourniquet and the methods of its use are well covered in standard first aid texts; however, certain points merit emphasis in the survival situation. A tourniquet should be used only after every alternate method has been attempted. If unable to get to medical aid within 2 hours, after 20 minutes, gradually loosen

the tourniquet. If bleeding has stopped, remove the tourniquet; if bleeding continues, reapply and leave in place. The tourniquet should be applied as near the site of the bleeding as possible, between the wound and the heart, to reduce the amount of tissue lost.

**b. Pain:**

(1) **Control of Pain.** The control of pain accompanying disease or injury under survival situations is both difficult and essential. In addition to its morale-breaking discomfort, pain contributes to shock and makes the survivor more vulnerable to enemy influences. Ideally, pain should be eliminated by the removal of the cause. However, this is not always immediately possible, hence measures for the control of pain are beneficial.

(2) **Position, Heat, and Cold.** The part of the body that is hurting should be put at rest, or at least its activity restricted as much as possible. The position selected should be the one giving the most comfort and be the easiest to maintain. Splints and bandages may be necessary to maintain the immobilization. Elevation of the injured part, with immobilization, is particularly beneficial in the throbbing type pain such as is typical of the "mashed" finger. Open wounds should be cleansed, foreign bodies removed, and a clean dressing applied to protect the wound from the air and chance contacts with environmental objects. Generally, the application of warmth reduces pain—toothache, bursitis, etc. However, in some conditions, application of cold has the same effect—strains and sprains. Warmth or cold is best applied by using water due to its high specific heat, and the survivor can try both to determine which is most beneficial.

(3) **Pain Killers.** Drugs are very effective in reducing pain; however, they are not

likely to be available in the survival situation. Hence, the importance of the above "natural" procedures. Aspirin, APCs, and such tablets are primarily intended to combat the discomforts of colds and upper respiratory diseases, and, at best, will just take the edge off severe pain. They should be taken, however, if available. If no aspirin is available, there are some parts of vegetation that can be used. For example, most of the willows have been used for their pain-relieving and fever-lowering properties for hundreds of years. The fresh bark contains salicin, which probably decomposes into salicylic acid in the human body. Wintergreen, also known as checkerberry, was used by some Indians for body aches and pains. The leaves are made into a tea. The boiled bark of the magnolia tree helps relieve internal pains and fever, and has been known to stop dysentery. To be really effective in control of pain, stronger narcotic drugs such as codeine and morphine are required. During active hostilities, morphine may be available in aircraft and individual first aid kits.

**c. Shock:**

(1) **Circulatory Reaction.** Shock in some degree accompanies all injuries to the body, and frequently it is the most serious consequence of the injury. In essence, shock is a circulatory reaction of the body (as a whole) to an injury (mechanical or emotional). While the changes to the circulatory system initially favor body resistance to the injury (by ensuring adequate blood supply to vital structures), they may progress to the point of circulatory failure and death. All aircrew members should be familiar with the signs and symptoms of shock so that the condition may be anticipated, recognized, and dealt with effectively. However, the best survival

approach is to treat ALL moderate and severe injuries for shock. No harm will be done, and such treatment will speed recovery.

(2) **Fluids.** Normally, fluids administered by mouth are generally prohibited in the treatment of shock following severe injury. Such fluids are poorly absorbed when given by mouth, and they may interfere with later administration of anesthesia for surgery. In survival medicine, however, the situation is different in that the treatment being given is the final treatment. Survivors cannot be deprived of water for long periods just because they have been injured; in fact, their recovery depends upon adequate hydration. Small amounts of warm water, warm tea, or warm coffee given frequently early in shock are beneficial if the patient is conscious, can swallow, and has no internal injuries. In later shock, fluids by mouth are less effective as they are not absorbed from the intestines. Burns, particularly, require large amounts of water to replace fluid lost from injured areas. Alcohol should never be given to a person in shock or who may go into shock.

(3) **Psychogenic Shock.** Psychogenic shock is frequently noted during the period immediately following an emergency; for example, bailout. Psychogenic shock, which occurs even without injury, requires attention to limit it, both in degree and duration. The degree of this post-impact shock varies widely among individuals but its occurrence is almost universal. In reality, the survivor has passed through two major emergencies almost simultaneously; the aircraft incident leading to the survival situation, and the situation itself. Should the survivor be injured (and the majority of them are), a third emergency is added. It is not uncommon, then, that

some psychogenic reaction with circulatory implications occurs. Resistance to this type of shock depends upon the individual's personality and the amount of training previously received. Treatment consists of stopping all activities (when possible), relaxing, evaluating the situation, and formulating a plan of action before the survival situation begins.

### d. Fractures:

(1) Proper immobilization of fractures, dislocations, and sprains is even more important in survival medicine than in conventional first aid. Rather than merely making the patient comfortable during transport to eventual treatment, in survival medicine, the initial immobilization is part of the ultimate treatment. Immobilizing body parts to help control pain was discussed earlier. In addition, immobilization in proper position hastens healing of fractures and improves the ultimate functional result. In the survival situation, the immobilization must suffice for a relatively long period of time and permit the patient to maintain a fairly high degree of mobility. Materials for splinting and bandaging are available in most survival situations, and proper techniques are detailed in most first aid manuals.

(2) The reduction of fractures is normally beyond the scope of first aid; however, in the prolonged survival situation, the correction of bone deformities is necessary to hasten healing and obtain the greatest functional result. The best time for manipulation of a fracture is in the period immediately following the injury, before painful muscle spasms ensue. Traction is applied until overriding fragments of bone are brought into line, (check by the other limb) and the extremity is firmly immobilized. Frequently, it is advantageous to continue traction after reduction to

ensure the proper alignment of the bones.

(3) As plaster casts are not available in the survival situation, improvising an immobilization device is necessary. This may be done by using several parallel, pliable willow branches, woven together with vines or parachute lines. Use care so that the extremity is not constricted when swelling follows the injury. In an escape and evasion situation, it may be necessary to preserve the mobility of the survivor after reduction of the fracture. This is difficult in fractures of the lower extremities, although tree limbs may be improvised as crutches. With companions, the use of improvised litters may be possible.

(4) Reduction of dislocated joints is done similar to that of fractures. Gentle, but firm traction is applied and the extremity is manipulated until it "snaps" back into place. If the survivor is alone, the problem is complicated but not impossible. Traction can still be applied by using gravity. The distal portion of the extremity is tied to (or wedged) into the fork of a tree or similar point of fixation. The weight of the body is then allowed to exert the necessary traction, with the joint being manipulated until the dislocation is reduced.

**e. Infection:**

(1) Infection is a serious threat to the survivor. The inevitable delay in definite medical treatment and the reality of the survival situation increases the chances of wound infection. Antibiotics may not be available in sufficient amounts in the survival situation. In survival medicine, one must place more emphasis on the prevention and control of infection by applying techniques used before the advent of antibiotics.

(2) Unfortunately, survivors have little control over the amount and type of infection

introduced at the time of injury. However, they can help control the infection by wearing clean clothes. Use care to prevent additional infection into wounds. Wounds, regardless of the type or severity, should not be touched with dirty hands or objects. One exception to this rule is the essential control of arterial bleeding. Clothing should be removed from wounds to avoid contamination surrounding skin areas.

(3) All wounds should be promptly cleansed. Water is the most universally available cleaning agent, and should be (preferably) sterile. At sea level, sterilize water, by placing it in a covered container and boiling it for 10 minutes. Above 3,000 feet, water should be boiled for 1 hour (in a covered container) to ensure adequate sterilization. The water will remain sterile and can be stored indefinitely as long as it is covered.

(a) Irrigate wounds rather than scrubbing to minimize additional damage to the tissue. Foreign material should be washed from the wound to remove sources of continued infection. The skin adjacent to wounds should be washed thoroughly before bandaging. When water is not available for cleaning wounds, the survivor should consider the use of urine. Urine may well be the most nearly sterile of all fluids available and, in some cultures, is preferred for cleaning wounds. Survivors should use urine from the midstream of the urine flow.

(b) While soap is not essential to clean wounds, a bar of medicated soap placed in a personal survival kit and used routinely would do much to prevent the infection of seemingly inconsequential injuries. External antiseptics are best used for cleaning abrasions, scratches, and the skin areas adjacent to lacerations. Used in deep, larger wounds, antiseptics produce further tissue damage.

(c) Nature also provides antiseptics which can be used for wound care. The American Mountain Ash is found from New-foundland south to North Carolina and its inner bark has antiseptic properties. The red berries contain ascorbic acid and have been eaten to cure scurvy. The Sweet Gum bark is still officially recognized as being an antiseptic agent. Water from boiled Sweet Gum leaves can also be used as antiseptic for wounds.

**f. The "Open Treatment" Method.** This is the only safe way to manage survival wounds. No effort should be made to close open wounds by suturing or by other procedure. In fact, it may be necessary to open the wound even more to avoid entrapment or infection and to promote drainage. The term "open" does not mean that dressings should not be used. Good surgery requires that although wounds are not "closed," nerves, bone, and blood vessels should be covered with tissue.

Such judgment may be beyond the capability of the aircrew member, but protection of vital structures will aid in the recovery and ultimate function. A notable exception to "open treatment" is the early closure of facial wounds which interfere with breathing, eating, or drinking. Wounds, left open, heal by formation of infection-resistant granulation tissue (proud flesh). This tissue is easily recognized by its moist red granular appearance, a good sign in any wound.

**g. Dressings and Bandages.** After cleansing, all wounds should be covered with a clean dressing. The dressing should be sterile; however, in the survival situation, any clean cloth will help to protect the wound from further infection. A proper bandage will anchor the dressing to the wound and afford further protection. Bandages should be snug enough to prevent slippage, yet not constrictive. Slight pressure will reduce discomfort in most wounds and help stop bleeding. Once in place, dressings should not be changed too frequently unless required. External soiling does not reduce the effectiveness of a dressing and pain and some tissue damage will accompany any removal. In addition, changing dressings increases the danger of infection.

### h. Physiological "Logistics."

Despite all precautions, some degree of infection is almost universal in survival wounds. This is the primary reason for the "open" treatment advocated above. The human body has a tremendous capacity for combating infections if it is permitted to do so. The importance of proper rest and nutrition to wound healing and control of infection has been mentioned. In addition, the "logistics" of the injured part should be improved. The injury should be immobilized in a position to favor adequate circulation, both to and from the wound. Avoid constrictive clothing or bandages. Applying heat to an infected wound further aids in mobilizing local body defense measures. Lukewarm saltwater soaks will help draw out infection and promote oozing of fluids from the wound, thereby removing toxic products. Poultices, made of clean clay, shredded bark of most trees, ground grass seed, etc., do the same thing.

### i. Drainage.

Adequate natural drainage of infected areas promotes healing. Generally, wicks or drains are unnecessary. On occasion, however, it may be better to remove an accumulation of pus (abscess) and insert light, loose packing to ensure continuous drainage. The knife or other instrument used in making the incision for drainage must be sterilized to avoid introducing other types of organisms. The best way to sterilize in the field is with heat, dry or moist.

### j. Antibiotics.

Antibiotics, when available, should be taken for the control of infection. Consensus is that the drug should be of the so-called "broad spectrum type;" that is, be effective against any microorganisms rather than specific for just one or two types. The exact amount to be included in survival kits will vary with the drug and basic assumptions as to the number and types of infections to be expected. Remember that antibiotics are potency-dated items (shelf life about 4 years), and including them in survival kits requires kit inspection and drug replacement with active medical stocks.

### k. Debridement.

(The surgical removal of lacerated, devitalized, or contaminated tissue.) The debridement of severe wounds may be necessary to minimize infection (particularly of the gas gangrene type) and to reduce septic (toxic) shock. In essence, debridement is the removal of foreign material and dead or dying tissue. The procedure requires skill and should only be done by nonmedical personnel in case of dire emergency. If required, follow these general rules. Dead skin must be cut away. Muscle may be trimmed back to a point where bleeding starts and gross discoloration ceases. Fat which is damaged tends to die and should be cut away. Bone and nerves should be conserved where possible and protected from further damage. Provide ample natural drainage for the potentially infected wound and delay final closure of the wound.

### l. Burns:

(1) Burns, frequently encountered in aircraft accidents and subsequent survival episodes, pose serious problems. Burns cause severe pain, increase the probability of shock and infection, and offer an avenue for the loss of considerable body fluids and salts. Direct initial treatment toward relieving pain and preventing infection. Covering the wound with a clean dressing of any type reduces the pain and chance for infection. Further,

such protection enhances the mobility of the patient and the capability for performing other vital survival functions. In burns about the face and neck, ensure the victim has an open airway. If necessary, cricothyroidotemy should be done before the patient develops extreme difficulties. Burns of the face and hands are particularly serious in a survival situation as they interfere with the capability of survivors to meet their own needs. Soaking certain barks (willow, oak, maple) in water soothes and protects burns by astringent action. This is a function of the acid content of the bark used.

(2) Maintenance of body fluids and salts is essential to recover from burns. The only way to administer fluids in a survival situation is by mouth; hence the casualty should ingest sufficient water early before the nausea and vomiting of toxicity intervenes. Consuming the eyes and blood (both cooked) of animals can help restore electrolyte levels if salt tablets are not available. NOTE: The survivor may also pack salt in personal survival kits to replace electrolytes (1/4 teaspoon per quart of water).

**m. Lacerations:**

Lacerations (cuts) are best left open due to the probability of infection. Clean thoroughly, remove foreign material, and apply a protective dressing. Frequently, immobilization will hasten the healing of major lacerations. On occasion (tactical), it may be necessary to close (cover) the wound, despite the danger of infection, in order to control bleeding or increase the mobility of the patient. If a needle is available, thread may be procured from parachute lines, fabric, or clothing, and the wound closed by "suturing." If suturing is required, place the stitches individually and far enough apart to permit drainage of underlying parts. Do not worry about the cosmetic effect;

just approximate the tissue. For scalp wounds, hair may be used to close after the wound is cleansed. Infection is less a danger in this area due to the rich blood supply.

**n. Head Injuries.**

Injuries to the head pose additional problems related to brain damage as well as interfering with breathing and eating. Bleeding is more profuse in the face and head area, but infections have more difficulty in taking hold. This makes it somewhat safer to close such wounds earlier to maintain function. Cricothyroidotemy may be necessary if breathing becomes difficult due to obstruction of the upper airways. In the event of unconsciousness, watch the patient closely and keep him or her still. Even in the face of mild or impending shock, keep the head level or even slightly elevated if there is reason to expect brain damage. Do not give fluids or morphine to unconscious persons.

**o. Abdominal Wounds.**

Wounds of the abdomen are particularly serious in the survival situation. Such wounds, without immediate and adequate surgery, have an extremely high mortality rate and render patients totally unable to care for themselves. If intestines are not extruded through the wound, a secure bandage should be applied to keep this from occurring. If intestine is extruded, do not replace it due to the almost certain threat of fatal peritonitis. Cover the extruded bowel with a large dressing and keep the dressing wet with any fluid that is fit to drink, or urine. The patient should lie on the back and avoid any motions that increase intra-abdominal pressure which might extrude more bowel. Keep the survivor in an immobile state or move on a litter. "Nature" will eventually take care of the problem; either through death or walling-off of the damaged area.

**p. Chest Injuries.**

Injuries of the chest are common, painful, and disabling. Severe bruises of the chest or fractures of the ribs require that the chest be immobilized to prevent large painful movements of the chest wall. The bandage is applied while the patient deeply exhales. In the survival situation, it may be necessary for survivors to wrap their own chest. This is more difficult but can be done by attaching one end of the long bandage (parachute material) to a tree or other fixed object, holding the other end in the hand, and slowly rolling body toward the tree, keeping enough counterpressure on the bandage to ensure a tight fit.

**q. Sucking Chest Wounds.**
These wounds are easily recognized by the sucking noise and appearance of foam or bubbles in the wound. These wounds must be closed immediately before serious respiratory and circulatory complications occur. Ideally, the patient should attempt to exhale while holding the mouth and nose closed (Valsalva) as the wound

is closed. This inflates the lungs and reduces the air trapped in the pleural cavity. Frequently, a taped, airtight dressing is all that is needed, but sometimes it is necessary to put in a stitch or two to make sure the wound is closed.

**r. Eye Injuries.**
Eye injuries are quite serious in a survival situation due to pain and interference with other survival functions. The techniques for removing foreign bodies and for treating snow blindness are covered in standard first aid manuals. More serious eye injuries involving disruption of the contents of the orbit may require that the lids of the affected eye be taped closed or covered to prevent infection.

**s. Thorns and Splinters.**
Thorns and splinters are frequently encountered in survival situations. Reduce their danger by wearing gloves and proper footgear. Their prompt removal is quite important to prevent infection. Wounds made by these

agents are quite deep compared to their width, which increases chances of infection by those organisms (such as tetanus) that grow best in the absence of oxygen. Removal of splinters is aided by the availability of a sharp instrument (needle or knife), needle nose pliers, or tweezers. Take care to get all of the foreign body out; sometimes it is best to open the wound sufficiently to properly cleanse it and to allow air to enter the wound. When cleaned, treat as any other wound.

**t. Blisters and Abrasions.**
Care for blisters and abrasions promptly. Foot care is extremely important in the survival situation. If redness or pain is noted, the survivor should stop (if at all possible) to find and correct the cause. Frequently, a protective dressing or bandage and(or) adhesive will be sufficient to prevent a blister. If a blister occurs, do not remove the top. Apply a sterile (or clean) dressing. Small abrasions should receive attention to prevent infection.

Using soap with a mild antiseptic will minimize the infection of small abrasions which may not come to the attention of the survivor.

**u. Insect Bites.**
Bites of insects, leeches, ticks, chiggers, etc., pose several hazards. Many of these organisms transmit diseases, and the bite itself is likely to become infected, especially if it itches and the survivor scratches it. The body should be inspected frequently for ticks, leeches, etc., and these should be removed immediately. If appropriate and possible, the survivor should avoid infested areas. These parasites can best be removed by applying heat or other irritant to them to encourage a relaxation of their hold on the host. Then the entire organism may be gently detached from the skin, without leaving parts of the head imbedded. Treat such wounds as any other wound. Applying cold wet dressings will reduce itching, scratching, and swelling.

# 7-10. Illnesses.

Many illnesses which are minor in a normal medical environment become major in a survival situation when the individual is alone without medications or medical care. Survivors should use standard methods (treat symptoms) to prevent expected diseases since treatment in a survival situation is so difficult. Key preventive methods are to maintain a current immunization record, maintain a proper diet, and exercise.

**a. Food Poisoning.** Food poisoning is a significant threat to survivors. Due to sporadic food availability, excess foods must be preserved and saved for future consumption. Methods for food preservation vary with the global area and situation. Bacterial contamination of food sources has historically caused much more difficulty in survival situations than the ingestion of so-called poisonous plants and animals. Similarly, dysentery or water-borne diseases can be controlled by proper sanitation and personal hygiene.

**b. Treatment of Food Poisoning.** Supportive treatment is best if the food poisoning is due to preformed toxin; staphylococcus, botulism, etc. (acute symptoms of nausea, vomiting, and diarrhea soon after ingestion of the contaminated food). Keep the patient quiet and lying down, and ensure the patient drinks substantial quantities of water. If the poisoning is due to ingestion of bacteria which grow within the body (delayed gradual onset of same symptoms), take antibiotics (if available). In both cases, symptoms may be alleviated by frequently eating small amounts of fine, clean charcoal. In PW situations, if chalk is available, reduce it to powder, and eat to coat and soothe the intestines. Proper sanitation and personal hygiene will help prevent spreading infection to others in the party or continuing reinfection of the patient.

# Backyard Medicine

## By Julie and Matthew Seal

## Agrimony

*Agrimonia eupatoria, A. procera, A. gryposepala*

Agrimony stops bleeding of all sorts, and is used in trauma treatment and surgery in Chinese hospitals. It helps relieve pain too, and has a long tradition as a wound herb as well as for treating liver, digestive, and urinary tract problems. Agrimony tightens and tones the tissues, and, in a seeming contradiction, also relaxes tension, both physical and mental. This is the herb for when you're feeling frazzled, when stress and tension or pain are causing torment.

You can hardly miss this tall and bright summer garden herb, which readily earns its old name of church steeples. The sticky burrs that cling to passers-by lie behind another name, cocklebur. Agrimony used to be a significant herb in the European tradition, being the Anglo-Saxon healing plant "garclive," but it is underused and underrated in modern western herbalism.

*Agrimonia eupatoria* is the "official" agrimony, but John Parkinson in *Theatrum Botanicum* (1640) preferred fragrant agrimony, *Agrimonia procera,* if available. The two can be used interchangeably. In Chinese medicine, *A. pilosa* is the species used, and its name, *xian he cao,* translates as "immortal crane herb," which gives an idea of the reverence in which it is held. It is used in surgery and trauma treatment to stop bleeding, and has been found to be effective against *Trichomonas* vaginal infections and tapeworms, as also for dysentery and chronic diarrhea. Dr Edward Bach chose agrimony as one of his thirty-eight flower essences. It is for people who soldier on, who say everything is fine when it is not, hiding inner turmoil behind a cheerful facade and ignoring the darker side of life. The out-of-balance agrimony person often resorts to alcohol, drugs, or adrenaline-producing sports to avoid dealing with life issues.

**Use Agrimony for . . .**

Contemporary American herbalist Matthew Wood has written more deeply about agrimony than anybody else. He uses it as a flower essence, herbal tincture, and homeopathic preparation, and has researched it in great detail,

expanding on the traditional picture of the plant. Wood calls agrimony "the bad hair day remedy"—imagine the cartoon picture of a cat that has had a fright or put its paw into an electric socket. He has found it works for people with mental and physical tension or work-related stress, with "pain that makes them hold their breath" and a range of other conditions.

**Agrimony Tea**

- eyewash, conjunctivitis
- gargle for mouth & gum or throat problems

Agrimony, from Woodville's *Medical Botany* (1790–3)

- in footbath for athlete's foot
- in bath for sprains & strained muscles

**Agrimony Tincture**
- appendicitis
- urinary incontinence
- potty training
- cystitis
- weak digestion
- diarrhea/constipation
- tension
- irritable bladder
- asthma
- childhood diarrhea
- burns

*. . . there are few of our wild flowers which are in more esteem with the village herbalist than the agrimony. Every gatherer of simples know it well.*

—Pratt (1857)

Agrimony is a great herb for treating intermittent fever and chills, or in alternating constipation and diarrhea, as it helps the body to recover a working balance between extremes, by releasing the tension and constricted energy that cause such problems.

Pain is very often associated with constriction, with one condition reinforcing the other. Agrimony can help release us from this self-perpetuating spiral, allowing body and mind to relax and restorative healing to begin as blood and energy flow are brought back to normal. Agrimony is a wonderful wound herb, as it rapidly stops bleeding and also relieves pain. It is thought that a high tannin and vitamin K content account for its remarkable coagulation properties. In the 1400s agrimony was picked to make "arquebusade water," to staunch bleeding inflicted by the arquebus or hand gun.

Agrimony works well for burns too put tincture directly on the burn and take a few drops internally; repeat until pain subsides.

Agrimony has an affinity for the liver and digestive tract, working to coordinate their functions. John Parkinson—the herbalist to King James II and King Charles I—wrote in 1640 that "it openeth the obstructions

of the Liver, and cleanseth it;
it helpeth the jaun-dise, and
strengthneth the inward parts,
and is very beneficiall to the
bowels, and healeth their inward
woundings and bruises or
hurts."All these are uses borne
out today and explained by
the herb's bitter and astringent
qualities.

Agrimony's other main
affinity is for the urinary tract,
being used to good effect to ease
the pain of kidney stones, irritable
bladder, and chronic cystitis. It
can be given safely to children
for bedwetting and anxiety about
potty training, and to the elderly
for incontinence.

## Harvesting Agrimony

Harvest when the plant is in
bloom in the summer, picking
the flower spike and some leaves.
For agrimony tea, dry them in
the shade until crisp, and then
strip the flowers and leaves off the
stems, discarding the stems. Store
in brown paper bags or glass jars,
in a cool dry place.

### Agrimony Tea

Use 1–2 teaspoonfuls of **dried agrimony** per cup of **boiling water,** infused for 10 to 15 minutes. The tea has a pleasant taste and odor, and was often used as a country beverage, especially when imported tea was expensive.

**Dose:** The tea can be drunk three times a day, or used when cool as an eyewash or gargle for gum irritations and sore throats.

## Agrimony Bath

Make a strong tea with a handful of **dried agrimony** infused in 1 pint of freshly **boiled water** for 20 minutes.

Poured hot into a foot bath, this soothes athlete's foot or sprained ankles; added to a hot bath it helps strained muscles after exercise, and general tension that has stiffened the muscles, back, and joints.

## Agrimony Tincture

To make agrimony tincture, pick the **flowers and leaves** on a bright sunny day. Pack them into a glass jar large enough to hold your harvest—clean jam jars work well—and pour in enough **brandy or vodka** to cover them. Put the lid on the jar and keep it in a dark cupboard for six weeks, shaking it every few days. Strain off the liquid, bottle, and label.

Amber or blue glass bottles will protect your tincture from UV light. If you use clear glass bottles, you will need to keep your tincture in a dark cupboard. It doesn't need to be refrigerated and should keep for several years, although it is best to make a fresh batch every summer if you can.

**Dose:** For tension or interstitial cystitis: 3–5 drops in a little water three times a day; as an astringent to tone tissues (as in diarrhea), half a teaspoonful in water three times daily.

The tincture can be used as a first aid remedy for burns. First cool the burn thoroughly by holding it under water running from the cold tap for several minutes. You can just pour a little tincture onto the burn, but for best results, wet a cotton ball with the tincture and hold it in place until the burn stops hurting.

## Birch

Birch has a multitude of historical uses but is less familiar for its undoubted medicinal benefits. The sap makes a clear and refreshing drink that can be preserved as a wine, beer, or spirit. The leaves produce a pleasant tea and an infused oil. In each form, birch is an excellent tonic and detoxifier, mainly working on the urinary system to remove waste products, as in kidney or bladder stone, gravel, gout, and rheumatism. It reduces fluid retention and swellings, and clears up many skin problems. Birch is one of the most useful of trees as well as one of the most graceful. From adhesives to wine, baskets to yokes, and boats to vinegar, it has been a boon to people in the cold north for thousands of years. Its medicinal qualities have been historically valued and should be better known today. Called the oldest tree in Britain, birch was a pioneer species when the ice caps retreated, moving in on the devastated land, growing quickly and then rotting to leave more fertile earth in which other species could take over. In its rapid life cycle birch pushes upward too fast to develop a strong heart wood, but this makes it perfect for making buckets and canoes.

As a youngster (writes Matthew), I was a suburban Hiawatha, and wanted to be a "Red Indian." I had read in my weekly comic, the *Eagle,* how my heroes had made birch bark canoes and wrote on bark paper. Birch was a common enough tree, but I never really got down to the canoe or the paper. Soccer was more important. But now these memories return, as Julie and I tap a birch in our garden. It is that time in spring after most of the frosts and before the birch buds and leaves emerge.

The tree is now forcing its sap upward in prodigious quantity, and you simply tap into the flow, remembering to be kind to the tree after you have taken your share by closing off the wound.

Birch sap is rich in fructose whereas maple has sucrose. Sucrose is sweeter to the taste and the maple yields more per tree, so maple syrup is by far the bigger commercial industry. On the other hand, birch sap is cool, refreshing and clear. It tastes even better when reduced by simmering down into a golden-brown ambrosia. It's the sort of drink the elves would envy!

**Description:** Deciduous trees that often hybridize, with whitish papery bark.

**Habitat:** Woods, heaths, moors, and gardens. Downy birch prefers wetter places.

**Distribution:** Silver birch or European white birch (*Betula pendula*) and downy birch (*B. pubescens*) are native to northern temperate regions of Eurasia, and found as introduced species in North America. Sweet birch (*B. lenta*) is native to eastern North America.

**Related species:** Worldwide, several birch species have medicinal value. In Ayurveda, Himalayan silver birch (*B. utlis*) is used.

**Parts used:** Sap, tapped in early spring; leaves, gathered in spring and early summer. The bark is also used.

**Use Birch for . . .**

Birch sap, birch water, or blood, had a folk reputation for breaking kidney or bladder stone and treating skin conditions and rheumatic diseases. It can be drunk in spring as a refreshing and cleansing tonic, clearing the sluggishness of winter from the system. The fermented sap also makes birch wine and country beers and spirits.

Besides being a source of tinder and paper, birch bark has been used for tanning leather, especially in Russia, and for

> **A stand of silver birch in the English Surrey hills, where the birch is so common it earned the name "Surrey weed".**

preserving nets and ropes. Another product of this gracious tree is an oil tar from the bark. This is used commercially in birch creams and ointments for chronic skin conditions. The fresh leaves or buds of birch offer a powerful but pleasant tea for general detoxing, urinary complaints, cystitis, rheumatic and arthritic troubles, and gout. Some herbalists add a pinch of sodium bicarbonate to improve the tea's ability to cut high uric acid levels. Any condition of fluid retention, such as cardiac or renal edema and dropsy, will be helped by the tea. Birch is rich in potassium, so that (like dandelion) it does not deplete the body of this mineral in the way that medical diuretics do.

Being such a good eliminator, birch tea is also effective as a compress applied directly to the skin for herpes, eczema, and the like. You can easily make your own birch leaf oil by infusing the leaves in olive or sweet almond oil. This goes into commercial cellulite treatments, and can be used as a massage oil to relieve muscle aches and pains, fibromyalgia, and rheumatism. Drink birch tea as well for maximum benefit.

Birch is regarded as safe medicinally and no side effects have been reported.

## Birch Leaf Oil

Pick the **leaves** in late spring or early summer, while they are still fresh and light green. Put them in a jar large enough to hold them and pour in enough **extra virgin olive oil or sweet almond oil** to cover them. Put a piece of cloth over the jar as a lid, held on with a rubber band. This will allow any moisture released by the leaves to escape. Put the jar in a sunny place indoors and leave for a month but stir it fairly regularly, checking to see that the leaves are kept beneath the surface of the oil.

Strain off into a jug, using a nylon jelly bag or a large strainer (if you use muslin, it will soak up too much of the oil). Allow to settle—if there is any water in the oil from the leaves, it will sink to the bottom of the jug. Pour the oil into sterile storage bottles, leaving any watery residue behind in the jug, and label. Using amber, blue, or green glass will protect the oil from ultraviolet light, so if you use clear glass bottles remember to store your oil away from light.

This can be used as a massage oil for cellulite, fibromyalgia, rheumatism, and other muscle aches and pains. It can be also used on eczema and psoriasis—but remember that these also need to be treated internally, so ask your herbalist for advice.

*. . . birch water is the hope, the blessing and the panacea of rich and poor, master and peasant alike . . . almost unfailingly cures skin conditions . . . and countless chronic ills against which medical science is so prone to fail.*

—*Baron Percy (c. 1800)*

**Birch leaf oil**
- cellulite
- detoxing massage
- aching muscles
- rheumatism
- eczema
- psoriasis

**Birch leaf tea**
- spring cleanse
- kidney stones

- urinary gravel
- cystitis
- gout
- arthritis
- rheumatism
- psoriasis
- eczema
- fluid retention
- fevers

**Birch sap**

- cleansing tonic

Our own crude birch tap: you can probably do better!

**Birch Leaf Tea**

Pick the leaves in spring and early summer while they are still a fresh bright green. They can be used fresh in season or dried for later use. To dry, spread the leaves on a sheet of paper or on a drying screen, which can be made by stretching and stapling a piece of netting to a wooden frame. Dry them in the shade, until crisp when crumbled. To make the tea, use 4 or 5 **leaves** per cup or mug of **boiling water**, and allow to infuse for 5 to 10 minutes.

**Dose:** Drink a cupful up to three or four times daily.

# Birch Sap

To collect the sap, drill a hole through the bark in the early spring, before the tree gets its leaves. Insert a tube into the hole—a straw with a flexible end works well—and put the other end in a bottle or collection bucket. After you have collected for about a week, make sure you plug the hole with a twig the right size so that the tree doesn't keep "bleeding." The sap is a delightfully refreshing drink as it comes from the tree, or it can be gently simmered down to taste to produce an amber ambrosia or further reduced to make a syrup.

# Poisonous Insects, Reptiles, and Plants

## Insects

My first experience with woodticks, jiggers, and Jersey mosquitoes was during the summer we spent at Bayville, near Toms River, NJ. In many ways Bayville, with its sand, its pines, its beautiful wood roads, and rare wild flowers, is an interesting and attractive place. The salty air is fine when the thermometer is self-respecting and keeps the mercury below 90° in the shade, but the oak underbrush harbors wood-ticks, the blackberry bushes cover you with jiggers, the woods are full of deerflies, and the vicious mosquito, whose name is Legion, is everywhere where he is not barred out.

## Wood-Ticks

I had been told of the ticks that infest the forests of the South, had heard bloodcurdling stories of how they sometimes bury themselves, entire, in the flesh of animals and men and have to be cut out, and my horror of them was great. In reality I found them unpleasant enough but, as far as we were concerned, comparatively harmless.

The woodtick is a small, rather disgusting-looking creature which, in appearance and size, resembles the common bedbug. It fastens itself upon you without your knowledge and you do not feel it even when it begins to suck your blood, but something generally impels you to pass your hand over the back of your neck, or cheek, where the thing is clinging, and, feeling the lump, you pull it off and no great harm done. The tick is supposed always to bury its head in the flesh, and it is said that if the head is left in when the bug is pulled off an ugly sore will be the result. We had no experience of that kind, however, nor, in our hurry to get rid of it, did we stop to remove the bug scientifically by dropping oil on it, as Kephart advises, but just naturally and simply, also vigorously, we grasped it between thumb and forefinger and hastily plucked it off. The effect of the bite was no worse on any of our party than that of the Jersey mosquito.

Often your friends will see a tick on you and tell you of it even while they have several, all unknown to themselves, decorating their own countenance. The name by which science knows this unlovely bug is *Ixodes leech*.

## Jigger. Redbug. Mite.

The tiny mite called by the natives jigger and redbug is more annoying than the woodtick, one reason being that there are so many more of him. He really does penetrate the skin, and his wanderings under the surface give one the feeling of an itching rash which covers the body. You won't see the jigger—he is too small, but if you invade his domain you will certainly feel him.

## Deerfly

The deerfly will bite and bite hard enough to hurt. It will drive its sharp mandibles into your skin with such force as to take out a bit of the flesh, sometimes causing the blood to flow, but the bite does not seem particularly poisonous, though you feel it at the time and it generally raises a lump on the flesh. The deerfly belongs to the family of gadflies. It is larger than a housefly and its wings stand out at right angles to its body. It will not trouble you much except in the woods.

## Blackfly

The Adirondack and North Woods region is not only the resort of hunters, campers, and seekers after health and pleasure, but it is also the haunt of the maddening blackfly. From early spring until the middle of July or first of August the blackfly holds the territory; then it evacuates and is seen no more until next season, when it begins a new campaign.

Under the name of buffalo-fly the blackfly is found in the west, where, on the prairies, it has been known to wage war on horses until death ensued—death of the horses, not of the fly. It is a small fly about one-sixth of an inch long, thick-bodied, and black. It is said to have broad silvery circles on its legs, but no one ever stops to look at these. Its proboscis is developed to draw blood freely, and it is always in working order.

The only virtue the blackfly seems to have is its habit of quitting operations at sundown and leaving to other tormenters the task of keeping you awake at night. When the blackfly bites you will know it, and it will leave its mark, when it does leave, which must generally be by your help, for it holds on with commendable persistence. If you would learn more of this charming insect, look for *Simulium molestum* in a book which treats the subject scientifically.

## No-see-um. Punky. Midge.

There is another pest of the North Woods which the guides call the no-see-um. It is a very diminutive midge resembling the mosquito in form and viciousness, but so small as to be almost invisible. Night and day are the same to the no-see-um; its warfare is continuous and its bite very annoying, but it disappears with the blackfly in July or August. By September the mountains and woods are swept clear of all these troublesome things, except at times and in some places the ever-hungry mosquito, which will linger on for a last bite in his summer feast.

The only way to relieve the irritation caused by the bites of these pests, including the mosquito, is to bathe the affected parts with camphor, alcohol, or diluted ammonia. When there are but one or two bites they may be touched with strong ammonia, but it will not do to use this too freely, as it will burn the skin.

## Gnats

In the mountains of Pennsylvania the most troublesome insects I found were the tiny gnats that persist in flying into one's eyes in a very exasperating fashion. They swarm in a cloud in front of your face as you walk and make constant dashes at your eyes, although to reach their goal brings instant death.

It is not much trouble to get one of these gnats out of your eye when it once gets in. All that is necessary is to take the eyelashes of the upper eyelid between your thumb and first finger, and draw the upper eyelid down *over* the under eyelid. The under eyelashes sweep the upper lid clear, and the rush of tears that comes to the eye washes the insect out.

## Bees, Wasps, and Yellow-Jackets

While honeybees and wasps can make themselves most disagreeable when disturbed, you can usually keep away from beehives and bee-trees as well as from the great gray, papery nests of the wasp; but the hornets or yellow-jackets have an uncomfortable habit of building in low bushes and on the ground where you may literally put your foot in a hornets' nest.

They are hot-tempered little people, these same hornets, as I have reason to know. Twice I have been punished by them, and both times it was my head they attacked. Once I found them, or they found me, in a cherry-tree; and the second time we met was when I stepped in their nest hidden on the ground. Their sting is like a hot wire pressed into the flesh. When angered they will chase you and swarm around your head, stinging whenever they can; but they may be beaten off if some friendly hand will wield a towel or anything else that comes handy.

If the stings of any of these stinging insects are left in the wounds they should be taken out with a *clean* needle or *clean* knife-blade. In any case mix some mud into a paste and plaster it on the parts that have been stung. If you are in camp and have with you a can of antiphlogistine use that instead of the mud; it is at least more sightly and is equally efficient in reducing inflammation.

Various things have been devised as protection against insect torments.

## Dopes

Then there are dopes to be rubbed over the face, neck, and hands. The three said to be the best are Nessmuk's Dope, Breck's Dope, and H. P. Wells's Bug-Juice. There is also a Rexall preparation which, I am told, is good while it stays on, but will wash off with perspiration.

## Nessmuk's Dope

In giving the recipe for his dope, Nessmuk says that it produces a glaze over the skin and that in preventing insect bites he has never known it to fail. This is the dope:

| Pine tar | 3 oz. |
|---|---|
| Castor oil | 2 oz. |
| Oil of pennyroyal | 1 oz. |

Simmer all together over a slow fire, and bottle.

This is sufficient for four persons for two weeks.

**Breck's Dope**

| Pine tar | 3 oz. |
|---|---|
| Olive (or castor oil) | 2 oz. |
| Oil of pennyroyal | 1 oz. |
| Citronella | 1 oz. |
| Creosote | 1 oz. |
| Camphor (pulverized) | 1 oz. |
| Large tube of carbolated vaseline | |

Heat the tar and oil, and add the other ingredients; simmer over slow fire until well mixed. The tar may be omitted if disliked or for ladies' use.

Breck tells us that his dope was planned to be a counter-irritant after being bitten as well as a preventer of bites.

**H. P. Wells's Bug-Juice**

| Olive oil | ½ pt. |
|---|---|
| Creosote | 1 oz. |
| Pennyroyal | 1 oz. |
| Camphor | 1 oz. |

Dissolve camphor in alcohol and mix.

Any dope must be well rubbed in on face, neck, ears, and *behind ears*, hands (on the backs), wrists, and arms; but be very careful not to get it *in your eyes*.

## Smudges

Smudges are said to afford relief in camp, but my own experience has been that the insects can stand them better than I. A smudge is made by burning things that make little flame and much smoke. Dead leaves, not too dry, will make a fairly good smudge, but a better way is to burn damp cedar bark, or branches, on piles of hot coals taken from the campfire and kept alive at different sides of the camp.

The accounts of extreme suffering caused by insect bites come from unusually sensitive people. All people are not affected alike. Two persons from one camp will tell entirely different stories of their experience with insects. The best way to encounter these, as all other annoyances, is to protect yourself as well as you can and then, without whimpering, make the best of the situation. All the pests described will not fall upon you at once, and, taken singly or even doubly, you will manage to survive the ordeal. If the pleasure of the trail did not over-balance the pain there would be fewer campers to relate their troubles.

## Snakes

The bite of a poisonous snake is by all means to be avoided, and the point is: You almost always can avoid it. With all the snakes in the United States, Doctor William T. Hornaday, director of the Zoological Park of New York City, tells us that out of seventy-five million people not more than two die each year of snakebites.

Snakes are not man-hunters; they will not track you down; they much prefer to keep out of your way. What you have to do is to keep out of theirs. In a region where poisonous snakes abound it is well to wear khaki leggings as a protection in case you inadvertently step too near and anger the creatures, for in such cases they sometimes strike before you have time to beat a retreat. According to Doctor Hornaday, the poisonous snakes of North America are:

The rattlesnake,

Water-moccasin,

Copperhead,

Sonora coral snake,

Harlequin snake.

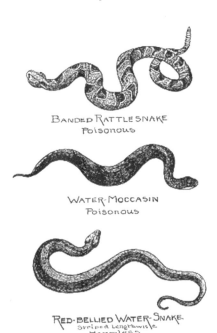

BANDED RATTLE SNAKE
Poisonous

WATER-MOCCASIN
Poisonous

RED-BELLIED WATER-SNAKE.
Striped lengthwise
Harmless

Poisonous and non-poisonous snakes.

## Rattlesnakes

The rattlesnake appears to vary in color and markings in the different localities where it is found, and there are fourteen or fifteen varieties, but all carry the rattles, shake them warningly, and coil before they strike. The rattlesnake does not want to fight and if you keep at a safe distance it will glide off in another direction, but it is safest not to venture within striking distance, which is said to be two-thirds the length of the snake, even if the snake has not coiled, for it moves quickly and strikes like a flash.

The rattles are at the extreme end of the tail and are composed of horny joints. The sound of the rattle is much like the humming of a locust (cicada). Rattlesnakes are often found sunning themselves on large rocks, and stone-quarries are the chosen winter quarters where whole colonies assemble. They are also found, during the summer, among underbrush and in stubble-fields, where they probably go to hunt field mice and other small mammals.

## Banded Rattlesnake

The mountains of Pennsylvania are a favorite resort of the rattlesnake, but, though I have passed many summers in Pike County, famous for its snakes, the only live one I ever saw in that locality was in a box at Rowland station. The men of our party occasionally killed one and brought it to camp as a trophy, but one of our weekend guests spent most of his time hunting the rattler that he might take its skin back to the city, yet without success.

It is the banded rattlesnake that is usually found in Pennsylvania. The color is yellowish and it is marked with irregular, wide bands of dark brown. Sometimes the snake is almost black, and it is thought that it turns dark with age.

## Diamond Rattlesnake

The rattlesnake marked in diamond patterns of gold outline

on brown is of the south and is oftenest found in Florida. This is a very large snake, and closely allied to it is the Texas rattlesnake, which is the same in markings and color, but paler, as if faded out.

## Massasauga

The massasauga is the rattlesnake occasionally found in the swamps from western New York to Nebraska, but it is rare. Its color is light brown with patches of dark brown its entire length.

## Copperhead

The copperhead is not a rattler, though its vibrating tail amid dry leaves will sometimes hum like one. (This is also true of the blacksnake.) Its bite is very poisonous. It is found amid rocks and in the woods, and is at home from New England and the Atlantic coast west to Indiana and south to Texas. This snake is seldom more than 3 feet long. Its color is light reddish-brown with bands of rich chestnut which are narrow on the back and wide at the sides. The underpart is whitish with dark spots on the abdomen. The head is generally coppery in color but not always. In Texas the colors of the copperhead are stronger, the bands and head are decidedly reddish, and the bands have narrow white borders.

## Harlequin Snake and Coral Snake

The harlequin snake and the coral snake are so similar in color and in habits, one description for both will answer our purpose. They are southern snakes, beginning in southern Indiana and extending south. They are quite poisonous, but of such retiring habits as hardly to be classed as dangerous. Most of their time is spent hidden under the sand and in the ground, but when they do come out their colors are so brilliant as not to be mistaken. On the harlequin snake the colors are bright coral-red, yellow, and black, which alternate in stripes

that encircle the body. Its head is always banded with a broad yellow stripe. The coral-snake is much the same in color, and only a close observer would notice the difference. The coral-snake is also found in Arizona.

## Water Moccasin, Cottonmouth

The water moccasin is ugly, and ugly all the way through. Its deadly viciousness is not redeemed by any outward beauty. Its average length is 3.5 feet, though it is occasionally longer. Its unlovely body is thick and the color of greenish mud; the sides are paler and have wide, blackish bands. There are dark bands from the eyes to the mouth and above them there are pale streaks. The top of the head is very dark. The abdomen is yellow with splashes of brown or black. Heavy shields overhang the eyes and give a sinister expression to their angry glare. When suddenly approached the moccasin opens wide its white-lined mouth, and one then understands why it is called cottonmouth.

This snake does not coil before its strikes, but vibrates its tail slowly and watches its prey with mouth open. The moccasin is decidedly a southern snake, and girls of the south know that its home is along the edges of bayous and in the swamps. It is frequently seen with its head and a small part of its body out of water while the rest is submerged, but at times it will be found on a water-soaked log or on underbrush and low boughs of trees that overhang the water. The bite is very poisonous.

## Other Snakes

There are many other snakes in the United States, but they are not venomous. Here is one thing to remember: You need never fear a snake found in this country which has *lengthwise stripes*, that is, stripes running from head to tail. Daniel C. Beard tells me that he has learned this from observation, and Raymond L. Ditmars, curator of reptiles in the New York Zoological Park, agrees with him.

While the lengthwise-striped snakes are harmless, others not striped in this way are harmless, too. The blacksnake, though he looks an ugly customer and, when cornered, will sometimes show fight, is not venomous and his bite is not deep. It is, therefore, wanton cruelty to kill every snake that crosses your path simply because it happens to be a snake. Kephart, in his book of *Camping and Woodcraft*, says in regard to identifying the poisonous snake:

"The rattlesnake, copperhead, and cottonmouth are easily distinguished from all other snakes, as all three of them bear a peculiar mark, or rather a pair of marks, that no other animal possesses. This mark is the *pit*, which is a deep cavity on each side of the face between the nostrils and the eye, sinking into the upper jaw-bone."

If, when one has been bitten and the snake killed, an examination is made of its head, it can be ascertained immediately whether the snake was venomous, and in this way unnecessary fright may be avoided.

## Beaded Lizard, Gila Monster

The only other venomous reptile found in the United States is the beaded lizard, called Gila monster (pronounced "heela"). Unless you visit the desert regions of Arizona and New Mexico, you will not be apt to run across this most interesting though poisonous reptile.

The Gila monster looks very much like a unique piece of Indian beadwork, with its fat body and stubby legs covered with bright-colored, bead-like tubercles, which form almost a Navajo pattern. Its length is about 19 inches, and its beads are colored salmon, flesh-pink, white or yellow, and black. Though it has the appearance of being stuffed with cotton, it is really formidable and very much alive. Its jaws are strong; when it bites it holds on like a bulldog,

and there is no way to force it to open its mouth except to pry the powerful jaws apart. While otherwise slow of movement, it will turn quickly from side to side, snapping viciously. The inside of the Gila's mouth is black, and when angry it opens it wide and hisses.

## Treatment for Snake Bites

If the unlikely should chance to happen and one of your party is bitten by a poisonous snake, first aid should be given *immediately*, and if a physician is within reach he should be summoned as quickly as possible. Much depends, however, upon what is done first. Anyone can administer the following treatment, and it should be done without flinching, for it may mean the saving of a life:

(1) As soon as the person is bitten twist a tourniquet very tightly above the wound, that is, between the wound and the heart, to keep the poison as far as possible from entering the entire system.

(2) Slash the wound or stab it with a *clean* knife blade and force it to bleed copiously. If there is no break in the skin or membrane of your mouth or lips and no cavity in any of your teeth, suck the wound to draw out the poison.

(3) Give a stimulant in small doses at frequent intervals to stimulate the heart and lungs and strengthen the nerves, but avoid overdoing this, for the result will be harmful.

(4) If you have with you an anti-venomous serum, inject it as directed by the formula that accompanies it.

Tie a loose bandage around the affected member, a handkerchief, neck scarf, or even a rope for a tourniquet, to check circulation. Every little while loosen the tourniquet, then tighten it again, for it will not do to stop the circulation entirely.

All authorities do not advise sucking the wound, but it is generally done, for with a perfectly sound and healthy mouth there is no danger, as the poison enters the system only by contact with the blood.

Some writers advocate cauterizing the wound with a hot iron; but, whatever is done, do quickly, and *do not be afraid*. Fear is contagious and exceedingly harmful to the patient. Remember that a snake bite is seldom fatal, and that a swollen arm or leg does not mean that the case is hopeless.

## Poisonous Plants

There are two kinds of poisonous plants: those that are poison to the touch and those that are harmless unless taken inwardly. Both may be avoided when you learn to identify them.

## Poison Ivy

We are apt to think that everyone knows the common poison ivy, but that some people are not familiar with it was shown when one beautiful autumn day a young woman passed along our village street carrying a handful

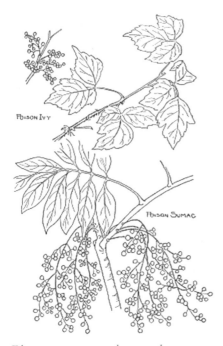

POISON IVY

POISON SUMAC

Plants poison to the touch.

escape a pestilence. We were left to close the incident by kicking the stuff into the street that some other equally uninformed person might not be tempted to pick it up.

If you do not know the poison ivy, remember this: It is the *three-leaved ivy*. Its leaves always grow in triplets as shown in illustration. The leaves are smooth, but not glossy; they have no teeth but are occasionally notched. Sometimes the plant is bushy, standing a foot or two high, again it is trailing or climbing. It loves fence corners and big rocks to clamber over; it will also choose large trees for support, climbing up to their tops. The flowers are whitish and the fruit is a pretty, green-gray berry, round and smooth, which grows in scant clusters.

Poison-ivy is found through the country from Maine to Texas and west to South Dakota, Utah, and Arkansas.

Some people are immune to ivy poison and, happily, I belong to the fortunate ones. Many persons are poisoned by it,

of the sprays of the vine, gathered probably because of their beautiful coloring. Noticing that she was a stranger, no doubt from the city, and realizing the danger she was running of poisoning herself or someone else, we hurriedly caught up with her and gave first aid to the ignorant in a few forceful remarks. The result was that, without a word, the young woman simply opened her hand, dropped her vines on the walk, and hurried off as if to however, and it may be that fear makes them more susceptible. On some the painful, burning eruption is difficult to cure.

## Poison Oak

The poison oak closely resembles the poison ivy, and is sometimes called by that name, but its leaves are differently shaped, being oval in outline with a few coarse, blunt teeth. They are also thicker and smaller than the ivy leaf. The poison oak is plentiful in cool uplands and in ravines, and is general throughout the Pacific coast from Lower California and Arizona to British America.

## Poison Sumach, or Swamp Sumach

Another member of the same family is the poison-sumach. They are all three equally poisonous and act by contact. The poison, or swamp, sumach is a high, branching shrub closely resembling the harmless species which grow on high, dry ground.

The poison variety chooses low, wet places. The leaves of the poison sumach are compound, with from seven to thirteen leaflets growing from one stem, as the leaves of the walnut tree grow; the stalks are often of a purplish color. The leaflets are oval in shape and are pointed at the tip. The surface is smooth and green on both sides and they have no teeth. The autumn coloring is very brilliant. The flowers are whitish-green and grow in loose clusters from a stiff middle stalk at the angles of the leaves. The fruit is a gray-green berry growing in scant, drooping clusters. This *gray drooping berry is the sumac poison sign*, for the fruit of the harmless sumach is crimson and is held erect in close pyramidal clusters.

Witch hazel (Pond's Extract) is used as a remedy for all of these poisons, but it is claimed that a paste made of *cooking-soda* and water is better. Alcohol will sometimes be effective, also a strong lye made of wood-ashes. Salt and water will give relief to some. It seems to depend upon the person whether the remedy, as well as the poison, will have effect.

## Yellow Lady's Slipper

Growing in bogs and low woods from Maine to Minnesota and Washington, southward to Georgia and Missouri, there is a sweet-scented, little yellow-and-brown flower called the yellow lady's slipper, the plant of which is said to have the same effect when handled as poison ivy. This flower is an orchid. The stalk, from 1 to 2 feet high, bears a single blossom at the top, and the leaves, shaped and veined like those of the lily-of-the-valley, grow alternately down the stem. The plant does not branch. Like the ivy, the yellow lady'sslipper does not poison every one.

I know of no other wild plants that are poisonous to the touch; the following will poison only if taken inwardly.

## Deadly Nightshade

To the nightshade family belong plants that are poisonous and plants that are not, but the thrilling name, deadly nightshade, carries with it the certainty of poison.

The plant is an annual and you may often find it growing in a neglected corner of the garden as well as in waste places. It is a tall plant; the one I remember in our own garden reached to the top of a five-foot board fence. Its leaves are rather triangular in shape,

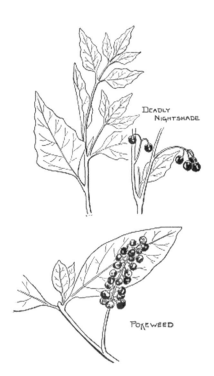

DEADLY NIGHTSHADE

POKEWEED

Plants poison to the taste.

they are dark green and the wavy edges are notched rather than toothed. The flowers are white and grow in small clusters. The fruit is a berry, round, black, and smooth, with calyx adhering to it. The berry clusters grow at the end of drooping stems. This must not be mistaken for the high-bush blueberry, for to eat the fruit would be most dangerous.

The antidotes for nightshade poison are emetics, cathartics, and stimulants. The poison should be thrown off the stomach first, then strong coffee be given as a stimulant.

## Pokeweed, Pigeonberry

Pokeweed comes under the heading of poisonous plants though its berries are eaten by birds, and its young shoots are said to be almost equal in flavor, and quite as wholesome, as asparagus. It seems to be the large perennial root that holds the poison, though some authorities claim that the poison permeates the entire plant to a certain extent.

The root is sometimes mistaken for that of edible plants and the young leaves for those of the marsh-marigold, which are edible when cooked. It is a tall plant with a stout stem and emits a strong odor. You will find it growing by the wayside and in rocky places. The leaves are oblong and pointed at the tips and base. They have no teeth. The small white flowers are in clusters. The fruit is a small, flat, dark-purple berry, growing in long, upstanding clusters on a central stalk. The individual stem of the berry is very short. The name inkberry was given to the plant because of the strong stain of the berry juice which was sometimes used for ink. Pokeweed is at home in various states, Maine to Minnesota, Arkansas, and Florida.

## Poison Hemlock

The poison hemlock is well known historically, being in use at the time of Socrates, and believed to have been administered to him by the Greeks. It is quite as poisonous now as in Socrates's day, and accidental poisoning has come from people eating the seeds, mistaking them for anise-seed, eating the leaves for parsley and the roots for parsnips. The plant grows from 2 to 7 feet high; its stem is smooth and spotted or streaked with purplish-red. It has large, parsley-like leaves and pretty clusters of small, white flowers which grow, stiff-stemmed, from a common center and blossom in July and August. When the fresh leaves are bruised they give out a distinctly mouse-like odor and they are very nauseating to the taste. Poison hemlock is common on waysides and waste places in New York, West Virginia, Pennsylvania, New Jersey, and Ohio. It is also found in New England and Michigan, Wisconsin, Illinois, Louisiana, and California.

The treatment recommended by professionals is emetics, warmth of hands and feet, artificial respiration, and the subcutaneous injection of atropine, administered by a physician.

## Water Hemlock

Water hemlock is similar in appearance and in effect. It is found in wet places and on the borders of swamps. The remedies are the same as for poison hemlock.

## Jimsonweed

The jimsonweed is very common in Kentucky. I have not seen so much of it in the east and north, but it appears to grow pretty nearly over the whole United States. It is from 1 to 5 feet in height, and an ill-smelling weed, though first cousin to the beautiful, cultivated datura, which is a highly prized garden plant. The stem is smooth, green, stout, and branching. The flower is large, sometimes 4 inches long, and trumpet-shaped. There are several varieties of this weed; on some the flower is white, on others the five, flaring, sharp-pointed lobes are stained with lavender and magenta. The calyx is long, close-fitting, and light green. The leaves are rather large;

they are angularly oval in shape and are coarsely notched. The fruit is a prickly, egg-shaped capsule which contains the seeds. It is these seeds which are sometimes eaten with serious results, and children have been poisoned by putting the flowers in their mouths.

Emetics should immediately be administered to throw the poison off the stomach, then hot, strong coffee should be given. Sometimes artificial respiration must be resorted to. In all cases of poisoning a physician should be called if possible.

The habit of chewing leaves and stems without knowing what they are should be suppressed when on the trail. It is something like going through a drug store and sampling the jars of drugs as you pass, and the danger of poisoning is almost as great.

## Toadstools

Unless you are an expert in distinguishing non-poisonous mushrooms from the poison toadstool, *leave them all alone*. Many deaths occur yearly from eating toadstools which have been mistaken for the edible mushrooms.

# Hiking and Navigating Terrain

# The Hiker's Kit

Only a few years ago, prior to the Spanish-American war, to be more definite, if one wanted a pack-sack, or boots, moccasins, blankets, or clothing for use on a hunting or a fishing trip in the woods, one likely as not got them from Port Arthur or Duluth or Marquette. And one had a lumberman's outfit, nothing else. I sometimes think the sportsmen would be better off today, at least as to their duffle, were they still in a large measure dependent upon the same source of supply. For lumbermen's duffle is made for service, whereas much that is sold to sportsmen today seems to me chiefly intended to be ornamental.

The Boy Scouts, of course, do not give their camping duffle anything like the wear and tear that the sportsman gives his. For the main part, their camping trips are comparatively tame, and the regular Scout uniform, common shoes, cheap blankets, and ordinary tents will do. There are two things, however, that the Scout should give special attention to—his pack-sack and his bed.

**Haversack and Knapsack**—A haversack is a bag with a single shoulder strap, made to carry at the side; a knapsack has two shoulder straps and is carried on the back, high up on the shoulder blades. Neither is well adapted for carrying the hiker's kit, and in fact both are sadly out of date.

Both of these bags were developed for the use of soldiers.

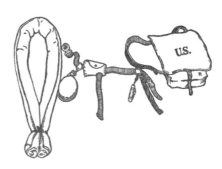

The scout's hiking kit, with blanket-roll separate from the pack-sack to show how it should be rolled.

The Century Dictionary says that "originally the military knapsack was meant for carrying food, but it has gradually become appropriated to a totally different purpose, as the transportation of clothes and the like, and food is carried in the haversack." This being the fact, the name should be discarded, for "knapsack" means "food sack." However, in this country the knapsack was discarded some years ago, and our infantry soldier carries all his equipment, except his rifle, in one complete highly developed harness, with everything except ammunition, canteen, and first aid pouch strapped in one compact roll, called the pack. And civilian hikers carry theirs in what is commonly called a pack-sack.

The best pack-sack made is one originated and patented by Poirier in Duluth, Minn., about twenty-five years ago. The North is the real home of the pack-sack, which is the white woodsman's improvement on the tumpline of the Northern Indians. With the latter, the Indian carries anything, from a backload of flour to a miscellaneous bundle folded ingeniously in pack-cloth, tent or blankets, puckered at the ends, with the tumpline serving for drawstrings, and tied in the middle with the loose ends of the line. The tumpline, of course, is simply the carrier, the pack-cloth, tent, or blankets serving in lieu of a sack.

**The Tumpline Pack**—To make the bundle as above described, the Indian first lays his pack-cloth on the ground, and piles his duffle on the middle of it. Next he takes the leather tumpline (which is some 15 feet long and about 2 inches wide for a foot in the middle where it goes across the wearer's head but otherwise little more than a heavy thong), and lays it with the headpiece at one end, and the two ends across the pack-cloth, one on each side the duffle and a foot or so from the edge. The ends of the cloth are now folded over the two end pieces of the tumpline and the duffle rolled up in the cloth, making a roll with the head piece out at one side and a tip-end of the tumpline sticking out each end of the bundle. To complete the job the Indian pulls up the ends of the tumpline, so puckering the folded-in ends of the pack-cloth and securing sufficient line to knot each end to the carrying loop, carry to the middle of the pack, twist once around the other end of the line, pass around the middle of the pack and tie.

The manner of carrying this pack is shown in an accompanying illustration, which also shows how any bag or bundle, or several of them, can be carried on top, without being fastened there. The headpiece goes across the top of the packer's head, toward the forehead. And take my word for it, one needs to get well used to this mode of packing before one attempts anything approaching a heavy load.

This method of packing, clever though it is, imposes too much hardship upon white men, and it is only used by them on short canoe carries or portages.

Many of the Indians, too, have largely given it up, using in its stead the white man's pack-sack. It has one excellent feature, however; in fording a swift stream or crossing on a log or in walking on treacherous ice, the packer has no fear of being drowned by his pack; for it is not strapped on him. The feature is retained in the Poirier pack above mentioned, by means of a headstrap, which is separate from the shoulder straps, and is shown hanging down in the illustration. Naturally it is intended that under such circumstances this pack is to be carried by the headstrap alone. For heavy packing over portages, however, both shoulder straps and headstrap are used, other duffle being piled up on top of the pack.

**The Poirier Pack-Sack**—The Poirier pack is a simple flat bag, made in four sizes, the largest 30 by 30 inches, and the smallest 18 by 18 inches. The shoulder straps lead from a common center near the top of the front of the sack, and attach to the two lower corners, a buckle in each strap (not shown in the illustration) provides for adjustment to fit the wearer. I fancy that when Poirier first brought out his pack the fit of the shoulder straps must have made a great hit. Formerly the soldier's knapsack had been the pattern after which pack-sacks were made, and of all the bunglesome contraptions, the old-fashioned army knapsack was about the worst. Whereas the shoulder straps of the Poirier pack-sack started from a common or "single-fire" center, between the shoulder-blades, like a pair of suspenders, those of the army knapsack went straight across the shoulders, starting from opposite corners of the bag. In early times they crossed the wearer's breast. Thus with the Poirier type of pack, the straps hugged the wearer "where he could stand it," while the army type of knapsack hung its weight close to the points of his shoulders. You will readily understand the difference if you place the point of your shoulder under the butt

of a heavy pole and lift it, then shift the weight closer to your neck. Before going further, I want to say that the pack worn by our infantry soldiers today is a highly developed affair and beyond criticism. Also that I believe the Swiss chamois hunters were the first, in modern times at least, to use the single-point suspension in connection with a pack.

Another good feature of the Poirier pack (the patent has expired and it is manufactured by various concerns) is the cut of the flap, and the three long straps that hold it down. These straps enable the pack-sack tripper to make his pack-sack large or small, according to the contents; therefore a snug pack is always assured. With the large sizes—too large for a boy—the blanket, poncho, and tent-cloth go inside, folded against the packer's back, to make the pack ride easy. With the child's size it is carried in the conventional roll, over the shoulder, or strapped in a bundle on the top of the pack.

Boy Scouts living in Minnesota or the Upper Peninsula of Michigan, where these packs are common, cannot do better than use them. I would recommend them for every Scout if it were not that I have worked out an excellent substitute, costing only half as much, which I will describe further along in this chapter.

**The Prospector's Pack**—The pack shown in the second position, which I call the prospector's pack, is one I have used for heavy packing, and like very much. I consider it superior to any pack made in the way it hugs the back, if well loaded and properly hung. But it is in some respects inferior to the Poirier pack. It is a homemade affair, consisting of a simple flat bag of heavy brown canvas in dimensions 24 x 3 x 36 inches, with canvas loops or "keepers" to hold the straps, and two 5 1/2-foot straps. I first had only the four canvas straploops on the back of the bag, but later made an improvement by putting two similar loops on the other side close to the bottom. By running the straps through these, they were secured against any possibility of slipping out of position, which formerly they had done, unless the corners of the bag were well filled, especially when taking the pack off or putting it on. I think a further improvement would be to rivet each strap to the bag on the bottom.

The blanket, rolled in the tent-cloth, 5 feet long, goes in this bag in the form of a letter U, the poncho or stretcher is folded and tucked down flat and smooth on the front side, or that which will be next the packer's back, and kit, grub etc., go in the middle of the blanket-roll U. Lastly, the upstanding ends of this are bent over together, one overlapping the other, and the top of the bag is folded down and secured by a strap passed vertically around the pack. I have used the same method of loading in connection with the Poirier pack-sack, and like it. It gives you a pack much easier to pack and unpack, that is more flat and rides better than if loaded with the blanket and the tent-cloth folded.

**The Grain-Bag Pack**—The third pack illustrated is the easiest to procure and the quickest made that I know of. And it is much used by men in the Northwest as an emergency pack-sack, or to serve where a regulation pack-sack is not had. I have used such a pack repeatedly, when the question of how to carry a back-load seemed perplexing—until I got hold of a grain-bag and a halter strap. The regular two-bushel cotton bag is what you want, not the clumsy "feed-bag" of burlap. Get a couple of walnuts, corn-cobs, or stones of similar size, and put one in each corner of the bag. Next, pile in your duffle, filling the bag half or two-thirds full. Tie the top of the bag upon itself, with a single knot now, tie your halter strap around the neck of the bag below this big knot, using also a single knot, tied in the center of the strap. Last, tie each end of the strap around a corner of the bottom of the bag, behind the walnut or stone, using a single knot as before. To adjust the straps, take up or let out through the knots tied to the corners.

**The Rucksack**—The fourth illustration shows the Swiss rucksack, which means literally back-sack. It is primarily a mountaineer's pack, and the shoulder straps start from a common center, as in the Poirier pack-sack. There are several different models, the one most commonly used being a single bag in size about 16 x 3 x 20 inches, closing at the top with a drawstring, the puckered opening being covered with a flap that buckles down. The model shown (rather imperfectly) in the illustration, is 18 by 22 inches, but a much larger bag when opened to its full capacity, the bag having a number of gores which can be let out by loosening a strap. The pockets on the back are handy for carrying camera, maps, etc. It is not, however, as practical an everyday pack as the Poirier type, and it costs three times as much; perhaps because it is a "fancy" bag.

**The Pack-Basket**—The last illustration in this row shows the Eastern pack-basket, which is much used by guides and sportsmen in the Adirondacks and Maine, and to some extent in the Maritime provinces of Canada. It is mostly used for a grub-pack, on canoe trips, but has nothing to recommend it for use on the trail. And the Poirier type of pack-sack double discounts it at its own game—portaging.

The first picture in the second row, showing different packs, illustrates my adaptation of the soldier's *haversack* (no longer used in the army and to be obtained for 75 cents from any dealer in condemned military supplies) as a pack-sack. This I will describe at length further along in this chapter.

**Other Pack Bags**—Next is an Eastern modification of the antiquated knapsack. This bag is carried by a canvas yoke, which fits the wearer better than the straps of a knapsack. Adjustable straps extend from the shoulder yoke to the bottom corners of the bag. A better pack-sack, also essentially Eastern, is the one named for "Nessmuk" or George R. Sears, author of a little book entitled "Woodcraft" which for many years was the only reliable handbook on camping and woodcraft. The "Nessmuk" pack-sack (erroneously called a "pack," since a pack is a pack only when it is packed), looks somewhat like the pack-sack previously mentioned, except for having a single point of suspension. The boxed sides, however, taper in at the top, and the top is puckered under the flap with a drawstring. The original Nessmuk pack-sack, I believe, did not have the shoulder straps meeting at a common center at the top of the bag.

The third illustration in this row shows the woodsman's "turkey," which is made with a grain-bag or a feed-bag and a short piece of rope. A small potato, a short section of corn-cob, or something of the like, is put in one corner of the bag, and one end of the rope tied behind it. Then the contents of the bag are piled in, and the bag is tied at the top with the other end of the rope. It makes a fairly comfortable one-shoulder pack, and is a trick worth knowing. The neck of the bag goes over the shoulder, so there need be no fear of the rope.

The last pack, made with a tumpline, has already been described. That immediately preceding it represents a duffle-bag or a pack done up in a tent, poncho, or blankets, carried with a pack-harness. This harness consists of two straps which go around the bag or bundle horizontally, and the carrying straps, which preferably should start at the top from a common center but in the Eastern manufactured article usually are attached, as illustrated, to the same sort of canvas yoke as is used on the pack mentioned above as a modification of the knapsack.

You now have a brief outline of the practical pack equipment used in the United States and Canada, with the exception of the pack I recommend for Boy Scouts, those of the soldiers, and a few mongrels that need not be discussed. I should like to describe the soldiers' pack as used in this country, it is so neat, practical, and interesting—I almost said unique. But I have not the space, and such a description would be of no practical value to the Scout, since the government does not allow anyone but a soldier to have the new army pack. Besides, it contains a number of features a Scout would not want. So now for the details of my Scout's pack-sack.

**The Haversack Pack-Sack**—I first described this pony pack-sack (as I then called it) in the June, 1911 number of *Recreation*, of which I was then the editor. And as that year the Boy Scout movement was sweeping over the country, and there was no practical Boy Scout pack-sack, many Scout Masters followed my suggestion. I am glad to say I have had many testimonials as to the satisfaction the little rig has given. Among the Scouts of my own troop, No. 1 of Mamaroneck, N.Y., it is voted the best equipment we have.

To begin with, I wanted a small pack-sack, suitable for carrying camera and lunch on an ordinary day's hike, yet large enough, if necessary, to carry the necessaries for a trip of two or three days away from any point of grub supply. I bought an ordinary soldier's condemned haversack, with a single shoulder strap, the haversack being made to carry at the hip. I unhooked the strap from the two D rings at the upper corners of the bag, and thought to cut it in two and make shoulder straps of it. (This I have since done with another haversack, and is done by the Scouts in my troop). But I wanted to make sure to have a broad strap over the shoulders,

where the weight would come, so used the old haversack strap for one shoulder strap, and got some leather and cut another one for the other shoulder. I got four iron D rings and four short pieces of leather strap, and secured a D ring to each lower corner of the front (back if you like, but I call it front because it is the side that goes forward) of the bag with rivets and stitching. The other two D rings I secured in the same fashion to the top of the bag, using, however, a 4-by-6-inch piece of sole leather as a reinforcement inside the bag and placing the rings in the center instead of at the corners. I then riveted and sewed my shoulder straps to these upper rings, and, using the brass hooks, four in all, from my haversack strap, adjusted my straps and hooked them to the lower D rings. I would have used a single ring at the top, attaching both straps to it, as on the Poirier type of pack-sack (see illustration) but did not have one and was in a hurry. Anyhow, I intended to put on a single ring later. This, however, I did not do until recently; and in the meantime, because of being not properly made in the first place, this bag, which I made simply for my own use, has been the cause of other bags also being made with the two-point suspension, instead of the proper single-point secured by using one large ring. While satisfactory enough for my own use, boys who borrowed this bag found that the straps were apt to slip off their shoulders if the bag were loaded lightly. To prevent this they crossed the straps at the top. And then when I would go to shoulder my pack I would find I couldn't get into it.

This bag, of course, is only large enough to carry cooking kit and grub, but no duffle. To get around this, I riveted on the five blanket straps, using one rivet to each, and reinforcing on the inside of the bag with a bit of strap. These straps are 20 inches long; be sure you do not make yours shorter. When the bag is used for a day's trip and no tenting is carried, they are rolled up, each in a neat little roll held by the buckle.

Tent-cloth and stretcher or tick will be described in the chapter on Tents and Tent Making. Your blanket should always be a double one, and of wool. Do not use a cheap, shoddy blanket; they are both uncomfortable and unhygienic, it being impossible to keep them dry.

**The Blanket-Roll**—To make up your blanket-roll, for strapping around the pack as shown in the illustration, first spread out your stretcher, or if using a combination tent (which you will find described in the chapter on Tents and Tent Making), spread that. Fold one end over so your cloth is 5 feet wide. Make a mark with a soft pencil and you will always know where to fold. If using stretcher and tarpaulin tent, now spread your tent on the stretcher, same size or smaller. Next, shake out your double blanket and fold it first the *long* way once, then fold this long strip on itself twice, or making three such folds in all, one on top of the other, in dimensions 3 by 5 feet. Lay this on the tent-cloth, and last of all spread on top your sweater and your pillow-bag, containing towel, handkerchiefs, clean socks, etc., which cannot go in the pack-sack. Now start on one of the long sides and roll, and roll tight. Do not include the stretcher or tent-cloth, whichever happens to be on the bottom. When your blanket is half rolled, pull the roll back to the edge of your outside canvas, and roll again, this time rolling in the canvas also. Make it tight; use your knees to help you. When you get within a foot of the edge of your canvas, stop and fold in half of it; then complete the roll, stopping when the folded edge of the canvas is almost underneath. Now bend the two ends up forming a U, with the folded edge of the canvas on the bottom or outside of the bend; see drawing. This will cause it to hold snug and neat. Strap your roll in place around the bag, and, if the bag is loaded, as it should be before the blanket-roll is strapped on, you are ready to hike.

As to the contents of the pack-sack, for the present I shall simply give a suggestion, in the form of a list, followed with a few explanatory notes. In the next chapter, however, I will give further attention to this subject.

The best mess-kit I have been able to secure for Boy Scouts consists of the following:

Frying-pan, stamped steel, 7¾ inches in diameter at top; handle cut off and fitted described below.
Bread-pan, retinned stamped steel, 7¾ inches diameter at top, 5¾ inches at bottom, 3 inches deep; detachable bale.
Cooking pot, retinned stamped steel, 5½ inches diameter, 3½ inches deep; bail handle and cover.
Tin plate, 7¾ inches diameter.
Tin cup, 3 by 3 inches, straight sides, holds ¾ pint.
Cooking knife, 4¾-inch blade, butcher pattern; serves all purposes.
Table fork, teaspoon, and tablespoon.

**The Mess-Kit**—The frying-pan I bought for 10 cents. I cut the patent "cold" handle off with a hacksaw, and with a hammer, pliers, and a vise as tools, bent the edges of the remaining 3½-inch stub around to the underside, forming a half-round base in which, after drilling three holes, I riveted a 2½-inch section of ¾-inch thin iron pipe. In this I push any convenient round stick, when commencing cooking operations, thus having a long cold handle, and I am not bothered with an awkward frying-pan handle in my pack. Almost every troop of Boy Scouts includes at least one person who has a breast-drill and can drill the holes for these rivets. Not having rivets handy, I cut off some wire nails, and for washers used some from worn-out automobile spark plugs. The piece of pipe also came from the scrap-box, having formerly served as a conduit for ignition wires on one of my cars. The bread-pan is called by dealers in household supplies a pudding dish, and can be duplicated in light tin for 10 cents. It will pay any troop, however, to order their mess-kits all at one time, through one dealer, and get retinned stamped (and of course seamless) steel. The cost for bread pans should not be more than 15 cents.

The cooking-pot is one listed in catalogues as a sauce-pot, and is hard to obtain in this size. If a number are ordered at once, as above suggested, they should not cost more than 35 cents each. This and the bread-pan should be obtained from a concern dealing in hotel and restaurant supplies; your local dealer can get them if you insist. Do not accept cheap kitchen tinware.

Cup, anywhere for 5 cents; same for plate.

Forks and spoons can be bought by the dozen, and will average 2½ cents each for a good quality. And a serviceable cooking (butcher) knife will cost 25 cents.

Thus for a dollar you can get together a mess-kit that is in every way superior to anything on the market. It will "nest" all in one little bag, or if you like you can carry it as follows: Put knife, fork, and spoons, each in a leather sheath, in the pockets at the sides of the pack-sack, and the plate in the pocket of the flap. Frying-pan in the frying-pan pocket that buttons (cut out the buttons) inside the bag; the bread-pan and the cooking-pot, the latter nested in the former and with a bag containing dishrag, soap, and dishtowel inside, down in the pack, bottom side in the hollow of the frying-pan in its bag and top side to fit in the hollow of the plate when the flap is buckled down. To make sure these nest as described, pack other things around and below them. And in order that the bottom of the frying-pan may not get too hard against your back, insulate it with your spare shirt, if on an extra-shirt hike, or your towel if not.

The other contents of the bag consist of a ditty-kit, a first aid can, and the food containers. The first is made as shown in an accompanying illustration, size to suit individual notions, and preferably of some strong goods such as brown denim or khaki. The contents are placed in the pockets, the flaps folded over, and the whole rolled up until closed by the flap, then secured with the straps. This is a rough and ready duplicate of the traveler's toilet roll, and contains toilet articles, needle and thread, waterproof match-safe (loaded), spool of adhesive plaster, extra first aid supplies, and other things, such as you might carry in your pockets.

**The First Aid Can**—The first aid can is a combination tin-and-cardboard mailing case 5½ inches long by 2¼ inches in diameter, costing 15 cents if you get it at retail from your druggist, or perhaps 5 cents if procured in dozen lots from a supply house. Like the other cans mentioned here and in the next chapter, it may be substituted by a baking-powder can. Personally, I like the screw top and the fact that this type of can does not rattle or dent. It contains 1 roller bandage, a triangular bandage, two antiseptic compresses of sublimated

The ditty-kit.

A practical mess-kit for scouts.

1. Frying-pans; 2. Bread-pans; 3. Pot; 4. Cup; 5. Plate; 6. Provision bags; 7, Provision cans; 8. Butter jar; 9. Lard tin; 10. Milk bottle; 11. Salt shaker; 12. Bread pan bail; 13. Knife-sheath; 14. Ditty-kit; 15. Dish-towel, gauze, assorted safety-pins, and a glass vial of tincture of iodine with rubber stopper.

If hiking in a snake country it is well, though not so necessary as is generally believed outside of snake country, to carry in addition a hypodermic syringe and the antidotes that go with it, a solution of potassium permanganate and another of strychnine. For directions for using these, consult your Scout Master. In passing, I may say that among the natives of real snake country, carrying a hypodermic is practiced to about the same degree that the carrying of a compass is practiced by the bushmen of the Canadian wilderness, which is to say that nobody but a tenderfoot or a stranger carries one.

The tin cup goes in the pack on top, where you can get it easily. Same applies to the pocket camera, if you have one. The 3¼ x 3 x 4½ size I find the most satisfactory, after trying many different ones. A good place to carry a map is in the pocket of the flap of the bag, along with the plate. There are, of course, a few extras which are desirable but not necessary. They all add to the load, and I think it best that they be distributed around among the party.

# Hiking Alone

It is a good thing for anyone to be entirely alone in the outdoors once in a while, and take stock of philosophy and other character resources. In fact, the stock may be found so low it would be embarrassing to be otherwise than alone. And under any circumstances the experience is refreshing, to say the least. Whether or not one gathers new reserve of confidence and energy, as one is pretty apt to, there is an overpowering feeling of getting well *rinsed*.

Now I suspect you are thinking of the long "lone" trips Daniel Boone made, and wondering how he survived feeling entirely washed away! The best thing for *you* is to try it on yourself. I mean for you to make a hike "by your lonesome."

And that immediately is a horse of another color. Hadn't thought of doing a thing like that, had you? Don't exactly like the idea, do you? Afraid?

**A Woodcraft Camp**—You were tempted to bring no tent-cloth, knowing you would find abundant white spruce saplings with which you could make a lean-to. Finally you compromised and brought a poncho. And now you set to work to make a lean-to with it. Instead of building a frame in the usual way or stretching the poncho by means of a series of short guy ropes tied to a supporting rope between two trees—a good stunt, by the way—you select a couple of small spruces that stand out by themselves on the edge of the open knoll where you have stopped, and are the right distance apart. You lop off the branches on the side of each that faces the other and stretch your shelter between them, in the form of a shed roof, pegged to the ground at the back. This not only furnishes your tent poles already placed, but the ends of your tent are already thatched and you have sufficient browse for your bed without going a step for it. A neat trick, you think, but there is a neater one still, which you will learn in due time if you follow woods ways.

It doesn't take long to make such a camp. Picking the browse—it should be done by hand, as there is a tendency to lop off *branches* instead of browse if you use a sheath knife or a belt ax—and shingling the bed constitute the larger part of it. You lay four poles on the ground, forming the boundaries of your bed, and wherever necessary stake them against rolling outward. Then, starting at the head of the prospective bed, you lay a row of the spruce fans, butts down, concave bend of stem up, tips overlapping the head pole. Row after row is added in the same orderly manner until you reach the foot. Then you start at the top and shingle another layer. A poncho spread on top would save your blankets somewhat, and keep down dampness, but why quibble, with bough beds so scarce these days!

**Camp Chores**—There is a spring you know about that needs digging out, and you think you will trench the lean-to. So you get out your "digger." And between this work and scouting for likely bass coves, making a forest range and working up firewood, noon comes before you realize it.

Lonely? No, not yet. Been too busy—and happy.

After dinner you get out your tackle and rig up, and for a half hour practice casting for accuracy, using a tournament weight instead of a lure. It is well to get your hand in, for you will be at a disadvantage in fishing from the shore—but, hold on! Why fish from the shore, even if there isn't a boat on the lake? You were going to wade, of course, but that amounts to almost the same thing. Now, a raft—

**Building a Raft**—Where is the Scout who does not know enough about pioneering to build a raft? A raft is in order, and what with cutting the necessary poles, and lashing them with wild-grapevines, fishing time will come and you will not get your swim. No matter, you'll get it first thing in the morning. Willow is selected because of its buoyancy and there being a good thicket of the sandbar variety close to camp. It is nearly valueless and you feel no qualms about cutting it. Luckily you find a couple of 5-inch trees which give you four good 6-foot logs. Dry wood would have been better. With some smaller poles lashed across them, and a couple of pieces of board picked up on the lake shore nailed (with old nails found in the boards) on top to furnish a smooth footing for bare feet, you have a good raft. But how it sinks when you get aboard! Not very buoyant after all. Logs are too small. But it will serve. And with your rod taken down and slung over your shoulder with a cord, you push out, using your pole in a manner that, to see you, would make an Illinois River duck hunter's "pusher" fall overboard, but getting there just the same. And you anchor successfully, 60 or

70 feet out from a likely cove, by pushing the pole down between the logs of your raft and ramming it into the mud. Now for action!

"Whizz!" goes the reel, and your lure, a salt pork imitation of a minnow, on a Seward "weedless" hook with a spinner on the shank and a weight on the trailer, plops into a little bay at the edge of the wild rice and rushes.

**The Gamest Fish That Swims—** "Splash! Slam!" Gee! Something doing in a hurry. Got one right off the bat. You struck the hook home with a strong twitch of the rod the instant you felt he had the lure, for he would detect the hook in short order and eject it. Up out of the water he goes, in a desperate attempt to throw the hook out. "Splash!" Letting a bass swim away with the bait and turn it around in his mouth and swallow it may be all right for the fisherman who baits with live minnows. But your way demands a fight from the first tug. You grind away on the multiplier, and don't let Mr. Bass get any slack line, not even when he jumps. Once again be jumps and shakes his head. He's a small-mouth for sure. Now you can see him in the water, darting from side to side, fighting his little best. How green he looks. And how you have to watch out now to prevent him from making you feel green, by darting under the raft. Let him get one hitch around that anchor pole, and—good night!

But that must not happen with the very first fish on a new rod. Gently but firmly you wear him down, then you slip the net into the water behind him, let him drop back into it, and with a lift he is yours. Yes, he's a small-mouth, "inch for inch and pound for pound the gamest fish that swims."

Mercifully—and prudently—you dispatch him while still holding him in the net, with the hook in his mouth. Keeping fish alive on a stringer is, next to taking more than can be used, the worst fool thing an angler can do; yet thousands persist in it and call it "keeping them." Who wants to eat fish, flesh or fowl that *died*, as such fish do die, slowly and painfully. A rap on the head with the ax handle does it. Then he is strung on a cord and slipped into the water, to trail from the raft. He weighs but little over a pound, but he pulled like a two-pounder. Another like him, and you'll have to quit, as you must not take more than you can eat for supper. You soon get him.

**Time to Eat Again**—For your supper fire you have cut and split an armful from a white ash windfall. It is dry, hard, and will burn down to good lasting coals. Burn just about as well if it were green. Chops and splits easily, yet you're glad you have a new straight 20-inch handle in your Scout ax. You sure can *chop* with it. But wait till you get a new head, a good one, of the proper wedge shape.

Your dinner was in reality a cold lunch, with only coffee to appease a rather strong desire for something hot. Now to eat!

Supper

Barley soup

Broiled small-mouth black bass

Macaroni and cheese

Baked potatoes

Raspberries and cream

Fresh bread and butter

Tea

That is the prospect. And a long evening to prepare and eat it. Broiling is simple enough. You brought a wire broiler along for the purpose, and you know enough to grease the broiler so it won't stick to the fish, which of course you split in halves, removing the spine. The berries are to be had for the picking, big, luscious red fellows such as Michigan's sandy soil produces, all you want of them right in camp. You figured on them too, and instead of any kind of dessert brought extra supplies of sugar and evaporated cream.

The macaroni and cheese is the only problem. But first you put the potatoes to baking, in the hot ashes—not embers—at one end of the fire. You have both your pot and your bread-pan on the fire, the former at the wide end hanging low from a dingle-stick, or camper's crane, and the latter sitting on the bed-sticks. When the former comes to a boil, you put in a teaspoonful of salt, and get out your little bag of macaroni. You have about a quarter of a pint, broken into short pieces. Nothing to do but dump it in the water and let it boil for about thirty minutes, so far as you can remember. "Well, here goes," you say aloud, and that is one more worry disposed of.

**Dressing Fish**—Then you go get your fish, which you left at the raft. To dress them—what on Earth makes you think that you can eat both of them?—you straddle a log, and commence by scaling the largest one. You hold him by the head, tail toward you, and with your fish knife scrape toward you; around the fins and gills you scrape at right angles, using the point of the knife. Both sides scraped, you sever head, belly fins, and side fins with three deft cuts, and when the head is removed the entrails come with it. You next cut out the vent, flop your fish, and cut deep down on each side his dorsal, and yank that out too. No need to do it, as you'd get the fin when you split him; but it's force of habit. Now you wash him, scrape off the slime that remains, wipe him dry with your "fish towel," split him in halves and remove his spine, and he is ready.

And he's enough, being larger than the first one caught.

# Determining Direction

In a survival situation, you will be extremely fortunate if you happen to have a map and compass. If you do have these two pieces of equipment, you will most likely be able to move toward help. If you are not proficient in using a map and compass, you must take the steps to gain this skill.

There are several methods by which you can determine direction by using the sun and the stars. These methods, however, will give you only a general direction. You can come up with a more nearly true direction if you know the terrain of the territory or country.

You must learn all you can about the terrain of the country or territory to which you or your unit may be sent, especially any prominent features or landmarks. This knowledge of the terrain together with using the methods explained below will let you come up with fairly true directions to help you navigate.

## Using the Sun and Shadows

The earth's relationship to the sun can help you to determine direction on Earth. The sun always rises in the east and sets in the west, but not exactly due east or due west. There is also some seasonal variation. In the northern hemisphere, the sun will be due south when at its highest point in the sky, or when an object casts no appreciable shadow. In the southern hemisphere, this same noonday sun will mark due north. In the northern hemisphere, shadows will move clockwise. Shadows will move counterclockwise in the southern hemisphere. With practice, you can use shadows to determine both direction and time of day. The shadow methods used for direction finding are the shadow-tip and watch methods.

**Shadow-Tip Methods.** In the first shadow-tip method, find a straight stick 1 meter long, and a level spot free of brush on which the stick will cast a definite shadow. This method is simple and accurate and consists of four steps:

**Step 1.** Place the stick or branch into the ground at a level spot where it will cast a distinctive shadow. Mark the shadow's tip with a stone, twig, or other means. This first shadow mark is always west—everywhere on Earth.

**Step 2.** Wait 10 to 15 minutes until the shadow tip moves a few centimeters. Mark the shadow tip's new position in the same way as the first.

**Step 3.** Draw a straight line through the two marks to obtain an approximate east-west line.

**Step 4.** Stand with the first mark (west) to your left and the second mark to your right—you are now facing north. This fact is true everywhere on Earth. An

alternate method is more accurate but requires more time. Set up your shadow stick and mark the first shadow in the morning. Use a piece of string to draw a clean arc through this mark and around the stick. At midday, the shadow will shrink and disappear. In the afternoon, it will lengthen again and at the point where it touches the arc, make a second mark. Draw a line through the two marks to get an accurate east-west line.

**The Watch Method.** You can also determine direction using a common or analog watch—one that has hands. The direction will be accurate if you are using true local time, without any changes for daylight savings time. Remember, the farther you are from the equator, the more accurate this method will be. If you only have a digital watch, you can overcome this obstacle. Quickly draw a watch on a circle of paper with the correct time on it and use it to determine your direction at that time.

In the northern hemisphere, hold the watch horizontal and point the hour hand at the sun. Bisect the angle between the hour hand and the 12 o'clock mark to get the north-south line (Figure 10-2). If there is any doubt as to which end of the line is north, remember that the sun rises in the east, sets in the west, and is due south at noon. The sun is in the east before noon and in the west after noon. Note: If your watch is set on daylight savings time, use the midway point between the hour hand and 1 o'clock to determine the north-south line. In the southern hemisphere, point the watch's 12 o'clock mark toward the sun and a midpoint halfway between 12 and the hour hand will give you the north-south line (Figure 10-2).

## Using the Moon

Because the moon has no light of its own, we can only see it when it reflects the sun's light. As it orbits the earth on its 28-day circuit, the shape of the reflected light varies according to its position. We say there is a new moon or no moon when it is on the opposite side of the earth from the sun. Then, as it moves away from the earth's shadow, it begins to reflect light from its right side and waxes to become a full moon before waning, or losing shape, to appear as a sliver on the left side. You can use this information to identify direction. If the moon rises before the sun has set, the illuminated side will be the west.

If the moon rises after midnight, the illuminated side will be the east. This obvious discovery provides us with a rough east-west reference during the night.

## Using the Stars

Your location in the Northern or Southern Hemisphere determines which constellation you use to determine your north or south direction.

**The Northern Sky.** The main constellations to learn are the

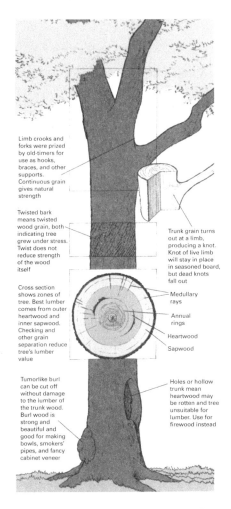

Limb crooks and forks were prized by old-timers for use as hooks, braces, and other supports. Continuous grain gives natural strength

Twisted bark means twisted wood grain, both indicating tree grew under stress. Twist does not reduce strength of the wood itself

Cross section shows zones of tree. Best lumber comes from outer heartwood and inner sapwood. Checking and other grain separation reduce tree's lumber value

Tumorlike burl can be cut off without damage to the lumber of the trunk wood. Burl wood is strong and beautiful and good for making bowls, smokers' pipes, and fancy cabinet veneer

Trunk grain turns out at a limb, producing a knot. Knot of live limb will stay in place in seasoned board, but dead knots fall out

Medullary rays

Annual rings

Heartwood

Sapwood

Holes or hollow trunk mean heartwood may be rotten and tree unsuitable for lumber. Use for firewood instead

Ursa Major, also known as the Big Dipper or the Plow, and Cassiopeia (Figure 10-3). Neither of these constellations ever sets. They are always visible on a clear night. Use them to locate Polaris, also known as the polestar or the North Star. The North Star forms part of the Little Dipper handle and can be confused with the Big Dipper. Prevent confusion by using both the Big Dipper and Cassiopeia together. The Big Dipper and Cassiopeia are always directly opposite each other and rotate counterclockwise around Polaris, with Polaris in the center. The Big Dipper is a seven-star constellation in the shape of a dipper. The two stars forming the outer lip of this dipper are the "pointer stars" because they point to the North Star. Mentally draw a line from the outer bottom star to the outer top star of the Big Dipper's bucket. Extend this line about five times the distance between the pointer stars. You will find the North Star along this line.

Cassiopeia has five stars that form a shape like a "W" on its side. The North Star is straight out from Cassiopeia's center star.

After locating the North Star, locate the North Pole or true north by drawing an imaginary line directly to the earth.

**The Southern Sky.** Because there is no star bright enough to be easily recognized near the south celestial pole, a constellation known as the Southern Cross is used as a signpost to the South (Figure 10-4). The Southern Cross or Crux has five stars. Its four brightest stars form a cross that tilts to one side. The two stars that make up the cross's long axis are the pointer stars. To determine south, imagine a distance five times the distance between these stars and the point where this imaginary line ends is in the general direction of south. Look down to the horizon from this imaginary point and select a landmark to steer by. In a static survival situation, you can fix this location in daylight if you drive stakes in the ground at night to point the way.

## Making Improvised Compasses

You can construct improvised compasses using a piece of ferrous metal that can be needle shaped or a flat double-edged razor blade and a piece of nonmetallic string or long hair from which to suspend it. You can magnetize or polarize the metal by slowly stroking it in one direction on a piece of silk or carefully through your hair using deliberate strokes. You can also polarize metal by

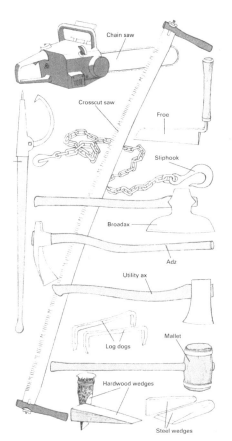

Chain saw

Crosscut saw

Froe

Sliphook

Broadax

Adz

Utility ax

Mallet

Log dogs

Hardwood wedges

Steel wedges

stroking it repeatedly at one end with a magnet. Always rub in one direction only. If you have a battery and some electric wire, you can polarize the metal electrically. The wire should be insulated. If not insulated, wrap the metal object in a single, thin strip of paper to prevent contact. The battery must be a minimum of 2 volts. Form a coil with the electric wire and touch its ends to the battery's terminals. Repeatedly insert one end of the metal object in and out of the coil. The needle will become an electromagnet. When suspended from a piece of nonmetallic string, or floated on a small piece of wood in water, it will align itself with a north-south line.

You can construct a more elaborate improvised compass using a sewing needle or thin metallic object, a nonmetallic container (for example, a plastic dip container), its lid with the center cut out and waterproofed, and the silver tip from a pen. To construct this compass, take an ordinary sewing needle and break in half. One half will form your direction pointer and the other will act as the pivot point. Push the portion used as the pivot point through the bottom center of your container; this portion should be flush on the bottom and not interfere with the lid. Attach the center of the other portion (the pointer) of the needle on the pen's silver tip using glue, tree sap, or melted plastic. Magnetize one end of the pointer and rest it on the pivot point.

## Other Means of Determining Direction

The old saying about using moss on a tree to indicate north is not accurate because moss

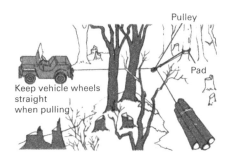

Pulley

Pad

Keep vehicle wheels straight when pulling

grows completely around some trees. Actually, growth is more lush on the side of the tree facing the south in the Northern Hemisphere and vice versa in the Southern Hemisphere. If there are several felled trees around for comparison, look at the stumps. Growth is more vigorous on the side toward the equator and the tree growth rings will be more widely spaced. On the other hand, the tree growth rings will be closer together on the side toward the poles. Wind direction may be helpful in some instances where there are prevailing directions and you know what they are.

Recognizing the differences between vegetation and moisture patterns on north- and south-facing slopes can aid in determining direction. In the northern hemisphere, north-facing slopes receive less sun than south-facing slopes and are therefore cooler and damper. In the summer, north-facing slopes retain patches of snow. In the winter, the trees and open areas on south-facing slopes are the first to lose their snow, and ground snow pack is shallower.

# Winter Travel in the Woods

What a change comes over the great forests of the North when winter reigns and holds all nature in his icy grip. The fleecy mantle of white covers hill and vale, stream and bush alike, bending to the ground the lower branches of the spruces and hemlocks, smoothing over the rough trails of the fall, and burying the logs, stumps, and underbrush from view until the following spring. The woods through which we traveled with ease and comfort when the ground was bare now has a forbidding appearance and it requires all the nerve we can muster to attempt to penetrate the dense, snow-laden growth, where we know that the first step will release a small avalanche of snow upon us. The bended branches and smaller growths of the thickets give a different appearance to the woods and distances seem shorter so that we find it difficult to keep to the old course, and wise is the trapper or other woods traveler who has blazed out his main trails before the coming of the snow. In this winter woods it would seem that only the wild creatures inhabiting it would be at home and perfectly familiar with the changed surroundings.

But the seasoned woodsman does not hesitate to travel the winter trail. If he is a trapper or spruce gummer the winter is his harvest time. He feels little of the storms which in more exposed country would keep one close indoors much of the time. On a still morning the cold may be intense and on all sides will be heard pistol-like reports from the freezing trees, but if he cannot keep warm by rapid walking, he treads down a spot of snow, pulls some loose bark from a white birch tree, places over it dead branches broken from the trunk of a nearby evergreen, and applies a lighted match to the oily birch bark. In a few seconds he has a roaring fire by the side of which he can rest and restore the chilled blood to its normal state. The Northern frost gives no warning; it creeps cautiously through the clothing and at once commences to freeze the flesh beneath and at such times a fire cannot be lighted too quickly.

One cannot travel the snowy bush in comfort and safety unless he wisely prepares for such travel, by wearing the proper clothing and carrying with him the most suitable equipment. Clothing must be of the correct weight: just heavy enough to keep the wearer warm while traveling but no heavier, as bulky clothing is tiresome to one who walks the trails. A long coat is bad for travel; it clings to the legs and interferes with stepping over logs. The outer clothing should be of a kind to which the snow will not cling, yet it must be soft. Wind proof cloth is not needed, in fact a medium thick but loosely woven cloth is warmer in

the woods than smooth, closely woven fabrics. The vest or waist coat is seldom worn in the forest, at least not by woodsmen. Woolen clothing, always, is the choice.

What I know on this subject I have learned from actual experience, and we are told that experience is the best teacher, but we could often save ourselves much discomfort if we would profit by the advice of others. However, knowledge acquired at the expense of time, health, comfort, and money is often less costly than ignorance. The clothing and outfits I recommend are those I have found best for my own use, but an article is most useful when properly used.

I consider the following the best dress for winter wear in the timbered country of the North and so dressed a healthy man may travel the wintry woods in comfort. Starting with underwear, I advise wearing pure woolen goods, always, of medium weight, and all in one piece. The soft, fine kind should be chosen.

## The Winter Trail

Wool absorbs the perspiration and is reasonably warm when damp or even wet. It never gets cold and uncomfortable like cotton underwear does, the nap does not flatten down, and it keeps the skin warm and induces a healthy circulation of the blood near the surface.

Wear woolen socks for the same reasons: two or three pairs, as required, and a pair of heavy knit wool stockings, knee length, over them. This is too much for warm weather, but I am talking of clothing for wear when it is cold. The amount of stockings required will depend somewhat on the constitution of the man who wears them; for one traveler can keep the feet warm with what would not be sufficient for another. Do not at anytime wear more socks than necessary, and wash them frequently, as it freshens the wool and makes them warmer. A number of pairs of medium-weight socks are better than one pair of very heavy ones. They are easier washed, easier dried, and more comfortable. Many bushmen wind a strip of woolen blanket about the foot, and this has the advantage of being cheaper than extra socks. I wear both the socks and the long stockings on the outside of the trousers, and the stockings should be held by a strap at the top. Stretch out the toes of the socks and stockings a little before putting the shoes or moccasins on over them and it will keep them from binding the toes.

The only footwear for winter travel when the weather is cold, especially for snowshoeing, is the buckskin moccasin. By "buckskin"

THE WINTER TRAIL

I mean Indian tanned moosehide, deer or caribou skin, or the white man's asbestol cordovan horsehide, the latter being the best wearing material, but not as soft and comfortable as the others. Caribou skin moccasins are my preference for snowshoeing, and I like the Ojibway pattern with pointed toe and cloth top; they are not as likely to cause sore toes as the Sioux pattern (the regular factory-made style) and the cloth top is warm and holds the snowshoe strings better than the buckskin top does.

Buckskin moccasins are not waterproof, in fact water will go through them almost as readily as through cloth, but waterproof qualities are not required in footwear for winter use in the North, as the snow never becomes damp until spring, and all water, except the smooth rapids, is well covered with ice. The only time when the traveler is likely to get wet feet is when snowshoeing over the ice on the lakes; then after a wind storm there is sure to be water under the snow on the ice.

A medium weight gray woolen shirt suits me best for woods wear. Trousers may be of almost any kind of strong, soft woolen material, and should be roomy, but fit well at the waist. I prefer to wear a belt rather than suspenders, but this is immaterial. If the snow clings to the trousers behind the knees, when snowshoeing, wear light overalls over them. I have never found anything better in coats than those made of mackinaw cloth, such as lumbermen wear. I like the plain colors best, blue black being my choice. All outside pockets should be covered with flaps to keep the snow out. Mackinaw is a soft, warm material and it will turn considerable rain. It has only one objectionable feature—the snow will cling to it, especially across one's back just above the pack sack, which the woodsman nearly always has with him; the warmth coming through the cloth causes it to collect the snow.

My choice of head dress is a good grade, long wool toque which can be drawn down over the forehead and ears. Over this I sometimes wear a sort of hood made of thin woolen cloth, which hangs down well over the collar of the coat and ties under the chin. This hood is very desirable, as it is a great protection from cold and snow. When walking through a snow-laden evergreen bush there is a constant shower of snow being released from the boughs and this hood keeps the falling snow from getting inside of the clothing, which it surely would do without this protection. It is also a shield against the cold wind when crossing frozen lakes, where the toque alone would not give sufficient protection. I steer clear of fur caps. They are too warm for walking, and I think it best to have no covering over the face, as any such arrangement will gather moisture from the breath and cause freezing. Unless one is exposed to a severe wind, holding the mittened hands against the face occasionally will prevent freezing in the coldest weather, providing we do not have to face the breeze.

The hands also need special protection from the cold and much could be written on this subject. I know of nothing better than mittens, not gloves, made of heavy woolen cloth, with a pair of cotton ones drawn over them. They are easier dried than a single pair of heavy ones; are easily made from old material, costing nothing, and are warm. They should be loose enough to pull off quickly, and the tops should come well up over the wrists inside the coat sleeves. Do not buy gauntlet gloves for the woods; they collect dirt and snow continually. No kind of leather gloves or mittens that I have ever worn will keep my hands warm unless they are very heavily lined and then they are stiff, so I prefer the cloth ones.

So much for cold weather clothing, but what shall we wear when the sun commences to travel his northern trail and the grip of Jack Frost weakens; when the snow melts during midday and our clothing seems uncomfortably warm. At such times we can discard the heavy

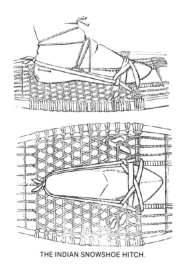

THE INDIAN SNOWSHOE HITCH.

shirt and substitute a lighter one; leave the overalls in camp and put the hood in the pack or the coat pocket, and wear fewer socks, with oil-tanned shoe pacs instead of buckskin moccasins. They are not as good for snowshoeing, but are waterproof if kept well oiled. Rubber shoes wear the filling of the snowshoe badly.

While I have been speaking of clothing for wear in the timbered districts of the Far North I realize that there are more of those who read this living in a less frosty climate, but for all of the Northern States this clothing is quite suitable and proper, with the exception of the hood and moccasins. The former is seldom needed in more open hardwood forest, and as snowshoes are not used much the shoe pac and rubber shoe are the footwear most often seen. For walking on bare ground or in shallow snow, both shoes have advantages and faults. The rubbers are heavier than the pacs and more protection to tender feet, but are more likely to tire the wearer, especially since rubber clings so fondly to all brush and weeds with which it comes in contact. But the pacs, while lighter and softer, will make tender feet sore on the bottoms, and they slip in snow more than do rubbers. My favorite rubber shoes for outdoor wear are those of ankle height, fastening with a lace or with strap and buckle.

Snowshoes can hardly be considered wearing apparel. An Italian who came over to Canada, when cold weather came, began to inquire about clothing for wear in that climate. When he asked what kind of footwear was best his informant told him that he thought snowshoes were the best when the snow came. Having no idea what snowshoes were he went to a store and asked to be shown some, and he was considerably surprised when he saw what they were. Snowshoes, however, are a part of the Northern woodsman's equipment, and a very necessary part. They are offered in a number of patterns by sporting goods dealers, and there are other styles made and used that are seldom or never seen in stores. Some are good; others are better, but each kind is good in some section of the country. It is not my object to go into detail in describing snowshoes, but I feel that I must say something about the patterns best adapted for use in the woods. They should be of about the standard shape, either round or square toe, as desired; for the average man, about 14 by 48 inches in size; frames of good straight grained wood, with the crossbars mortised in without weakening the bows. The tail should be fastened with rawhide, counter-sunk, and not a screw or

rivet; and the filling throughout should be of good rawhide thoroughly stretched, rather fine and close in the ends and coarse and open in the centers. The toe should be large and quite broad, the tail narrow, and they should balance at a point just a few inches behind the center of the space between the crossbars. With such shoes you can travel fast on loose snow or hard; they turn easily; the broad flat toe takes a good grip and makes hill climbing easy, and it also stays nearly on the surface of the snow while the narrow tail cuts down and as a consequence they lift easily for the next step. If the filling is too close in the center the snow will pack under the foot; if the toes are too small they cut down and loose snow falls on top, making them heavy to lift; if the tail is too heavy it is difficult to turn with them; if the toe is upturned they slip on a crust or hard trail, make the feet sore, and are not good for climbing hills. Unless you know just what you are doing it is a good rule to avoid extreme styles.

If you are a "Down East" man you will undoubtedly select some kind of snowshoe boot, harness, fastening, or whatever you choose to call it. Most of these give satisfaction, but I have used the Indians' method mostly, the same being a tie or hitch with a piece of ⅝-inch lamp wick, about 4 feet long. The toe strap is separate and is fastened by weaving the ends in and out of the filling at the sides of the toe opening. The way of tying to the foot is shown in the illustration more plainly than I can describe it. Both strings are tied together above the heel, and when properly adjusted it is not necessary to untie for putting the shoe on or removing it from the foot; a simple twist will do it. I have used snowshoes for a week or more without undoing the fastening, and it is very nice in extreme cold weather to be able to put on or remove shoes without baring the hands.

If you are simply traveling through the woods aimlessly, with no intention of making future use of the trail, it makes little difference how you go, but if you are a trapper and are breaking out a trap line you will, of course, aim to strike the good places for sets without walking farther than necessary, and you should make your trail with a view of using it afterwards, avoiding steep ascents and dense thickets. If possible, get over your trail the second time before the packed snow hardens and the trail will be smoother. Blaze your trail on trees and brush as you go along. I think it best to mark the brush by cutting them half off and bending them away from the trail. If you must mark trees, mark two sides and then you can follow the marks either way, and you can also indicate the turns in the path. My objection to marks on trees are that they cannot be seen as plainly as cut brush, especially after a driving snowstorm, when the snow clings to the trunks of trees, and that the drooping, snow-laden branches often hide the spots just when you need to see them most. A foot of fresh fallen snow may completely obliterate your trail, but if it is well marked you can follow it still, and the beaten bottom makes easier traveling, no difference how much snow has fallen over it.

Breaking out fresh trails is hard work, and slow. You can break trail away from camp six hours, and return over the broken trail in two. In a snowy climate it is advisable, whenever possible, to travel each permanent trail at least once in ten days to keep it in good condition; but the trapper will want to get over the ground oftener than that anyway.

As snowshoes are costly and their life depends much on the care they receive I will give some rules covering this point that is always well to observe. In breaking out a fresh trail avoid snags which show through the snow or little protuberances which indicate snags beneath the surface; also beware of places where the snow appears to be held up by brush or sticks beneath. I once broke a new snowshoe frame by stepping into a concealed hole; the whole trail dropped down and my snowshoe caught on a snag of a nearby stump, breaking a section out of the frame. It is the stringing, however, that is usually cut out by the snags. Be careful also when crossing logs to see that the shoes are not supported solidly at the ends while the middle is free to go down; such treatment will either break the frames or bend and strain them, and if they assume a curved shape they are unsightly and tiring to the feet, also hard to use in hill climbing. I always like to get started on the trail as early in the morning as possible, so that I can travel a few miles before daylight, and I camp early in the evening so I can get wood and make a comfortable camp before dark. In the early spring, when the snow melts during the day and clings to the snowshoes, the only time one can travel is in the morning until about ten o'clock, and late in the evening. At night, if the moon shines, one can make good time, but through the day is the best time for resting at this season. When the snow sticks, the snowshoes get wet and heavy and damp snow packs on top and clings to them, and when these troubles come it is best to cut wood, build a good fire, and camp by it until evening. Stand the snowshoes up in the snow where the sunshine and the warm wind will dry them, make some tea and eat your lunch, then roll into your blanket and rest until the sun gets low, when you can resume your journey.

It is difficult traveling, at the best, and the strength of the traveler is heavily taxed.

Always he has the heavy pack and the snowshoe trail seems endless. The home camp is ever a welcome sight. It means greater comfort and usually a day of rest to wash and mend the clothing, and admire the drying furs, the harvest of the traps. There are days of awful cold, and the deep, loose snow seems almost too much to endure; yet with all the hardships and privations there is an unexplainable fascination connected with the free, wild life in the woods and in tramping the winter trail.

# Traveling in the Pathless Woods

Everybody admires the man who can travel in the woods without getting lost. Such a man always commands respect among his less accomplished associates. The sportsman never ceases to wonder at the ability of his guide to find his way unfailingly through the dense bush, and the white guide also admires and wonders at the Indian's accomplishments in the same line. To the uninitiated the feats of the woodsman seem like a sixth sense—instinct, they call it. But it is not instinct, but simply the application of knowledge which comes to those who are forced by circumstances to be observing in such matters. The man who can take an outfit on his back and travel a month in the wilderness, living without a particle of aid from his fellow men, is a woodsman, and he possesses a knowledge of woodcraft which would make a better world if it could be imparted to all mankind.

I was born and grew to manhood in one of the wildest and roughest districts of Pennsylvania. Northeast from my home I could travel 30 miles without seeing a human habitation, and northward the wild, uninhabited mountains reached a like distance, broken at one place only by a narrow valley in which there were a few small farms. Little by little I learned to know these mountains and the narrow valleys between. There was not a stream within 10 or 15 miles where I had not fished for trout and trapped for mink and 'coons, and I had hunted every swamp and red brush flat for deer, bears, and grouse. I knew every place where blueberries grew in sufficient numbers to make the gathering profitable, and often I wandered long distances merely for the pleasure of mountain travel. I soon got the reputation of being an accomplished woodsman, an honor which I did not deserve, for I knew nothing whatever about travel in real wilderness. The long mountains paralleling one another made it easy to get about without losing the sense of direction, and I kept my compass points merely by familiarity with the ground on which I traveled.

When at the age of twenty-three I went into the wilderness of Canada, I was up against an entirely different proposition. Before me were hundreds of miles of unbroken bush, spotted with lakes that at first looked all alike to me, and cut by small streams which flowed about from lake

A COMPASS OF A PRACTICAL TYPE.

to lake in the most haphazard fashion imaginable. I had never traveled with the sun as a guide and knew nothing regarding the use of a compass, both of which are essential for wilderness travel.

My first move was to file on a piece of government land. The land guide helped to locate me and while we were looking about I saw him look at his compass, then he remarked that it was just noon and we would make some tea. I was surprised to see him get the time of day from a compass and asked him how he knew it was noon. "Because the sun is directly south," he answered, "and it is in that position only at noon." And then he explained to me how a compass could be used as a watch, with fair accuracy, and how a watch could be made to answer very well as a compass.

The woodsman told me that I could not travel in that country without a compass, and I soon found that such was the case. I borrowed a compass from a friend, a small, slip-cover instrument with a stop to hold the needle stationary when not in use. But I found that the slip-cover was inconvenient; dust got in at the stop opening and hampered the movement of the needle; and finally the compass slipped through a hole in my pocket and was lost. By these experiences I learned that the most practical form of compass for a woodsman was an open-face, watch-shaped instrument, without a stop, and with a ring by which it could be fastened to the coat or vest like a watch. Such an instrument does not have the long life of the finer stop compass, but it costs only a dollar or thereabouts, and after a year or two of use can be thrown away and a new one purchased. Of course, if a stop compass can be found that has no outside opening to admit dust it is better still.

An Indian seldom carries a compass, but he travels mainly by the "lay of the land." He learns the country just as I learned the mountains of Pennsylvania, and as a rule he has little idea of direction. Sometimes he travels by sun, in fact the sun answers for both watch and compass. But when the sun is invisible and the ground unfamiliar he sometimes meets with trouble and "loses his wigwam." But he is much less apt to get lost than a white man, under similar conditions, for when he loses his bearings he doesn't lose his head, in fact he doesn't consider it a serious matter at all. He simply makes camp and the next day he travels on until he rights himself again. The Indian also, when forced to it, uses means of getting his bearings which only Indians and veteran woodsmen know how to use.

For my own part I travel mostly by the sun when on strange ground, verifying my directions occasionally by reference to the compass. I also study landmarks and make use of them constantly, for to travel by compass alone is slow and difficult.

Comparatively few people who have never used a compass know how the instrument works;

, I once knew a man who thought that the needle pointed towards home when the owner lost his bearings. But it doesn't do any such thing unless by chance the home lies north.

On the peninsula of Boothia Felix, which juts into the Arctic Sea northwest of Hudson's Bay, is the magnetic north pole, and the needle of the compass, when free to revolve, points to this particular part of the earth. It does not point directly towards the magnetic pole in all parts of the world, for the magnetic currents which converge there do not flow in straight lines. In fact, there is an area in Asia, where the compass needle is deflected and points to a smaller local magnetic pole. But for bush travel all that is necessary is to consider that the blue end of the compass needle points north, and to call this point north always, the opposite direction, of course, being south.

Perhaps I should not say that the needle always points north, for it may lose its magnetism with age or the pivot on which it swings may become dulled, or again the needle may be deflected by a metal object being brought too near. If the needle behaves queerly, maybe you are holding it too near your gun, or some metal object in your belt or pocket may be attracting it. All objects of iron or steel become magnetized to a certain extent and will attract the needle if brought too near. But aside from such outside influence, and that of wear, the compass is a perfectly reliable instrument. Sometimes it tells us that the sun rises in the northwest, in which case we should believe it without question, for if we go contrary to the teachings of the instrument we will find that ninety-nine times out of one hundred the compass is right and we are dead wrong. One of the greatest mistakes a man can make when he gets turned around in the big timber is to doubt his compass, but many people will take a chance on their very unreliable instinct rather than to trust a perfectly trustworthy instrument which was brought into the woods to serve them on just such occasions. But one need never be in doubt, for if the needle swings freely and settles down in the same position each time, he may be sure that the instrument is all right.

By referring to the drawing, which shows a very common type of compass, it will be noted that the dial is graduated in degrees, on its outer edge, with the principal points marked with letters. These letters mean north, east, south, west, northeast, southeast, etc. To make the compass work perfectly it must be held level and steady until the needle stops swinging, then the compass can be turned easily, so that the blue end of the needle stands over the letter "N." When this is done all the points of the compass are shown. The only way a compass can be used is to show these directions, and, of course, the user should know which way he wants to go. Usually a man in the woods knows some familiar landmark; it may be a stream, a lake, a mountain, or even the railroad which he left

when he entered the woods, and he will know whether he is north, south, east, or west of this landmark, so there is little excuse for getting completely lost. But if he is so hopelessly muddled that he doesn't know for the life of him whether he is in the Grand Canyon or a Canadian swamp the compass will not help him very much. If he is traveling north of his landmark he can return to it by going south, and the compass will tell him quickly which direction is south.

Suppose you have made a camp in the wilds and have set out to explore the surrounding country. For the sake of illustration I have drawn a map

A ROUTE TRAVELLED BY COMPASS.

of some of my old-time hunting ground, showing the location of one of my camps. The first move would be to learn the country in the immediate vicinity of camp. The stream by the side of the camp flows east and this would be the first with which to get acquainted. A trip along the stream both ways from camp will serve to familiarize one with the stream and nearby country, so that he would have a good landmark, and he could hardly cross this stream knowing that it was the same one which flows by the camp. He would also know, if he were to reach this creek, whether the camp lay up stream or down. This then would serve as a base from which to operate. We will say now that he wishes to see some of the country north and northwest of camp. He sees in the distance a high hill with a peculiar bunch of trees on its summit. By referring to the compass he finds that the position of this hill is a little east of north. Then facing in that direction he notes that the sun is behind his right shoulder, for it

is morning and the sun is in the southeast. Replacing the compass in his pocket he starts toward the tree-crowned hill which he has chosen as an objective point. As long as the hill is in sight he has clear sailing, but when the forest hides his landmark from view he keeps traveling straight ahead, maintaining his same position with reference to the sun. But the sun is also moving and he dare not go far without again looking at the compass and noting the changed position of the sun. This, you will see, is traveling by landmark, by compass, and by sun, and it will be found a very practical way.

But a man cannot travel straight in the average wilderness country, for nature imposes obstacles. Lakes, swamps, unfordable streams and other natural obstructions force detours, all of which must be kept in mind and a general straight course maintained.

Presuming that in spite of the unavoidable detours the traveler has kept a reasonable straight course and has reached the high hill with its peculiar clump of trees, he will know now that since his course has been a little east of north his camp must be just that much west of south from this hill. It would be an easy matter for him to retrace his steps to camp if he wished to do so.

From the top of the hill the explorer studies the topography of the surrounding country, and notes the lakes; the hollows, which indicate water courses; the swamp and clump of evergreen bush. Perhaps he sketches a map of what he sees, the details to be added as the country is learned more thoroughly.

To the northwest he sees what appears to be a fairly large lake, and as this looks interesting he sets out in that direction, traveling as before, by sun, compass and marker. Sometimes he can pick a mark a half mile distant and at other times he must be content to make use of a dead tree standing a hundred yards or less away. But near or far, they all serve the same purpose.

Having reached his objective he finds that what appeared to be a large lake is in reality a chain of small lakes or ponds and he draws them into his map.

Then he sets out down stream, noting that it flows in a southwesterly direction, and occasionally he takes a compass bearing to make sure that this course has not changed. After traveling about a mile he decides to return to camp. By carefully considering the distance traveled in each direction he concludes that he is now about two and a half miles northwest of camp, therefore he must travel southeast, so he starts in that direction. When about a quarter of a mile from camp he recognizes the surroundings and changes his course a little at the point marked by the arrow, and goes straight to camp.

In the same way the camper would explore the country for a few miles east, west, and south, and when he has become reasonably well acquainted with this ground he is ready to push his explorations to greater distance, knowing that he can without difficulty return to familiar ground, and then easily find his camp, for he could not cross the section of country with which he is now familiar without recognizing it.

To travel in a straight line by compass, and to keep your bearings regardless of how or where you go, is easy, if the rules I have given are followed; but people do not always know these rules, or for one reason or another they do not observe them. As a result they get lost. What to do in such a case I can't tell; but one thing that should not be done is to get frightened and travel desperately first in one direction, then in another, always more or less in circles, as men do when they wander aimlessly.

I am a firm believer in that "ounce of prevention" adage, for prevention is better than cure every time. This policy has carried me through hundreds of miles of wilderness without once getting lost. I have never

been lost, although many times I have lost my bearings for awhile when traveling in company with somebody who was leading the way, or when trying to travel in unfamiliar country without using the methods I have been describing. I have never gone astray when using a compass, or when traveling by any of the other ways I have mentioned.

A short time ago I was talking about bush travel with a friend and after he had listened to my chatter for awhile he asked, "What would you do if you were to get lost?" "I wouldn't get lost," I answered, "for the rules I have been explaining to you are to prevent that and will always do so if followed. I always follow them." "That sounds all right," he argued, "but you know people do get lost sometimes and I want to know what a man should do if he gets lost. You say that you first get acquainted with the country near camp, then explore farther, etc., but here now is something different. I go into the woods to hunt deer, with a few fellows.

We know nothing of the country and are dependent on our guides. They have led us into camp and we scarcely know how we came. Well, the next day, I set out to look for game, alone, intending to hunt close to camp. I go first this way and then that way, looking at the likely places, and after awhile it dawns on me that I don't know which direction to go to reach camp. In other words, I am lost. Now what should I do?" I will confess that the question was too much for me. Having never been lost, I had no experience of this kind from which to draw. I recalled stories of people who were lost but couldn't think of anything that would help a lost man find his way. There are many ways to find the compass points, but when a man doesn't know what direction he wants to travel, what good is there in knowing which is north and east?

I suggested to my friend that a man would surely always have some point in mind with which he was acquainted and would know approximately which direction this place lay. "If he does he isn't lost," he replied. "And even if he knows that the railroad runs north and that he is east of it, the railroad may be fifty or a hundred miles away, while he may be only a mile or two from camp."

The only practical thing I could suggest was this: When a man suddenly discovers that he has lost his bearings and doesn't know which way to go to reach camp or familiar ground, he should above all things avoid getting excited and "losing his head." It is not at all a serious matter and if he will keep cool and use judgment he will come out all right. First let him note carefully his surroundings so he will know the place when he sees it again. Then he can set out in what seems to be the most probable direction to familiar ground, but he must travel in a straight line by the method I described in the last chapter. After traveling a reasonable distance, if no familiar ground is reached he should return to the starting point and try another direction. If all this fails, the various points of the compass having been tried, he should come back to the starting point and camp there until his friends find him. I am presuming that he has lost his bearings under the conditions named by my friend and that he has companions some where not many miles distant. The campfire may help his friends find him and if he fires his gun it may also do some good. It is a very good plan to agree on some sort of a signal to use in case some member of the party loses his way but I know this is seldom done, for nobody cares to let his friends know that he feels the remotest possibility of getting lost. I never leave camp without having with me a good quantity of matches. I always carry a light ax and if the weather is cold I put a blanket in my packsack. Thus, if anything happens to prevent my getting back to camp I am reasonably outfitted for camping out a night.

In my talk about travel by compass I have spoken of keeping direction by the sun and thus doing away to a great extent with frequent reference to the compass. Doubtless the reader has been wondering what he should do on days when the sun is invisible. Fortunately there are few such days unless it is during a rain when of course very little traveling is done. But there are days when fog or clouds obscure the sun for hours and then travel is slow because one must make frequent reference to the compass. The only safe way is to select some conspicuous object in the line of travel each time a compass bearing is taken and to take a new bearing when this object is reached. A dense fog is the worst possible condition for then not only is the sun invisible but one cannot see far enough to choose objective points. I seldom attempt to travel under such conditions but when I do, if I make a half or three-quarters of a mile an hour, providing I have no stream, lake shore, or trail to follow, I consider that I am getting along very well. Blinding rain or snow storms also make travel very difficult. I have

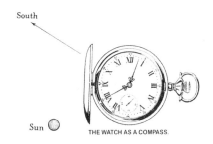

South

Sun

THE WATCH AS A COMPASS.

traveled in a heavy snowstorm by making use of the wind as a guide, in conjunction with the compass. The wind seldom changes during a steady rain or snow storm, and anyway the compass would apprise the wayfarer of a change in the wind before he had gone far out of his course.

There are ways of learning the directions without a compass which may be used in case of emergency. First there is the sun. In theory it rises in the east and sets in the west; but in reality it only behaves so on or very near the equator. As we are in the northern hemisphere the sun is of course south of the east and west line all the time, and in winter it is farther south than in summer, because the earth wabbles back and forth throughout the seasons and the northern portion leans

away from the path of the sun in winter. As a consequence the sun rises somewhat south of the east in summer and sets a little south of west. In winter it rises still farther south and its path across the sky is always to the south of us. At noon it is straight south. Thus it will be seen that if one knows approximately the time of day he can easily figure out the compass points. Directions by the sun can be learned with much greater accuracy if one has a watch, for knowing the time of day exactly he should know just how far the sun is from the zenith at that time and thus easily locate the true south. Having found it he has but to face in that direction and the north will then be behind him, the east on his left, and the west on his right side.

But there is a much better way of getting the compass directions by means of a watch and it is done in this way. Holding the watch so that the hour hand points to a line perpendicular to the sun, count half way from this hour to twelve and this will be south; in other words half way between the hour hand and the figure twelve is south. Count forward from the hour hand to twelve in the forenoon, but in the afternoon the south is half way between the hour hand and twelve, counting back towards twelve. While I may not have made my point clear I believe that the drawing will convey the idea more distinctly. The time shown is 8 p.m. and with the hour hand pointed towards the sun, south would be midway between 8 and 12 or in line with Fig. 10.

When the sun is invisible and no compass or other ordinary means of locating directions is available it is advisable to stay in camp if possible. But it is well to know means of finding directions under such conditions for one never knows what may happen and a little knowledge along this line can do no harm even if it is never used. We sometimes read or hear from woodsmen of such means and usually they are given as safe and reliable methods. But they should never be taken too

seriously. For instance we are told that moss grows only on the north side of trees, while the larger branches are on the south side. This is true in a general way but conditions have their effect and the shelter of the other trees or nearby hills may reverse the order more or less. But the fact that the sun's rays never directly reach the north side of a tree encourages the growth of moss on that side, while the almost constant sunshine by day, on the south side, causes the sap to flow there more vigorously and thus gives a greater growth to the branches on the south side. In prairie country the prevailing wind, usually from the north, will give a permanent incline to the grass, which may help one to locate directions.

It is seldom necessary to travel at night unless in the north when the snow is soft during the day and travel is better at night. But then the traveler usually has a snowshoe trail to follow or he will have some other way of keeping his directions. If not he can travel by the north star in the same way that he keeps his bearings by the sun during the day. The difference is that the north star does not move across the sky as does the sun, and it is always in the north. To find this star first locate the group which constitutes what is commonly known as the dipper. The two stars forming the side of the bowl farthest from the handle are in line with the north star and it is above the open side or top of the dipper bowl.

I have remarked that a man traveling without guidance of any kind always moves in a circle and I think the readers are all well acquainted with this fact. I don't know why we do so, but one theory is that one leg is longer than the other and naturally takes a longer step. Others think the trouble is caused by one leg being stronger than the other. But

★ North Star

★    ★    ★
      ★      ★

Dipper

★    ★

THE STAR THAT MARKS THE TRUE NORTH.

whatever the cause it is a fact that a man wandering aimlessly in the woods will in a short time cross his own trail. This fact was never brought home to me so forcibly as one time when I tried to travel without a compass on a cloudy day. It was early spring and I was traveling on snowshoes, so there was no danger of getting lost, for I had my trail to follow back to camp. I was trying to travel south and was setting a line of traps. I had traveled quite a distance straight south as I supposed when I saw before me a fresh snowshoe trail. I thought at once that some Indian trapper must have invaded my trapping ground. I stepped into the trail and was surprised to find that my snowshoes fitted perfectly into the tracks; then the truth dawned upon me—I had been traveling in a circle. Feeling very foolish I started forward again, resolved to keep a straight course. I found the place where I had made the first turn to the right and here I left the trail and started south again. After traveling perhaps a half mile I again saw a fresh trail ahead and knew at once that I had made another circle. Once more I attempted to strike a straight course south and I traveled the remainder of the way without completing a circle. When the time came to return to camp I had just one trap left and I set it at the end of the trail in a ravine which led down from a hillside. A few days later when I went to look at the traps I climbed to the top of the hill where I had set the last trap, a distance of about 100 yards, and was very much surprised to see below me the lake on which my camp was situated, and the cabin itself not more than a mile away.

To travel straight by that questionable sense known as instinct is absolutely impossible, notwithstanding the stories we hear of Indians, foresters, and others who habitually travel this way. Instinct is a very unreliable guide and something more tangible is needed. So when you hear stories of a man who can go anywhere and find his way without failure from one part of

the woods to another, it may be wise to pretend credulity, but you may be sure that the story teller is either elaborating or his hero has a very thorough knowledge of the woods and a very reliable, altogether scientific method of keeping his bearings.

The surest way to get lost is to try to travel on strange ground without any guidance whatever, and this is perhaps most easily accomplished by letting some other person lead the way until you have completely lost your bearings. It is a strange fact that few people pay any attention to where they are going if somebody else leads the way and this probably results in more cases of people losing their bearings than all other things combined. I have lost all sense of direction in a very short time by letting some other person lead the way, and this in a farming community. Another easy way to get lost is to follow a game trail, for in such cases the trail and the probability of sighting the game so interests and completely fills one's thoughts that he seldom gives any thought to directions or distance traveled.

To sum up the whole matter of bush travel, one thing stands out as being of the utmost importance and that is to keep the compass points constantly in mind and at the same time have familiar ground from which to start operations. With these two essentials there will be no worry about getting lost to mar one's pleasure and he can travel anywhere he chooses in the big woods.

# Finding, Cooking, and Preserving Food

# Tracks, Trailing, and Signaling

## By Ernest Thompson Seton, Chief Scout

"I wish I could go West and join the Indians so that I should have no lessons to learn," said an unhappy small boy who could discover no atom of sense or purpose in any one of the three R's.

"You never made a greater mistake," said the scribe. "For the young Indians have many hard lessons from their earliest day—hard lessons and hard punishments. With them the dread penalty of failure is 'go hungry till you win,' and no harder task have they than their reading lesson. Not twenty-six characters are to be learned in this exercise, but one thousand; not clear straight print are they, but dim, washed-out, crooked traces; not indoors on comfortable chairs, with a patient teacher always near, but out in the forest, often alone and in every kind of weather, they slowly decipher their letters and read sentences of the oldest writing on Earth—a style so old that the hieroglyphs of Egypt, the cylinders of Nippur, and the drawings of the cave men are as things of today in comparison—the one universal script—the tracks in the dust, mud, or snow.

"These are the inscriptions that every hunter must learn to read infallibly, and be they strong or faint, straight or crooked, simple or overwritten with many a puzzling, diverse phrase, he must decipher and follow them swiftly, unerringly if there is to be a successful ending to the hunt which provides his daily food.

"This is the reading lesson of the young Indians, and it is a style that will never become out of date. The naturalist also must acquire some measure of proficiency in the ancient art. Its usefulness is unending to the student of wild life; without it he would know little of the people of the wood."

## There Are Still Many Wild Animals

It is a remarkable fact that there are always more wild animals about than any but the expert has an idea of. For example, there are, within 20 miles of New York City, fully fifty different kinds— not counting birds, reptiles, or fishes—one quarter of which at least are abundant. Or more particularly within the limits of Greater New York there are at least a dozen species of wild beasts, half of which are quite common.

"Then how is it that we never see any?" is the first question of the incredulous. The answer is: Long ago the beasts learned the dire lesson—man is our worst enemy; shun him at any price. And the simplest way to do this is to come out only at night. Man is a daytime creature; he is blind in the soft half-light that most beasts prefer.

While many animals have always limited their activity to the hours of twilight and gloom, there are not a few that moved about in daytime, but have given up that portion of their working day in order to avoid the arch enemy.

Thus they can flourish under our noses and eat at our tables, without our knowledge or consent. They come and go at will, and the world knows nothing of them; their presence might long go unsuspected but for one thing, well known to the hunter, the trapper, and the naturalist: wherever the wild four-foot goes, it leaves behind a record of its visit, its name, the direction whence it came, the time, the thing it did or tried to do, with the time and direction of departure. These it puts down in the ancient script. Each of these dotted lines, called the trail, is a wonderful, unfinished record of the creature's life during the time it made the same, and it needs only the patient work of the naturalist to decipher that record and from it learn much about the animal that made it, without that animal ever having been seen.

It is hard to overvalue the powers of the clever tracker. To him the trail of each animal is not a mere series of similar footprints; it is an accurate account of the creature's life, habit, changing whims, and emotions during the portion of life whose record is in view. These are indeed autobiographical chapters, and differ from other autobiographies in this—they cannot tell a lie. We may get wrong information from them, but it is our fault if we do; we misread the document that cannot falsify.

## When to Learn Tracking

The ideal time for tracking, and almost the only time for most folk,

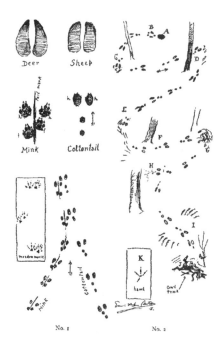

Deer, Sheep, Mink, Cottontail, Hawk, Owl, Meadow Mouse.

is when the ground is white. After the first snow the student walks forth and begins at once to realize the wonders of the trail. A score of creatures of whose existence, maybe, he did not know, are now revealed about him, and the reading of their autographs becomes easy.

It is when the snow is on the ground, indeed, that we take our four-foot census of the woods. How often we learn with surprise from the telltale white that a fox was around our hen house last night, a mink is living even now under the wood pile, and a deer—yes! there is no mistaking its sharp-pointed un-sheep-like footprint—has wandered into our woods from the farther wilds.

Never lose the chance of the first snow if you wish to become a trailer. Nevertheless, remember that the first morning after a night's snow fall is not so good as the second. Most creatures "lie up" during the storm; the snow hides the tracks of those that do go forth; and some actually go into a "cold sleep" for a day or two after a heavy downfall. But a calm, mild night following a storm is sure to offer abundant and ideal opportunity for beginning the study of the trail.

## How to Learn

Here are some of the important facts to keep in view, when you set forth to master the rudiments:

*First*—No two animals leave the same trail; not only each kind but each individual, and each individual at each stage of its life, leaves a trail as distinctive as the creature's appearance, and it is obvious that in that they differ among themselves just as we do, because the young know their mothers, the mothers know their young, and the old ones know their mates, when scent is clearly out of the question.

Another simple evidence of this is the well-known fact that no two human beings have the same thumb mark; all living creatures have corresponding peculiarities, and all use these parts in making the trail.

*Second*—The trail was begun at the birthplace of that creature and ends only at its death place; it may be recorded in visible track or perceptible odor. It may last but a few hours, and may be too faint even for an expert with present equipment to follow, but evidently the trail is made, wherever the creature journeys afoot.

*Third*—It varies with every important change of impulse, action, or emotion.

*Fourth*—When we find a trail we may rest assured that, if living, the creature that made it is at the other end. And if one can follow, it is only a question of time before coming up with that animal. And be sure of its direction before setting out; many a novice has lost much time by going backward on the trail.

*Fifth*—In studying trails one must always keep probabilities in mind. Sometimes one kind of track looks much like another; then the question is, "Which is the likeliest in this place."

If I saw a jaguar track in India, I should know it was made by a leopard. If I found a leopard in Colorado, I should be sure I had found the mark of a cougar or mountain lion. A wolf track on Broadway would doubtless be the doing of a very large dog, and a St. Bernard's footmark in the Rockies, 20 miles from anywhere, would most likely turn out to be the happen-so imprint of a gray wolf's foot. To be sure of the marks, then, one should know all the animals that belong to the neighborhood.

These facts are well known to every hunter. Most savages are hunters, and one of the early lessons of the Indian boy is to know the tracks of the different beasts about him. These are the letters of the old, old writing.

## A First Try

Let us go forth into the woods in one of the northeastern states when there is a good tracking snow, and learn a few of these letters of the wood alphabet.

Two at least are sure to be seen—the track of the blarina and of the deer mouse. They are shown on the same scale on page 283.

In Fig. 3 is the track of the meadow mouse. This is not unlike that of the blarina, because it walks, being a ground animal, while the deer mouse more often bounds. The delicate lace traceries of the masked shrew are almost invisible unless the sun be low;

they are difficult to draw, and impossible to photograph or cast satisfactorily but the sketch gives enough to recognize them by.

The meadow mouse belongs to the rank grass in the lowland near the brook, and passing it toward the open, running water we may see the curious track of the muskrat; its five-toed hind foot, its four-toed front foot, and its long keeled tail are plainly on record. When he goes slowly the tail mark is nearly straight; when he goes fast it is wavy in proportion to his pace.

The muskrat is a valiant beast; he never dies without fighting to the last, but he is in dread of another brookland creature whose trail is here—the mink. Here he was bounding; the forefeet are together, the hindfeet track ahead, and tail mark shows, and but four toes in each track, though the creature has five on each foot. He is a dreaded enemy of poor Molly Cottontail, and more than once I have seen the records of his relentless pursuit. One of these fits in admirably

as an illustration of our present study.

## A Story of the Trail

It was in the winter of 1900, I was standing with my brother, a business man, on Goat Island, Niagara, when he remarked, "How is it? You and I have been in the same parts of America for twenty years, yet I never see any of the curious sides of animal life that you are continually coming across."

"Largely because you do not study tracks," was the reply. "Look at your feet now. There is a whole history to be read."

"I see some marks," he replied, "that might have been made by some animal." "That is the track of a cottontail," was the answer. "Now, let us read the chapter of his life. See, he went in a general straight course as though making some well-known haunt, his easy pace, with eight or ten inches between each set of tracks, shows unalarm. But see here, joining on, is something else."

"So there is. Another cottontail."

"Not at all, this new track is smaller, the forefeet are more or less paired, showing that the creature can climb a tree; there is a suggestion of toe pads and there is a mark telling evidently of a long tail; these things combined with the size and the place identify it clearly. This is the trail of a mink. See! he has also found the rabbit track, and finding it fresh, he followed it. His bounds are lengthened now, but the rabbit's are not, showing that the latter was unconscious of the pursuit."

After 100 yards the double trail led us to a great pile of wood, and into this both went. Having followed his game into dense cover, the trailer's first business was to make sure that it did not go out the other side. We went carefully around the pile; there were no tracks leading out.

"Now," I said, "if you will take the trouble to move that wood pile you will find in it the remains of the rabbit half devoured and the mink himself. At this moment he is no doubt curled up asleep."

As the pile was large and the conclusion more or less self-evident, my brother was content to accept my reading of the episode.

## What About Winter Sleepers

Although so much is to be read in the wintry white, we cannot now make a full account of all the woodland four-foots, for there are some kinds that do not come out on the snow; they sleep more or less all winter.

Thus, one rarely sees the track of a chipmunk or woodchuck in truly wintry weather; and never, so far as I know, have the trails of jumping mouse or mud turtle been seen in the snow. These we can track only in the mud or dust. Such trails cannot be followed as far as those in the snow, simply because the mud and dust do not cover the whole country, but they are usually

Dog tracks, front and back
Cat tracks, front and back
Uppermost, well-developed human foot
Middle, a foot always cramped by boots
Bottom, a bare foot, never in boots
Muskrat tracks, (1/3 life-size)

as clear and in some respects more easy of record.

## How to Make Pictures of Tracks

It is a most fascinating amusement to learn some creature's way of life by following its fresh track for hours in good snow. I never miss such a chance. If I cannot find a fresh track, I take a stale one, knowing that, theoretically, it is fresher at every step, and from practical experience that it always brings one to some track that is fresh.

How often I have wished for a perfect means of transferring these wild life tales to paper or otherwise making a permanent collection. My earliest attempts were in free-hand drawing, which answers, but has this great disadvantage—it is a translation, a record discolored by an intervening personality, and the value of the result is likely to be limited by one's own knowledge at the time.

Casting in plaster was another means attempted; but not one track in ten thousand is fit to cast. Nearly all are blemished and imperfect in some way, and the most abundant—those in snow— cannot be cast at all.

Then I tried spreading plastic wax where the beasts would walk on it, in pathways or before dens. How they did scoff! The simplest ground squirrel knew too much to venture on my waxen snare; around it, or if hemmed in, over it, with a mighty bound they went; but never a track did I so secure.

Photography naturally suggested itself, but the difficulties proved as great as unexpected, almost as great as in casting. Not one track in one thousand is fit to photograph; the essential details are almost always left out. You must have open sunlight, and even when the weather is perfect there are practically but two times each day when it is possible—in mid-morning and mid-afternoon, when the sun is high enough for clear photographs and low enough to cast a shadow in the faint track.

## The Coon That Showed Me How

Then a new method was suggested in an unexpected way. A friend of mine had a pet coon which he kept in a cage in his bachelor quarters up town. One day, during my friend's absence the coon got loose and set about a series of long-deferred exploring expeditions, beginning with the bachelor's bedroom. The first promising object was a writing desk. Mounting by a chair the coon examined several uninteresting books and papers, and then noticed higher up a large stone bottle. He had several times found pleasurable stuff in bottles, so he went for it. The cork was lightly in and easily disposed of, but the smell was far from inviting, for it was merely a quart of ink. Determined to leave no stone unturned, however, the coon upset the ink to taste and try. Alas! It tasted even worse than it smelt; it was an utter failure as a beverage.

And the coon, pushing it contemptuously away, turned to a pile of fine handmade, deckle-edge, heraldry note paper—the pride of my friend's heart—and when he raised his inky little paws there were left on the paper some beautiful black prints. This was a new idea: The coon tried it again and again. But the ink held out longer than the paper, so that the fur-clad painter worked over sundry books, and the adjoining walls, while the ink, dribbling over everything, formed a great pool below the desk. Something attracted the artist's attention, causing him to jump down. He landed in the pool of ink, making it splash in all directions; some of the black splotches reached the white counterpane of the bachelor's bed. Another happy idea: The coon now leaped on the bed, racing around as long as the ink on his feet gave results. As he paused to rest, or perhaps to see if any places had been neglected, the door opened, and in came the landlady. The scene which followed was too painful for description; no one present enjoyed it. My friend was sent for to come and take his coon out of there forever. He came and took him away, I suppose "forever." He had only one other place for him—his office and there it was I made the animal's acquaintance and heard of his exploit—an ink and paper, if not a literary affair.

This gave me the hint at the zoo I needed, a plan to make an authentic record of animal tracks. Armed with printer's ink and paper rolls I set about gathering a dictionary collection of imprints.

After many failures and much experiment, better methods were devised. A number of improvements were made by my wife; one was the substitution of black paint for printer's ink, as the latter dries too quickly; another was the padding of the paper, which should be light and soft for very light animals, and stronger and harder for the heavy. Printing from a mouse, for example, is much like printing a delicate etching; ink, paper, dampness, etc., must be exactly right, and furthermore, you have this handicap—you cannot regulate the pressure. This is, of course, strictly a zoo method. All attempts to secure black prints from wild animals have been total failures. The paper, the smell of paint, etc., are enough to keep the wild things away.

In the zoo we spread the black pad and the white paper in a narrow, temporary lane, and one by one drove, or tried to drive, the captives over them, securing a series of tracks that are life-size, properly spaced, absolutely authentic, and capable of yielding more facts as the observer learns more about the subject.

As related here, all this sounds quite easy. But no one has any idea how cross, crooked, and contrary a creature can be, until he wishes it to repeat for him some ordinary things that it has hitherto done hourly. Some of them balked at the paint, some at the paper, some made a leap to clear all, and thereby wrecked the entire apparatus. Some would begin very well, but rush back when half-way over, so as to destroy the print already made, and in most cases the calmest, steadiest, tamest of beasts became utterly wild, erratic, and unmanageable when approached with tracklogical intent.

## Trying It on the Cat

Even domestic animals are difficult. A tame cat that was highly trained to do anything a cat could do, was selected as promising for a black track study, and her owner's two boys volunteered to get all the cat tracks I needed. They put down a long roll of paper in a hall, painted pussy's feet black, and proceeded to chase her up and down. Her docility banished under the strain. She raced madly about, leaving long, useless splashes of black; then, leaping to a fanlight, she escaped up stairs to take refuge among the snowy draperies. After which the boys' troubles began.

## Drawing Is Mostly Used

These, however, are mere by-accidents and illustrate the many practical difficulties. After these had been conquered with patience and ingenuity, there could be no doubt of the value of the prints. They are the best of records for size, spacing, and detail, but fail in giving incidents of wild life, or the landscape surroundings. The drawings, as already seen, are best for a long series and for faint features; in fact, the drawings alone can give everything you can perceive; but they fail in authentic size and detail.

Photography has this great advantage—it gives the surroundings, the essential landscape and setting, and, therefore, the local reason for any changes of action on the part of the animal; also the aesthetic beauties of its records are unique, and will help to keep the method in a high place.

Thus each of the three means may be successful in a different way, and the best, most nearly perfect alphabet of the woods, would include all three, and consist of a drawing, a pedoscript, and a photograph of each track, and a trail; i.e., a single footprint, and the long series of each animal.

My practice has been to use all whenever I could, but still I find free-hand drawing is the one of the most practical application.

When I get a photograph I treasure it as an adjunct to the sketch.

## A Story of the Trail

To illustrate the relative value as records, of sketch and photograph, I give a track that I drew from nature, but which could not at any place have been photographed. This was made on February 15, 1885, near Toronto. It is really a condensation of the facts, as the trail is shortened where uninteresting.

At A, I found a round place about 5 x 8 inches, where a cottontail had crouched during the light snowfall. He had leaped out and sat looking around; the small prints in front were made by his forefeet, the two long ones by his hind feet, and farther back is a little dimple made by the tail, showing that he was sitting on it. Something alarmed him, causing him to dart out at full speed, and now a remarkable change is to be seen: The marks made by the front feet are behind the large marks made by the hind feet, because the rabbit overreaches each time; the hind feet track ahead of the front feet; the faster he goes, the farther ahead those hind feet get; and what would happen if he multiplied his speed by ten I really cannot imagine. This overreach of the hind feet takes place in most bounding animals.

Now the cottontail began a series of the most extraordinary leaps and dodgings as though trying to escape from some enemy. But what enemy? There were no other tracks. I began to think the rabbit was crazy—was flying from an imaginary foe—that possibly I was on the trail of a March hare. But I found for the first time some spots of blood. This told me that the rabbit was in real danger but gave no clue to its source. I wondered if a weasel were clinging to its neck. A few yards farther, I found more blood. Twenty yards more, for the first time on each side of the rabbit trail, were the obvious marks of a pair of broad, strong wings. Oho! Now I knew the mystery of the

cottontail running from a foe that left no track. He was pursued by an eagle, a hawk, or an owl. A few yards farther and I found the remains of the cottontail partly devoured. This put the eagle out of the question; an eagle would have carried the rabbit off boldly. A hawk or an owl then was the assassin. I looked for something to decide which, and close by the remains found the peculiar two-paired track of an owl. A hawk's track would have been as K, while the owl nearly always sets its feet in the ground with two toes forward and two toes back. But which owl? There were at least three in the valley that might be blamed. I looked for more proof and got it on the near-by sapling—one small feather, downy, as are all owl feathers, and bearing three broad bars, telling me plainly that a barred owl had been there lately, and that, therefore, he was almost certainly the slayer of the cottontail. As I busied myself making notes, what should come flying up the valley but the owl himself—back to the very place of the crime, intent on completing his meal no doubt. He alighted on a branch 10 feet above my head and just over the rabbit remains, and sat there muttering in his throat.

The proof in this case was purely circumstantial, but I think that we can come to only one conclusion: that the evidence of the track in the snow was complete and convincing.

## Meadow Mouse

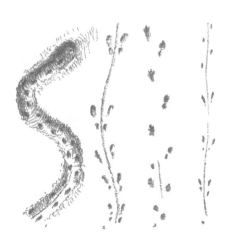

TRACKS
1. Blarina in snow
2. Deermouse
3. Meadow mouse
4. Masked shrew

The meadow mouse autograph illustrates the black-track method. At first these dots look inconsequent and fortuitous, but a careful examination shows that the creature had four toes with claws on the forefeet, and five on the hind, which is evidence, though not conclusive, that it was a rodent; the absence of tail marks shows that the tail was short or wanting; the tubercules on each palm show to what group of mice the creature belongs. The alternation of the track shows that it was a ground-animal, not a tree-climber; the spacing shows the shortness of the legs; their size determines the size of the creature. Thus we come near to reconstructing the animal from its tracks, and see how by the help of these studies, we can get much light on the by-gone animals whose only monuments are tracks in the sedimentary rocks about us—rocks that, when they received these imprints, were the muddy margin of these long-gone creatures' haunts.

## What the Trail Gives— The Secrets of the Woods

There is yet another feature of trail study that gives it exceptional value—it is an account of the creature pursuing its ordinary life. If you succeeded in getting a glimpse of a fox or a hare in the woods, the chances are a hundred to one that it was aware of your presence first. They are much cleverer than we are at this sort of thing, and if they do not actually sight or sense you, they observe, and are warned by the action of some other creature that did sense us, and so cease their occupations to steal away or hide. But the snow story will tell of the life that the animal ordinarily leads—its method of searching for food, its kind of food, the help it gets from its friends, or sometimes from its rivals—and thus offers an insight into its home ways that is scarcely to be attained in any other way. The trailer has the key to a new storehouse of Nature's secrets, another of the Sybilline books is opened to his view; his fairy godmother has, indeed, conferred on him a wonderful gift in opening his eyes to the foot-writing of the trail. It is like giving sight to the blind man, like the rolling away of fogs from a mountain view, and the trailer comes closer than others to the heart of the woods.

*Dowered with a precious power is he,*
*He drinks where others sipped,*
*And wild things write their lives for him*
*In endless manuscript.*

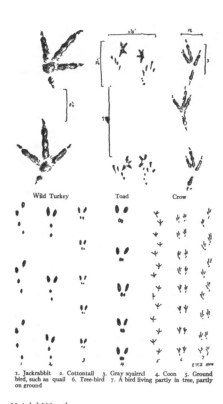

Wild Turkey          Toad          Crow

1. Jackrabbit   2. Cottontail   3. Gray squirrel   4. Coon   5. Ground bird, such as quail   6. Tree-bird   7. A bird living partly in tree, partly on ground

Wild Turkey

Toad

Crow

1. Jackrabbit

2. Cottontail

3. Gray squirrel

4. Coon

5. Ground bird, such as quail

6. Tree-bird

7. A bird living partly in tree, partly on ground

## Horses' Track

*N.B—The large tracks represent the hind feet.*

These are the tracks of two birds on the ground. One lives generally on the ground, the other in bushes and trees. Which track belongs to which bird?

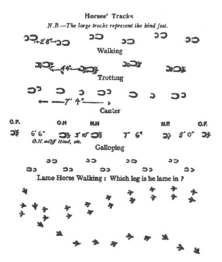

Walking, Trotting, Canter, Galloping

Lame Horse Walking: Which leg is he lame in?

# 23 Tactics for Hunting Success

## Tip #1: Got Guts?

Coyote problems have become more prevalent in the past decade. This is particularly true for deer hunters throughout the Northeast. To significantly reduce the numbers of resident and, especially, transient coyotes preying on deer in your area, use this practical and effective method. It is particularly effective for those who own or lease hunting property.

If you shoot a deer, don't leave the gut pile in the woods. Carry a folded heavy-duty trash bag in your day pack and, after removing the deer's entrails, put them into the bag. Tie the bag tightly to prevent leakage. Then either stuff it into the deer's chest cavity while dragging the deer out or use an ATV to remove the bag even if you have to return to get it soon after dragging the deer out.

While the scent of the blood left behind might attract a coyote or two, they will quickly move out of the area once they discover there isn't anything to eat. By simply removing the innards, you dramatically decrease the chance of attracting a pack of coyotes.

For the first couple of years that we owned our property in upstate New York, we routinely left gut piles in the woods. The practice often ended with us seeing coyotes near or at the gut-pile site. Once we started to remove the entrails from the woods, coyote sightings dropped quickly and noticeably. Since then, the number of coyote sightings on our lands has reduced by more than 95 percent.

We not only remove deer innards, but we also remove all

Deer entrails left out in the field are coyote magnets. They often attract more than one coyote, leading to fights over who gets to eat first. The sounds and odors left by coyotes often make resident deer nervous.

traces of turkey, small game, and waterfowl using smaller plastic bags, of course.

## Tip #2: Where to Aim to Make a Quick Kill

I'm often asked by hunters, "What part of a deer's body is best to aim at to make a quick and humane kill?" There are two primary areas on a deer's body—the neck and the shoulder—that, when hit by a projectile, will cause the deer to fall immediately and expire quickly.

A shot made to the middle of the neck will almost always sever the neck vertebrae, instantly dropping the deer in its tracks. It is most effective when the deer is standing still at a distance between 20 and 40 yards. When a deer is shot in the neck, there is also little loss of edible, quality meat. The remaining meat on the body is left unscathed, which provides the hunter with a delectable game animal.

It should be noted, however, that the neck of a deer is a small target area. It is not wise to shoot a deer in the neck when it is moving or if it is far from the hunter. Even when a deer is at close range, a neck shot should only be taken by hunters who are skilled and proficient shooters. This is not a shot for novice hunters or shooters.

The shoulder is another highly effective body part to aim at. It is my favorite place to aim, particularly when the deer is more than 30 yards away. The problem with this shot is that the bullet must hit the shoulder squarely in the middle of the scapula to be effective. A shoulder shot shatters the bone and often pierces both lungs, damaging them severely. This results in the animal being instantly immobilized and imparts a quick, humane kill. Like a neck shot, this is not a shot that should be taken by a neophyte. A hunter has to master the art of taking a shoulder shot, particularly at longer distances.

All serious hunters should make every effort to accurately shoot at a deer's shoulder. However, before making a shoulder shot, hunters must become familiar with the skeletal structure of a deer to achieve accurate bullet placement. Hunters who don't take the time to learn the anatomy of their quarry often end up aiming behind the shoulder. With this shot, the bullet ends up hitting the main vital area of the lungs and heart. While this hit will inevitably kill, it will not be as effective as an instantly disabling shoulder shot.

Unlike the neck shot, the shoulder shot damages meat.

Cody with a dandy mule buck he took at Bear Track Outfitters in Wyoming. Cody's well-placed shoulder shot took this buck down at 195 yards. Shoulder shots are reliable for making quick kills.

But, when you want to drop an animal in its tracks, it provides the best opportunity to do so. Plus, it is a larger target zone than the neck.

One last point about shooting the shoulder of big game is to make sure the bullet used is designed to break bone reliably. One excellent bullet choice is Winchester's Super-X Power Max Bonded load, available at affordable prices in a variety of calibers and bullet weights and specifically designed for whitetail deer. I also like Winchester's line of X-P 3 bullets, particularly the AccuBond CT or E-Tip; they are a little more expensive but well worth the money. Visit www.winchester.com for a complete line of deer cartridges.

Remington also makes a quality line of deer cartridges in its Core-Lokt, UMC, and AccuTip lines. The AccuTip is a super-accurate, polymer-tipped big game bullet that delivers devastating terminal performance. Visit www.remington.com for more information.

## Tip #3: Urinating in the Woods

Many years ago, I did my own nonscientific research about this. For three seasons I intentionally urinated in the woods in places where I could see a deer's reaction if it passed my marking area. Sometimes I urinated close to my stand, other times 50 to 100 yards from it.

Rather than getting into all the various reactions I noted over the three years, I will be brief and say sometimes it spooked the hell out of deer, especially if they came upon the scent when it was fresh. I noticed this was particularly true of mature bucks. With that said, however, there were times they tolerated the odor. However, those times occurred much less frequently than the times they showed concern or worry about the smell.

Since that time, I no longer urinate in the woods. If a male hunter cannot hold his urine, then taking along a wide-necked bottle to pee in is a good idea. If you do use a bottle to pee in, make sure to wash it out each day. Otherwise, pee at least 100 yards from your stand with the wind taking the odor away from the area from which you expect to see deer.

Some hunters have told me they regularly pee in buck scrapes and it has helped to attract bucks. If it really worked, I'm happy for them, but I wouldn't recommend it.

## Tip #4: Use a Decoy!

I could write at least one chapter, if not an entire book, on using decoys to enhance hunting success. Decoys serve several functions—they attract deer, hold their attention, relax them, and, during the rut, entice bucks into checking them out. Most importantly, a decoy will help distract a deer's attention from the hunter. For bow hunters, this is a crucial element because it helps them draw their bows undetected.

While I use full-sized deer decoys, I also include other nontraditional decoys in my deer hunting. These include fake apples and corn, a deer tail, plastic grass, a turkey decoy, and I even used a mounted doe head years ago. All these unorthodox decoys have worked to attract deer to my stand many times. Few hunters realize, or perhaps refuse to accept, their effectiveness.

Used properly, a buck or doe full-sized decoy can be a useful tool to attract bucks, particularly during the peak chase period of the primary rut.

Another type of decoy includes fertilizing oak trees and other natural vegetation. I also create mock scrapes and rubs to decoy deer. Some other tactics I use that act as decoys are a variety of deer scents, calls, and antler rattling.

All these decoying tactics work to attract deer. For those who want more detailed information about using all the decoys I mentioned in this tip, please visit my website at www.deerdoctor.com. You'll also find full chapters on the subject of decoying in my first book *Whitetail Strategies: A No-Nonsense Approach to Successful*

*Deer Hunting,* and the subsequent, *Whitetail Strategies: The Ultimate Guide.*

## Tip #5: Calling and Rattling

I use deer calls and ratting antlers as tactics to bring deer as close as possible to my stand. When I call or rattle, I try to make the vocalizations and noises as realistic as possible. By doing so, it creates a natural-seeming illusion and helps pacify a deer by putting it at ease.

Countless hunters think they have to use deer calls and rattling antlers loudly for a deer to hear them. Deer have excellent hearing. Mother Nature purposely designed their large, funnel-shaped ears to pick up sound waves from long distances. In one study about how far deer could hear, researchers determined that they could regularly hear rattling antlers from more than a quarter-mile away. They are much more capable of hearing sounds than humans are.

When using antlers or deer calls to attract deer, make the calls sound realistic by not making them too loud, and you will have more success.

An experience I had with a buck I was watching in a field in Saskatchewan, Canada, backs up what the researchers found. I blew a grunt call at him and, at a distance of about 250 yards away, the buck instantly picked up his head and looked my way. On another occasion, I called to a doe in a field on my farm that was exactly 176 yards from my blind. I made a soft blat—it was hardly audible to me—and the doe picked up her head and trotted toward my stand. I suspect that deer can hear calls for 300 or more yards and rattling from a quarter of a mile or more away.

Because of this, a majority of the time it is unnecessary to make loud vocalizations or rattles. With that said, however, there are several variables regarding how far a deer can hear. On a particularly quiet day, this range is extended even farther. Factors that can affect a deer's hearing include wind direction, humidity, temperature, natural ambient sounds, and sounds of man, such as road noise from vehicles or passing ATVs. In suburban areas, this could also include children, barking dogs, or tool use by homeowners.

Most often, however, making deer vocalizations and rattling too loudly will sound unnatural to deer. Louder-than-normal sounds will often lead to deer becoming uncomfortable and unresponsive to your efforts. Keep your calls low to increase your success.

## Tip #6: Keep Deer Scents Fresh

If you think all doe estrous scent is collected fresh and taken from numbered estrus does, please send me your name and address—I have a bridge to sell you! I have manufactured my own deer scent, Love Potion No. 9: A Fatal Attraction of Pheromones, for more than twenty years. All sexually attractive deer scents contain preservatives.

Think about that for a moment. If I sold 200,000 bottles of Love Potion No. 9 to a store, such as Walmart, I would get back

Kate took this awesome Texas buck using an adult estrus blat vocalization. She kept the volume low to sound natural and sexually alluring to the big buck.

This buck was taken using Love Potion No. 9. To keep your deer scent fresh, store it in a cool, dry area out of direct sunlight.

whatever bottles they didn't sell after deer season passed. Smaller outdoor stores usually don't have a return policy, so they keep the leftover bottles until the following season. Again, no big deal since the scent contains a preservative to prevent it from oxidizing. Most scents are also placed in amber or dark bottles to help slow oxidation. As long as estrus or other deer scents are kept in a cool, dry place, they will retain their freshness over long periods of time.

## Tip #7: Ditch It

Mature bucks are wary creatures. As such, they are destined to become trophy-class animals simply because their fight-or-flight behavior can be heightened to extreme levels. They react instantly to anything new or worrisome within their environment. It is this neurotic behavior that often saves them from making fatal mistakes.

Most mature bucks will bed in out-of-the-ordinary places to conceal themselves. They will often choose an area in thick cover that is in plain view of predators. By doing so, they allow themselves a much better view of approaching danger, which provides them ample time to escape.

They seek this type of cover more often when foul weather is imminent. Places in which I have often found mature bucks bedded down, particularly in heavy rainstorms, include ditches, sloughs, or swales in farm fields, small blowdowns, high grassy areas, cattails, gullies, stream bottoms, and drainages.

When the ground is wet or damp, hunters can quietly stalk

along without being heard. In these conditions, I often abandon my deer blind or tree stand in favor of still-hunting. I slip along using a crosswind to hide my scent. Most deer usually bed facing downwind, which affords a stealthy approach from the side and out of view of the buck. Rather than using a straight line of approach, meander side to side as you move along.

The key to success when still-hunting is to spot the deer before it sees you. You'll be surprised how often this ends with the hunter getting a close shot at an unsuspecting buck. On occasions, the buck may wind the hunter and spook, offering a jump shot. This type of hunting calls for either hunting with a scope set at its lowest setting or iron sights. A small, light firearm you can quickly raise to your shoulder is the best choice. This tactic works equally well for bow hunters, too.

## Tip #8: Track 'Em Down

I live in upstate New York, where our firearm season often begins

and ends with snow. During a fresh snowfall, I sometimes head to a piece of state land of 1,200 acres that borders my cousin Leo's farm. I look for a large set of tracks, about 2½ to 3 inches long, that leaves Leo's land and heads into the state ground and I follow them. I usually do this after the

You can almost be assured when finding a large splayed track, such as this one, in snow or dry ground that it was left by an adult buck. Be forewarned, an adult doe can also leave a splayed track. Most times, however, it is an excellent indicator that it was left by a mature buck.

primary rut has waned. That way, I'm hopefully following a buck whose sole interest isn't chasing a doe.

When the tracks start to meander back and forth, I know I have entered the buck's core area where he will find a good place to bed down. I slow my pace and look carefully at my surroundings as I cautiously move forward. This is when I take only a few steps at a time. Each time I stop, I remain as still as possible, only moving my eyes while I try locate the buck. Before I move again, I slowly take a peek behind me, and only then do I move forward a few more paces and repeat the whole process.

## Tip #9: How Your Scent Is Carried

Researchers claim that deer can detect odors better than the average dog and, depending on what research you read, they can smell fifty to one hundred times better than a human. The nose of a whitetail has up to 297 million olfactory receptors. Dogs have 220 million, while humans max out at a mere five million receptors. In research, test dogs are able to detect odors from one to two parts in a trillion. A dog's ability to not only detect scent but also separate one scent from another is mind-boggling. That is why a dog can detect cancer in a human and even scent the onset of death approaching.

A large portion of a deer's brain is dedicated to analyzing odors via two giant olfactory bulbs attached to the brain that decode every aroma encountered. The bulbs weigh around sixty grams, four times as much as human olfactory bulbs. In other words, a deer's sense of smell is nearly one-third better than a dog's.

It is virtually impossible to keep a deer from detecting human odor. With that said, hunters who realize the importance of reducing their scent will see and bag more deer.

The savvy hunter will also benefit by understanding how deer use the elements to smell what is going on in their environment moment by moment. Deer constantly monitor the air to analyze particles. They can quickly separate what odors are nonthreatening and which ones indicate potential danger.

There are many factors that affect how odors are carried on air currents. They include wind speed, air temperature, and moisture. For instance, on warm moist days in a still environment, a deer's ability to smell odors from molecules is enhanced.

- Falling rain and snow force scent molecules to the earth quickly, where they are diluted at ground level by the moisture.
- Mist and fog, particularly heavy fog, also block scent molecules from being dispersed long distances.
- When the humidity is high and temperatures range from 55 to 75 degrees, these are optimal conditions for a deer to use its sense of smell. Deer often

become more in tune to odors in these conditions.

- Low humidity, between 10 and 20 percent, causes the deer's nasal passage to become dry, hampering its ability to detect scent molecules.
- When temperatures are high, there is more air convection movement. The currents carry scents high into the air, making them more difficult for deer to pick up.
- Deer are also handicapped in very cold temperatures. The cold air pushes scent molecules downward, where they quickly disperse.
- Air movement or currents play a big part in a deer's ability to use its olfactory senses. An ideal scenting conditions are when the humidity is between 25 and 75 percent, the temperature is between 45 and 90 degrees, and there are slight winds of 10 to 20 miles per hour. Under these conditions, a deer will be able to detect odors, including human scent, for a half mile or more.

## Tip #10: Doe Clues

Always pay close attention to a doe. Her body language is often a clue as to what is going on around her. If she constantly looks around or in one direction, she may be getting anxious about approaching deer, particularly if one is a buck.

A doe that is flagging her tail continuously from side to side as she watches her behind probably has a buck following her.

When a relaxed doe, maybe feeding or simply ambling by, suddenly comes to an abrupt stop and cups both ears in a particular direction, something has alerted her and is probably heading her way. If she begins to eat or slowly move again, she has most likely determined the noise isn't dangerous. If you see a doe behaving this way, other deer will probably appear in short order. Sometimes, the savvy hunter gets an opportunity to spot a buck long before it gets close simply by being attentive to a doe's actions.

## Tip #11: Walking on Crusted Snow

Once fresh snow becomes crusted, it is difficult for hunters to approach their stands without alerting deer to their presence. Under these conditions, the deeper a hunter goes into his hunting land, the greater the odds are that deer will flee. When quiet, soft snow turns into crunchy, loud snow, it is time to change tactics.

Instead of heading to your stand before dawn, wait until mid-morning when the sun has had a chance to soften the hard surface of the snow. It will substantially lessen the noise made by each step you take, thus allowing a stealthier approach. Select the stand that is located the farthest away from bedding areas, even if it isn't positioned in a prime location. This will help reduce the noise made by your approach and lessen the possibility of deer being spooked by your noisy footfalls.

## Tip #12: Walk Out of Step

Other than the sounds made by human voices, deer are most alerted by a hunter's footfalls. As hunters walk to their stands, the sounds made by their footfalls are rhythmic and repetitive. Deer are instantly aware of the noise and recognize it as potential danger. To prevent alerting deer during your approach, change the way you walk in the woods. Make each of your footsteps land more quietly on the ground by placing your heel on the ground first. Then take a couple quick but short steps forward. Stop for several seconds before you begin to walk again. Start the next step on your tiptoes and walk slowly for several steps. Repeat this until you reach your stand. This tactic will prevent you from making a cadenced walk. It will confuse deer, providing a better opportunity for you to reach your stand undetected, or at least preventing deer from fleeing the area.

## Tip #13: The Eyes Have It

To see more deer when you are still-hunting, it is important to not concentrate your attention on one specific location. Without moving your head too much, use your eyes to slowly and carefully scan from left to right and back again. You'll be surprised how often this will help you spot a motionless deer or one that is skulking away from you.

## Tip #14: Other Hunters

Whenever you spot a hunter moving through your location, whether you're still-hunting or in a tree stand, it is time for you to come to full alert. Watch behind the other hunter, as well as the direction he or she is moving. Many times a buck will circle behind a hunter or try to quietly sneak off. In either case, you might get an opportunity to take a shot at a buck that is unaware of your presence because it is concentrating solely on escaping the other hunter. Over the years, I have had many hunters inadvertently send bucks my way as they walked by my hunting location.

## Tip #15: Check the Cover Twice

When still-hunting, a hunter's visual perspective changes dramatically every few steps. The key to successful still-hunting is to see a buck before he spots you. Even though you may have carefully scanned the cover ahead of you and didn't see a deer, that can change with a few steps. Natural vegetation that might have hidden a buck from your view moments ago might now have changed enough to reveal a deer. The savvy still-hunter knows to check the cover ahead of him more than once.

## Tip #16: Don't Walk Along the Skyline

When you're walking to a tree stand or still-hunting in steep terrain, walk below the peak of the ridge. By not silhouetting yourself against the skyline, your presence and movement will be much harder for a deer to detect.

## Tip #17: Snip Dense Cover

When moving through dense underbrush, use a small set of pruning shears to snip briars, branches, and brittle twigs as you move forward. These will create noise by catching on your clothing or snapping as they break against your body. Silently snipping them will allow you to move noise-free through even the thickest cover.

## Tip #18: He May Not Have Seen You

If you spot a deer that is looking back at you, remain motionless but at the ready. Many times a deer may look as if it has seen you, but it really hasn't. By standing alert and very still, the deer will not sense danger and will eventually return to whatever it was doing.

## Tip #19: Take Your Boots Off

When approaching a ledge to check if there is a buck bedded in the cover below, remove your boots. Take the last dozen steps before the cliff's edge in your stocking feet. Your silent approach will give you a better chance of catching a bedded buck with his guard down.

## Tip #20: Belly Crawl

Deer are masters at detecting a standing or crouching hunter, even from long distances. One of the most underutilized tactics to close the distance between hunter and quarry is the belly crawl. It will make your approach almost invisible. Crawling on your belly is a top-notch tactic when trying to get close to deer in open areas.

## Tip #21: Tick, Tock

When still-hunting, forget about the time. Remove your watch and put it in your daypack. Then, you won't be tempted to constantly check to see how long you have been stalking your quarry. It will keep you focused on the hunt rather than how long you've been at it.

## Tip #22: Take Boot-Length Steps

The most successful still-hunters know to move at a tortoise's pace. They don't take regular strides—instead, they keep their steps short so they won't lose their balance.

## Tip #23: Walk With a Crosswind

Many hunters know to keep the wind in their face as they move along. However, walking with a crosswind is even better and will help you see more deer.

# Fishing Bait

## The Hellgrammite

The most active and prolonged wriggler of all live baits is the hellgrammite, an exceedingly effective bass bait. Because of the extreme toughness of the larva, its constant wriggle and continued life after being hooked, it is much sought by the angler. Large perch and chub cannot resist it. Pickerel have been known to take it, but other baits for that fish are superior. Walleyed pike, big catfish, and eels will take it, but trout will not touch it. I have tried it in pools where large brown trout abide near where bass lie, and the bass have always responded to it.

The hellgrammite is the aquatic larva of a fly, the horned corydalus (*Corydalus cornutus*), somewhat resembling and closely allied to the dragonfly. It is supposed to exist for several years in the larval state under loose rocks on or just below the waterline of rivers and other waters of low temperature. Here its life is spent in devouring other smaller insect larvæ, and during this period it is most suitable for baiting purposes. But this repulsive-looking, yet harmless, creature is used as bait in all three stages of its life. First in its larval—*creeper* stage; then in the dormant *pupa* stage, and last after the final change into the adult *flying* insect. The corydalus is a large, fierce-looking insect with four gauzy wings which, when at rest, lie flat over the body, which is a cinnamon color on the belly, dark brown at the sides, and dull black at the head and thorax. It begins its flight after dusk and, like the creeper, is entirely nocturnal in its habits. I have never seen it in flight during the daytime in New York regions. This fine, large insect is very abundant on Montana streams,

Rainbow-trout *salmo iridens*.

where it is used extensively by anglers who hook them alive to fish at the surface for the big rainbows. These big rainbows run up to fourteen pounds' weight, and they are so adroit in nipping the insect from the hook that several experts requested me to make an artificial from specimens sent me in "spirits," which I did, and named it the "Winged Hellgrammite." Its body measures over 2 inches in length, the wings extending half an inch beyond the tail, and with the two long black horns at the head the entire insect measures 3¾-quarter inches long.

The artificial hellgrammite creeper differs somewhat in having a row of short-pointed feelers along each side of the abdomen. The belly is grayish cream-color, the back dark brown with black shiny head and thorax. The artificial of this creeper has been found exceedingly good in many swift and still waters for large or small-mouth bass and walleye. A smaller and decidedly different species, the artificial of which I have named the "Trout Hellgrammite," because I found it frequently in the stomachs of brook-trout in widely different localities, is described in detail elsewhere along with the other creepers that trout take as food. The hellgrammite creeper is very easily captured and may be kept a considerable time in damp grass and rotten wood at low temperature.

## The Crawfish

In placing the crawfish second in value as a bait, I do so because it is equally effective in swift streams and in placid lakes over almost the entire continent of North America. Indeed wherever bass abide, a five, medium-sized, light brown crawfish is resistless in any condition of weather or season. This freshwater crustacean is very prolific in all brooks and streams of a low temperature, and frequently in lakes. Its habit is mostly nocturnal, and it burrows holes in the pebbly sand as a protection from its enemies. Its abode can easily be identified by the little mound of fresh sand beside its hole, and if we are quick in our movements we can scrape them out a few inches down, wait a few minutes for the water to run clear, and capture them. It requires practice to do it with success, for they are nimbleness personified, running equally fast backward or forward. Indeed, their capture, like any other bait, is quite a difficult undertaking,

filling up the off days or early hours when bass are not in a biting humor.

While the crawfish is an expert swimmer, it rarely leaves the bottom to swim in mid-water or near the surface, but crawls slowly in search of food among the stones and sand. It feeds mostly on small fish, dead or alive, and. like marine crustaceans, is very pugnacious, with frequent combats among its own kind or with other creatures it happens to meet. It is rarely seen by day, and little is really known of its natural habits except in confinement. As a bait, its best qualities are the lively kicking movement and hardihood after being hooked, and the prolonged time it takes while swimming downward from the surface after the cast. Bass will dash after it on its journey down, and it is generally perfectly aware of them, so, on reaching the bottom, it will instantly crawl under a stone out of reach. The amateur soon learns that it is best to keep this nimble bait swimming free from the bottom.

It swims along entirely with its tail, the numerous legs being used only to balance the body, and it is for that reason I have, after many trials, succeeded in making the artificial with a disjointed tail to move up and down from the body, giving a lifelike appearance to the lure if played property in working the angler's rod-tip. In its natural environment the crawfish grows rapidly, casting its shell several times in one season. When very young, it is pale yellow in color, growing a darker brown with age. For my own part I prefer this bait to be light cinnamon color, not over 2 inches long with the tail stretched. Many anglers consider a 4-inch dark colored crawfish is most effective in either lake or stream.

## The Cricket

Next after the crawfish I consider the cricket third in value, because it is eagerly taken by all game-fish, both in lake or stream. Its jumping propensities in meadows through which meanders a trout stream lead to sure disaster, for all kinds of fish congregate in certain fruitful places to await these leaps of death. So soon as the cricket alights on the surface, it kicks and spins rapidly around, making its way to shore. But its landing-place is invariably down the gullet of trout or chub; indeed any fish will take it that happens to be in sight. If properly hooked it makes a most effective live bait by reason of the continued rumpus made at the surface. The cricket never sinks, alive or dead, and especially in placid water is an easy prey, due to its frantic efforts to get back on land, which are so very obvious that fish cannot fail to see them quite a distance away.

Large, full-grown specimens are not common until late in the fall after the trout season closes, and for that reason they are not so popular for trout as for bass. Sometimes they come out during July. When they do, I consider them superior to any other bait (except minnows) for brown trout during the daytime. My artificial cricket made in three different sizes of cork bodies was highly successful with brown trout as early as June 3, of last year. This is one of the few instances where the artificial is of greater service than the natural bait, as it is also more durable, for the cricket, when hooked, is very tender, and is easily flipped off, besides being repeatedly nipped from the hook by the fish. A very few casts will find this bait limp and almost lifeless. For trout fishing the smallest size is much the beat. Bass seem to prefer a good big size, running up to the surface after it as they do after a fly. In Lake George I caught bass on crickets in water 30 feet deep. The most fruitful hunting-ground for crickets is under corn shucks and piles of decaying weeds or other vegetation. If the reader will carefully examine the representation of the artificial cricket he will consider it, as I do, the best imitation of all my nature lures. It looks still more natural when placed in the water. After a little practice the vibrant rod-tip can be skillfully made to

give the lure all the actions of the natural insect, with a result that is exceedingly interesting both in the manner it is made to act and the way trout are seen to take it.

## The Lamprey

This most excellent bass bait is another of limited service. Bass and chub seem to be the only fish that take it with any degree of certainty. Its peculiar wriggle while swimming is its best point, for it is an awful pesky live bait to get snagged on the bottom. We are obliged to keep the live lamprey on the move all the time or good-bye to our tackle. The lamprey-eel (often known as the "lamper") belongs to a very low order of animals, having no bony skeleton, no gills, ribs, or limbs, and being a naked eel-shaped creature with a sucker mouth, the lips of which are fringed with fine hairs. It inhabits the fresh cold waters of rivers and brooks, and gets its living by attaching itself to other fishes, feeding on them by scraping off the flesh with its rasp-like teeth. Adults attain to a weight of several pounds and 2 feet in length.

This creature is the only one I would never think of breeding or transplanting for food purposes, indeed its destruction and extinction from our streams would be a most desirable thing. Like the common eel it is nocturnal in its habits, moving about the deeper parts of the bed of rivers in sluggish places which are haunted by suckers and other coarse fish. It is only the very young that is used for bait, the best size being about 5 inches long. These are usually found in black muddy sand close to the shore of slow-moving backwaters of rivers, and a shovel is all that is necessary to capture them. Dig deep, best under several inches of water, and throw the mud upon the dry bank, then search through it with the hands for the wrigglers. They are more slippery and agile than the eel, and of all live bait the most difficult to impale on the hook. A dead one is no attraction to the bass; its wriggle only is the attraction.

By the time this is in print I shall have perfected a floating lamprey; at present my artificial, while very natural in appearance, is the only non-floating bait I have made. It wriggles all right, but must be kept moving or it sinks to the bottom, with the same difficulty to recover as the natural bait. I shall work on this bait till I succeed in producing a lamprey that wriggles and at the same time floats in suspension about mid-water or near the bottom, according to where it is fastened on the leader. In many rivers the lamprey as a bait is most attractive to bass, and if the artificial is made as I think it ought, it will be one of the best baits for bass fisherman to use.

## The Green and Brown Frogs

I do not place the frog so far down on the list because of its being inferior to the others as an effective bait, but by reason of its limited availability. The frog is not always, everywhere effective.

In certain waters it is supreme, either for bass, pickerel, pike, or muskellunge. Large chub, perch, walleyed pike take the frog, at times. I have often fished brown-trout waters with frogs caught on the banks of the stream, but failed every time, though I have ocular proof of trout taking frogs. I witnessed a big captive brown trout gobble four fair-sized green frogs in less than as many minutes, in one case tearing the limbs from the body; a second after, the body vanished likewise. There are certain special waters in which the frog, green or brown, is an irresistible bait for bass and pike.

In the temperate zone, east or west, there are a large number of species of astonishing variety as to size, shape, and color. The most abundant, covering a wider range, is the black-spotted, green leopard-frog; also the brown, banded pickerel frog; it is to these two kinds I have devoted much time in the last several years in developing a perfect artificial imitation so as to give the angler a worthy substitute for the live frog. In all my long fishing career I do not know of a more painful or cruel pastime than casting out a live frog hooked by the lips. If not taken by the fish in the first few casts, the frog turns over on its back, swells up like a rubber ball, and is then worse than useless. In that condition some anglers take it from the hook, give it a short

**Various creatures that game-fish (Darwin from living specimens).**

a) Young lamper-eel: b) Adult crawfish: c) Green leopard-frog: d) June grasshopper: e) Common red-legged grasshopper: f) Nymph-creeper: g) Brown hairy caterpillar: h) Cricket: i) Caddis-creeper and case: j) Trout-hellgrammite creeper: k) Brown pickerel-frog: l) Bass-hellgrammite creeper: m) Base winged hellgrammite.

respite by hooking a new one. A far more effective way to fish a frog is to just drop it on the water, sit still and wait while froggie wends its own path without restraint till it happens to meet its doom in the shape of a savage fish on the lookout for just such a gastronomic tidbit as the bass considers it to be.

The ideal frog water is a weedy, shallow lake, and although very prolific, they are never abundant where game-fish abide. Being both land and water creatures they live in constant danger of being devoured, not only by fish, but by reptiles, birds, and animals which take the frog as part of their diet, from the smallest tadpole to the big bullfrog. Along the riverside an observing angler will find many more frogs than he would imagine, particularly about grassy slopes and shallow backwaters. I have noticed that their color is similar to their environment. You observe most often the brown frog near rocky, stony shores, and the green frog mostly abide among the green weeds and grasses of both lakes and streams. This fact is well to remember in the choice of color to use for bait, for the reason that fish naturally are more apt to prefer a bait similar to their daily diet. Between the two species, brown or green, there seems to be no preference; one is just as effective as the other, but I do think if brown is common in a certain locality, it is wisdom to use that color, natural or artificial. The habits of the frog are so well known it is not necessary to give details. My artificial is unsuitable for trolling. Like the natural frog it should be cast lightly in open spaces between weeds and lilypads, or just made to skip along the surface of open water. In a running stream frogs do not often swim across, but when they do, they strike rapidly along with the water flow. They are most effective when cast at the sides where the water is fairly deep and are visible to the fish lying below in the middle of the stream.

# The Brook Trout's Rival

When the German brown trout was introduced in the brook trout streams of Pennsylvania some years ago, fly-fishermen condemned the act because they believed the brook trout (*S. fontinalis*) was superior to the brown trout as a game fish. Deforestation, rendering the streams too warm for the brook trout, has changed the fly-fisherman's feeling in the matter. The brown trout can thrive in warm water, and with the brook trout's gradual extermination the brown trout is being welcomed as the next best thing. A correspondent at Reading, PA, signing himself "Mourner"— he mourns the passing of the true brook trout—declares the brown trout strikes harder than the brook trout and after being hooked, unlike the brook trout, makes two or three leaps out of the water, but is not so gamey and cunning as the brook trout and tires out much quicker. The German species has been popular because it attains a larger size quickly and destroys almost every fish in the streams, including the brook trout. "The fly-fishermen who for years have matched their skill, cunning, artifice, and prowess against the genuine brook trout that since creation dawned have inhabited the mountain brooks that flow down every ravine," says Mourner, "have had forced on them, as never before, the sad truth that, like the deer, bear, quail, woodcock, and grouse, brook trout are slowly but surely passing. There never was a fish so gamy, elusive, and eccentric, so beautiful and so hard to deceive and capture by scientific methods as the native brook trout. No orator has yet risen to fully sound its praises; no poet to sing its merits as they deserve; no painter to produce its varied hues. The brook trout was planted in the crystal waters by the Creator 'when the morning stars sang together' and *fontinalis* was undisturbed, save as some elk, deer, bear, panther, or wildcat forded the shallows of his abode, or some Indian or mink needed him for food. In this environment the brook trout grew and thrived. Much warfare made him shy and suspicious until he became crafty to a degree. The brook trout successfully combated man's inventive genius in the shape of agile rods, artificial flies and other bait calculated to fool the most wary, and automatic reels, landing nets, and other paraphernalia designed to rob a game fish of 'life, liberty, and the pursuit of happiness.' But it was not until the tanner and acid factory despoiler turned poisoned refuse into the streams and the dynamiter came upon the scene and the sheltering trees were cut away by the lumberman, letting in the sun and warming the water to a nauseous tepidity, that the brave trout faltered, hesitated, and then quit the uneven conquest.

Carp and bass were planted in the streams to further endanger the brook trout's existence. Next the California trout and the German brown trout, who prey upon the true brook trout's progeny, followed, till finally, beaten, baffled, dismayed, poisoned, routed, and overwhelmed by the superior numbers and size of a cannibalistic race, he gradually began his retreat. It is good-bye to the brook trout now. With him it was either cool pools, solitude, and freedom, or extermination. The waters that pour down into larger streams are sad memories now of his school playgrounds. No more will the sportsman's honest hunger be appeased by the brook trout's fine-grained flesh from hardening waters of nearby mountain brooks. But memory of the brook trout cannot be wrested from those who knew him at his best, and braved personal danger from rattler, bear, and wildcat to win him from the crystal waters. The brook trout has been butchered to make a carp's holiday. Gone he may be now, but he will live forever in the dreams of all true fishermen as the real aristocrat of the mountain streams. The like of him will not soon be seen again." The Fish Commission has mastered the science of the artificial propagation of the brook trout—millions are now produced with little trouble and expense—and the stocking of waters is a common practice, but the Fish Commission can't propagate forests and woodland streams. Mourner must know that the brook trout itself is not hard to save; it is the preservation of its wild habitat that is the great puzzle. If the United States Forestry Department will protect the trout streams from the greedy lumberman, the factoryman, and acid maker, the Fish Commission will have no trouble in saving the brook trout.

# Trout on Barbless Hooks

Dame Juliana Berners, who wrote the earliest volume on gentle fishing (1500), was the first celebrated example of the artful and merciful woman fisher, and Cleopatra the first female to make notorious the coarse and ungodly method in fishing for pastime. Sweet Dame Berners believed in angling—the desire of fair treatment to the quarry, correct tackle, a love of the pursuit superior to greed for number in the catch, and a heavenly admiration of the general beauties of nature in the day as well as in the play; and brutal Cleopatra believed in mere fishing, the killing of the greatest number, regardless of means, mercy, or method.

Our modern Dame Bernerses and Cleopatras in the fishing fold are many. The wife who aids the net fisherman—the marine farmer whose calling emulates the professional duties of Jesus' disciples, Peter. Andrew, James, and John—does not count. Her part in fishing, while by no means angling, is as honest as the work of the upland farmer's helpmate, and God Himself will not condemn little children, male or female, who fish indiscriminately, "because they do not know." Fishing for the modern market is just as honorable as market fishing was in the ancient days when Jesus praised the net fishermen and made them His nearest and dearest friends, and angling—merciful ungreedy fishing with humane tackle and a clear conscience—is even more righteous than net fishing, because, while the main result of the Angler's pursuit is the same as the marketman's—fish taking— the angler's method of capture is far less cruel, and his creel of fish is far less in number than the boatful of the marketman.

The distinction in angling and fishing is made by the modes employed in the taking, the killing, and the disposing of the fishes. Any fisherman who uses tackle appropriate to the various species, who is not greedy in his catch, who plays his game with mercy, who dispatches it with the least suffering, who disposes of it without wanton waste, and who is thankful to the Maker for the ways and means for all these conditions, is an angler. And cannot woman be as artful and gentle in pursuits and as appreciative in feeling as man? Surely. England and Scotland and Ireland are famous for their women anglers, and Maine, the Adirondacks, California, and Canada boast of the finest female fly-casters in the world. There are more women anglers in these last-named territories than there are men anglers in all other parts of the United States. A woman, Mary Orris Marbury, wrote the best volume scientifically descriptive of trout, bass, and salmon flies of modern times, and Cornelia

Crosby, a daughter of the Maine wilderness, is the fly-fishing enthusiast of America.

Great minds, male and female, have gentle hearts. Izaak Walton handled a frog as if he loved him. Cowper would not unnecessarily hurt a worm. Lincoln upset his White House Cabinet to rescue a mother pig from a mire. Webster neglected the Supreme Court to replace a baby robin that had fallen from its nest. Moses, John the Divine, Washington, Thoreau. Audubon, Wilson, and even Napoleon and Cæsar the mighty mankillers were all of tender hearts, and all of these were—anglers. Christ was only a fisher of men, but He loved and associated with the fishers of fishes. Walton, the father of fishers and fishing, angled for the habits of fishes more than for their hides. The capture of a fish was insignificantly incidental to the main notion of his hours abroad— his divine love of the waters, the fields, the meadows, the skies, the trees, and God's beautiful things that inhabit these. 'Tis the soul we seek to replenish, not the creel. So a Long Island dairyman's daughter views the theme, and she handles the mother and baby trout as if she loved them. *Salvelinus fontinalis*, little salmon of the streams, the angler's dearly beloved brook trout—this is the dairymaid's special delight. She breeds these rainbow-hued beauties and broods over them, she feeds and fondles them, and they are to her what David's holy, fleecy flock were to him—his blessed charge by heavenly day and cardinal care at night. They feed from her hand, and play like kittens with her fingers. Cleopatra cleaved her fishes with a murderous hand and hook. Audrey cuddles her trout with a magnanimous mind and heart.

The trout, with all its famous beauty of color, grace, and outline, all its army of admirers, all the glory of its aqua-fairyland habitat, all its seeming gentility of breeding and character, is none the less a little villain at the killing game, like the less admired feline and canine and serpentine species,

for he will devour the daintiest and gaudiest butterfly that ever poet sang of. Fledgling robins and bluebirds, orioles and wrens are meat and drink to him. Young chipmunks and squirrels that lose their balance in the storm fall into his ready maw. The bat, the bee, the beetle and ladybug are rich morsels to his gastric eye, and the golden lizard, the umber ant, the silvery eel, the crawling angleworm, the chirping cricket, creeping spider, the grasshopper, the hopping frog, and e'en the heavenly hummingbird are but mealtime mites to him. Perhaps the knowledge of this life-destroying trait in all the fishes made Cleopatra indifferent to the gentler mode of fishing, just as it had a softer influence over Audrey, for she, though loving both the fishes and their victims, was induced to angle and thus punish, but never kill, her finny favorites. She had heard of the artificial dry fly anglers of Europe using the barbless hook that held the trout without pain or injury, and this she made herself, tying up dozens of somber-hued and lustrous patterns on the bent bit of bronze that formed the snare. The ruly trout who gently waver in the deep pool, satisfied with the food supplied by their fair mistress, and who behave themselves when they swim abroad in the general ponds and streams, are not molested, but the rebellious urchins who, disdaining the bits of liver and worm fed to them in plenty, go forth to slay the happy ladybug and butterfly, are made the game of the barbless hook.

Audrey has five or six thousand trout in the pond and the stream flowing into it. The surrounding country is wildly beautiful, the water being surrounded by great trees of elm, hickory, maple, beech, chestnut, walnut, and dogwood, under which is spread a rich green lawn, with here and there patches of wild shrubs, vines, and ground flowers. Rustic benches circle the water-edge oaks, and sleek deer, as tame as Belgian hares, browse on the rich grass and eat dainty morsels from the palms of their human friends. Cleopatra's marble perch basin was cold and deadly in its artificial atmosphere. Audrey's woodland trout preserve is warm and lifelike in its natural loveliness.

# The Identification and Classification of the Sea Trout

"I am the wiser in respect to all knowledge and the better qualified for all fortunes for knowing that there is a minnow in that brook."—Thoreau.

There is still considerable argument about the identification and classification of the sea trout. Some authorities still claim the sea trout is a distinct species; others declare it to be the brook trout, *Salvelinus fontinalis*, that goes to sea from the fresh water ponds and streams.

The squeteague (*vulgo* weakfish, wheatfish, sea bass, white sea bass, carvina, checutts, shecutts, yellowfin, drummer, bluefish, squit, suckermang, succoteague, squitee, chickwit, gray trout, sun trout, salmon, salmon trout, shad trout, sea trout, saltwater trout, spotted trout, etc.) is not a trout of any sort; so this species need not be considered in this sea trout discussion.

My personal theory concerning the sea trout is that any trout that goes to sea is a sea trout, and that more than one species of trout go to sea—whenever they have the opportunity.

The small-stream trout that visit the ocean do so mainly in search of a change in food; the sea-going trout of large rivers are impelled to leave their fresh water retreats for the ocean waters also to satisfy a desire for new varieties of food, but more so because of an instinct that warns them of the danger of remaining in the freshwater rivers during certain periods of the year—the coldest seasons when the waters freeze to the river bottom, and in the melting time, when the ice thaws into huge sharp-edge chunks, and the mass of ice, swift-running water, and rocks turn the rivers into raging, roaring floods that would cut and bruise the trout unmercifully.

Nature makes these large-river brook trout in the calm periods of spring, summer, and autumn, and sea trout in severe winter weather and during dangerous flood time.

The broad streams of the west coast of Newfoundland—Fishels River, Crabs River, Big and Little Codroy Rivers, Big and Little Barachois Rivers, and Robinson's River—afford the best evidence of trout migrating to the sea to escape the fury of the flood, and any of the little trout streams in any part of the world where the streams flow into salt water will afford the student means of observing the trout's fondness for marine excursions in search of a change of diet.

Just as the different species of trout are widely contrasting in colors, shapes, sizes, traits, etc., while in their natural habitat—fresh water—so are they confoundingly different in these matters while sojourning in salt water.

The true brook trout (*Salvelinus fontinalis*) is of various shades, shapes, and sizes, these depending upon the character of the water he inhabits. In shallow, swift streams of a light color pebble bottom the specimens in general are likely to be thin, narrow, and of a bright gray hue, though, of course, there are individual specimens in this condition of water that are exceptions to the rule—a few old specimens who have sheltered themselves for years in dark, deep, steady spots under the protruding bank of the stream, or along the side of a sunken tree stump, etc. This autocrat of the eddy is fat, stocky, and dark in color, just the opposite of his younger relatives of the swift-running part of the stream.

The brook trout of deep, still dark-bottom ponds are fatter, darker, broader, of duller color, and of slower motion than their brothers of the rapid waters. The trout's shape, weight, size, and color are influenced by its food, its age, its activity, its habitat, and its habits. Its color corresponds to the color of the water bottom, and will change as the water bottom changes. If removed to a new water, where the bottom color is different from the bottom color of its first abode—lighter or darker, as the case may be—it will gradually grow to a corresponding shade, blending with its new habitat just as its colors suited the stones and grasses and earthy materials of its native domain.

The landlocked trout, if imprisoned in a deep, dark, muddy-bottom, shaded woodland pool, will be dull in color, stocky in shape, and of sluggish habits. The trout confined to a bubbling fountain pool, with a bottom of golden sand, at the foot of a waterfall, in the full glare of the sun, will be of albino character.

Perhaps no other fish offers specimens of its own kind so deeply in contrast as *fontinalis*. This is scientifically and interestingly illustrated in many ways—color, size, shape, form, action, environment, etc. For example, consider the big, fat, long, strong, copper-color brook trout that, having access to salt water, gormandizes upon the multitudinous food of the sea—shrimp, killifish, spearing, spawn, crab, etc.—and the tiny, active, silvery albinolike brook trout that is locked in a small foamy basin under a dashing waterfall, feeding only upon minute crustacea and the insect life that is carried to its watery prison. These two specimens are not freakish individuals of their species—like the blunt-nose specimen and the various other deformities—but are quite common contrasting representatives of their tribe.

If we were to display in a group side by side one of each of the shape-and-color-differing specimens—one large copper-shade, sea-going brook trout, one tiny silvery, fountain-locked brook trout, one ordinary-environed brook trout, one blunt-nose brook trout, etc.—the fact of their being of an identical species would be correctly appreciated by the scientific man only.

I am not resorting to poetic license or theorizing or delving into ancient precedents to carry my point of natural history, for I once captured one of the big, sea-going specimens, and my friend, James Cornell, angling in an adjacent stream the same day, brought to creel a little silvery beauty of the foamy waterfall. Shape, form, tint, weight— every mood and trait—were of astounding contrast in these two specimens, yet both were of the same species, the true brook trout; my dark, strenuous three-pounder taken in the open, brackish creek as I cast from the salt meadowland sod banks, and Cornell's albino like gamester succumbing to the fly in the foamy fountain of a deep woodland brook; both specimens widely separated in appearance, habits, and habitat, but still both legitimate brothers of the family *fontinalis*—little salmon of the streams.

Trout in the sea feed on shrimp, the spawn of herring, and on the entrails of cod and other species of fishes thrown away by market fishermen.

If the sea-going trout did not eat the spawn of the herring, herring would be too plentiful for Nature's even-distribution arrangement. The sea trout is gorged with herring spawn, which lies in heaps like so much sawdust on the shores and shallow places of the ocean. Cod spawn and milt float on the water's surface; the spawn of the herring sinks.

The sea trout fresh from the streams is plump, has bright red spots, and is in ordinary color when it goes to sea; when it returns to the streams, though bigger (longer) and stronger, it is comparatively thin, and is of white or silver-sheened shade.

Prof. George Brown Goode (*American Fishes*): "The identity of the Canadian sea trout and the brook trout is still denied by many, though the decision of competent authorities has settled the question beyond doubt."

Eugene McCarthy (*Familiar Fish*): "Many anglers are now

turning their attention to catching sea trout, either on account of the novelty of the sport or because they believe that they are taking a new variety of fish. That there is novelty in such fishing cannot be denied, but that the fish is new in any way certainly can be. . . . There is no doubt that the sea trout and the brook trout are one and the same fish. It is broadly claimed that any of the trout can live as well in salt water as they can in fresh water, and everything seems to prove the claim to be correct. All trout grow to a larger size in salt water than in the brooks or rivers, and they lose their spots in the sea, becoming pale and silvery in color. Brook trout were originally found at a distance not greater than 300 miles back from the ocean in waters tributary to it. Where conditions of temperature were favorable, they invariably sought salt water. When transplanted to, or found in, inland waters, they have adapted themselves to fresh-water conditions as well. All members of the trout family require cold water

for their habitat, averaging about 68 degrees or less. Therefore, they must either seek the cold water of the ocean, or, if barred from that by long stretches of warm-river waters, they must seek the cold, small tributaries high up in the hills. While trout are found in the highland streams south of New York as far as South Carolina, they are not able to seek the sea on account of the warm, intervening waters. On Long Island (NY) streams all trout are sea-going. From that point along the coast northward sea trout are rarely, if ever, found until the northern shores of Maine and New Brunswick are reached. All rivers flowing into the St. Lawrence as far west as Quebec, as well as those entering the Saguenay and those of the Labrador coast, are especially noted for most excellent sea trout fishing, and are the favorite resorts of anglers. . . . In all ways the sea trout corresponds with the brook trout when taken in fresh water. If taken in salt water, there will only be the variation of coloring. . . . ouananiche . . . and sea trout . . . with the exception of salmon . . . afford the greatest sport that the angler can find. . . . Exactly the same tackle is used (for sea trout) as for ouananiche, trout, or bass, and the same flies, both in kind and size. . . . When the fish begin to leave the sea and ascend the rivers, the bright colorings not only return, but actually appear to be more beautiful than those of the trout that always remain in fresh water. . . . But little attention, comparatively speaking, has been given to sea trout, principally because their nature was not understood, and, in fact, but little has been said or written in regard to them to arouse interest. The lessees of the sea trout streams on Long Island are very enthusiastic over the fishing they secure, as are those sportsmen who have sought it in Canada. The Canadian rivers are now more quickly and easily reached than formerly, and as the fish are rapidly acquiring fame they are bound to become much sought after by anglers.

However, sea trout fishing is but fishing for brook trout under different conditions, and amid varied surroundings. They offer, however, two extra inducements—they are more plentiful and usually average larger."

Charles Hallock (*Sportsman's Gazetteer*) refers to the common theory that sea trout (Canada) are merely a clan or detachment of the brook trout which have temporarily left their freshwater haunts for the sea; then Mr. Hallock asks: "But, if we must accept this as a postulate, we must be permitted to ask why the same peculiarities do not attach to the trout of Maine. Cape Cod, and Long Island? Why do we not discover here this periodical midsummer advent and 'run' of six weeks' duration; and why are only isolated individuals taken in the saltwater pound nets and fykes of Long Island, etc., instead of thousands, as in Canada? Moreover, the Canadian sea trout are never taken in the small streams, but only in rivers of considerable size, and the same trout uniformly return to the same river, just as salmon do—at least, we infer so from the fact that six-pounders are invariably found in the Nouvelle, and varying sizes elsewhere. Besides, we must be able to answer why a portion only of the trout in a given stream should periodically visit the sea at a specified time, while an equal or greater number elect to remain behind in fresh water; for we may suppose that, having equal opportunities, all have the same instincts and desires."

But, trout of different localities do not have equal opportunities; therefore, they have not the same instincts and desires. Local conditions of Nature everywhere guide the instincts and govern the desires of every living thing. So, the trout of Maine, the trout of Cape Cod, the trout of Long Island—influenced by local conditions—are all vastly different in opportunities, instincts, desires, etc. The Eskimo biped, the African biped—the bipeds of all countries—are all species of the animal man, but who dare suggest that they all have equal (similar) opportunities and the same instincts and desires?

Even individuals of the trout of one community are profoundly separated in character from their immediate brothers and sisters. Trout vary in their tastes and antics as they vary in color, shape, and size. There are hundreds of natural trout flies and hundreds of artificial trout flies, imitations of the living insects, used as lures in fishing. Why so many patterns? Because the trout, like man, is in love with a variety of foods at different times, and both man and trout change in their tastes by the month, the week, the day, the hour, and the minute.

The angler does not have to use the hundreds of fly patterns at one fishing, but he does experiment with a variety of the lures to find the particular patterns the fish is responsive to at the moment. One or two patterns would suffice—if the angler could select the particular species the trout are rising to without trying all the patterns until he discovers the killing patterns. A chef might please his master with one or two of the forty courses billed if he knew what the man wanted. Sometimes the angler can judge the appropriate fly to use by observing Nature in seeing trout rise to the live fly; but there are times when trout are not rising, times when they are tired of the fly upon the water, and times when the real fly is not on the wing.

General rules are of no service without a deep regard for general conditions, local and otherwise. All trout must not be judged alike even if they be of one species and in one little pool. Individuals of man, though of one race and in one district, are not all alike in their habits any more than they are in their shades, shapes, and sizes.

The conditions of the large rivers of Newfoundland are different from the conditions of the small streams of Maine, Long Island, and Cape Cod; hence the differing desires of the trout in these differing waters. There is

no similarity in the quiet, tiny trout brooks of Long Island and the broad torrential rivers of Newfoundland, and it is only natural that the fishes of these deeply contrasting waters should be widely separated in character— instinct, desires, color, shape, size, etc. So I do not hesitate to express a belief that the sea trout, no matter where we find it, is just our own fond *fontinalis* incognito.

Between Halifax and Sydney, Nova Scotia, there are many wild sea trout rivers where the fish have never seen a human being. Angle from the middle of June to the end of August. In June large sea trout are caught in salt water at the mouth of rivers on the artificial fly and minnow bait. The best east shore sea trout streams are St. Mary's, Musquodoboit, Tangier, Cole Harbor, Petpeswick, Quoddy, Sheet Harbor, Moser's River, Halfway Brook, Smith Brook, Ecum Secum, Isaac's Harbor, and about Guysboro.

Southwest of Halifax great sea trout fishing may be had at Ingram River, Nine Mile River,

Hubley's. Indian River, and about Liverpool, Chester, and the salmon country about Medway.

In New Brunswick beautiful and prolific sea trout waters may be reached from the towns of New Castle (Miramichi River and branches—May and June). Chatham (Miramichi River, Tabusintac River, Bartibog River, Eskeldoc River), Bathhurst (Nepisguit River, Tetagouche River, Caroquet River, Pokemouche River), and Campbellton, in the Baie de Chaleur River, Restigouche River, and the Cascapedia, Matapedia, Upsalquitch, Nouvelle, Escuminac rivers.

My choice of sea trout flies includes: Brown Hackle, Claret, Cinamon, Codun, Jenny Lind, Parmachenee Belle, Montreal, Grouse, Silver Doctor. Use sober-hued patterns in fresh water; bright patterns in salt water. Hooks: Nos. 7 to 12.

# Hooking the Trout

"Give plenty of time for the fish to swallow the hook," says O. W. Smith, in *Outdoor Life* (December, 1914), addressing the croppie (strawberry bass) angler.

It is not un-anglerlike to catch any fish hooked beyond the lips? Angling has its gentle qualities as well as its practical ends. It's different in mere fishing. I don't believe any angler would purposely hook his game otherwise than in the lip—a nerveless center where there is no pain—though the plain fisherman may resort to any method in his pursuit.

I remember some years ago when two fishermen caught the same fish (a large fluke), one hook being in the fish's mouth and the other hook on the inside of the fish's stomach, it was decided after a long discussion that the fish really belonged to the man whose hook held to the mouth; the swallowed hook was judged as illegitimate.

Fishes hooked in the mouth do not suffer any pain. I've recaught many a once-lost specimen with my snell in its lip; these in both fresh water and salt water. Incidents of this character furnish one of the many proofs that mouth-hooking the fish is perfectly humane. Two friends witnessed my catch (July 11, 1915) of a Long Island 2¼-pound brook trout that had a fly and leader (my first cast) dangling from its mouth, the gear he broke away with a few minutes before his actual capture.

There is no need of subjecting fishes to any pain in angling. Hook them in the lips, and kill them the very second they are taken from the water. Letting them die slowly not only pains the captured fishes, but injures them as food.

Be a sportsman in angling as well as in hunting. The chivalric gunner, unlike the market shooter, does not pot his quail huddled stationary on the ground; he gallantly takes it on the wing—gives it a fair chance. So the angler, unlike the trade fisher, gives his game fair play. I catch quite my share of many species of fishes, but I only rarely suffer them to swallow the bait, and this by accident. Even pickerel and fluke (plaice) can be abundantly taken by being hooked in the lips. I never allow the pickerel or the black bass to swallow the bait; I hook them in the lip as I hook my trout—on the wing, as it were.

# Angling

"... which, as in no other game
A man may fish and praise His name."
—W. Basse.
"I chose of foure good dysportes
and honeste gamys, that is to
wyte: of huntynge: hawkynge:
fysshynge: and foulynge. The best
to my symple dyscrecon why then
is fysshynge: called Anglynge with
a rodde: and a line and an hoke."
—Dame Juliana Berners, *The
Treatyse of Fysshynge wyth an Angle,*
*1496.*

"If the bending rod and the
ringing reel
Give proof that you've fastened
the tempered steel.
Be sure that the battle is but begun
And not till he's landed is victory
won."
—Author Unknown.

**Fair and Foul Angling**—
Anybody can catch a trout with a
worm. This is the bait of the boy
and the boatman. The angler gives
the trout a fair battle with the
artificial fly. Comparing live-bait
fishing to artificial fly angling is
like comparing blacksmithry to
jewel working, bronco breaking
to genteel horsemanship, or
buccaneering to yachting.

**Refinement of Angling**—Angling
is fishing governed by rules of
chivalry—correct tackle, limit in
the catch, and humane treatment
of the game.

**Landing the Fish**—"The surest
way to take the fish is give her
leave to play and yield her line."
Quarles, *Shepheard's Eclogues,* 1644.
Subdue a big fish before you try
to land him. Don't be in a hurry.
Give him line, but keep it taut (not
tight), and don't become excited.
Don't try to yank him out of his
element or pull him through the
line guides. Raise the rod tip over
the back of your head, and don't
grab the line—guide the game into

the landing net or up to the gaff. Take your time. Be glad if the fish escapes. His life is as important as yours—to him, at least. Besides, you'd soon tire of fishing if you never lost a fish. "The play's the thing" in angling, anyway, because, as an angler, you can buy fish cheaper than you can catch them, if you play fair—if you're not of the gentry that judge the day by quantity instead of quality. Some of the greatest anglers are the poorest fish killers, but to them one fish correctly captured on chivalric tackle means more than a tubful of butchered victims means to the unenlightened bungler. Contrast and conditions count for something in everything. If there were no cloudy days we'd never correctly value the sunshine. Method in the pursuit, appropriateness of the equipment, and uncertainty in the catch, wholly distasteful to the selfish neophyte, are thoroughly appreciated by the angler.

**Ancient Angling**—One of the most ancient literary works on fishing, perhaps the most ancient of all really known volumes on the subject, is *Hauleutics of Oppian*, the work of a Greek poet, AD 198, from which many articles on fishing and angling, thought to be modern, have been taken. Athenæus tells us that several writers wrote treatises or poems on fishing centuries before the Christian era.

**Old Angling Books**—1486—*The Booke of St. Albans*; by Dame Juliana Berners. 1590—*Booke of Fishing with Hook and Line*; by Leonard Mascall. 1596—*Hawking. Hunting, Fowling and Fishing*; by W. C. Faukener. 1606—*Booke of Angling or Fishing*; by Samuel Gardner, D.D. 1651—*Art of Angling*; by Thomas Barker (the second edition of this book, published in 1657, was issued under the title of *Barker's Delight*). 1652—*Young Sportsman's Delight and Instructor in Angling*, etc.; by Gervase Markham. 1653—*The Compleat Angler, or the Contemplative Man's Recreation*, etc.; by Izaak Walton (the second edition, almost rewritten by the author, appeared in 1655). 1662—*Experienced Angler, or Angling Improved*; by Robert Venables. 1676—*Angler's Delight*, etc.; by William Gilbert. 1681—*Angler's Vade Mecum*; by Chetham. 1682—*Complete Troller*; by Nobles. 1696—*The True Art of Angling*; by J. S.

**Carrying the Rod**—Joint your rod only when you reach the place of angling, and take it apart again when you are ready to leave the water for camp, unless the camp is on the edge of the lake or stream. When angling along thickly wooded banks, carry the rod in front of you, tip first, pointing the tip through the bushes you penetrate; never pull it after you. Fasten the hook on one of the reel bars, and then thrust the rod's tip through the branches or shrubbery ahead of you when you move along, casting here and there. This is not necessary when one only moves a step or two, for then, if there be open space, the rod and line may be held clear of the underbrush and branches. In all cases keep the rod ahead of you. When disjointed, the rod pieces may be held together by small rubber bands until the rod case is made use of, but don't lay the rod away with the rubber bands intact, as the rubber will bend the tip out of shape, dislodge the wood coating, disturb the whipping, and tarnish the ferrules. Dr. E. F. Conyngham of Bonner, MT, doesn't like my notion of carrying the rod tip first. The doctor says he favors carrying it butt first with the tip trailing behind. "I have fished with a fly for trout and salmon nearly forty years in Europe and this continent," says the doctor, "and never yet saw an expert angler carry a rod in the way described by Mr. Bradford. That is just the proper caper to break tips. The rod in going through brush should be carried butt forward; then the tip will trail as easily as the tail on a dog, and furthermore, you can walk at good speed without interference. In my many years of fly fishing I have had one broken tip; a woman knocked it down and stepped on it. Luckily it was lancewood, so I could repair it. What would have been my predicament had the rod been of split bamboo?" Very good, Doctor. I may be wrong but, I learned my way from my fathers of the angle—Seth Green. John Harrington Keene, Frederick Mather, William C. Harris, *et al.*—when I was being taught first lessons in fly-fishing. Seth Green, John Keene, and Harris personally advised me to carry the fly rod tip in front of me, and each of the trio personally showed me the method on the trout streams. Harris and Keene always carried their fly rods tip first, and I have seen both these experts along the streams many times during many years of personal fishing with both of these anglers. However, Dr. Conyngham must not be denied his view on the subject. Just as there are famous wing shots who shoot with one eye closed and other experts who give trigger with both eyes open, so in angling, there are many practiced hands who disagree on the various ways and means in fishing. I favor keeping my tip in front of me, and while I shall never change this method, I refrain from condemning Dr. Conyngham's contrastive way of carrying his tip. Charles Zibeon Southard agrees with both the Doctor and me. He advises carrying the tip ahead in the open and behind in the brush.

**The Angling World**—"Angling takes us from the confusion, the filth, and the social and moral degradation of the big cities and places us in close contact with one of the most important divisions of human labor—the cultivation of the soil, which is the real foundation of all national wealth and true social happiness. Everything connected with the land is calculated to foster the best and noblest feelings of the soul and to give the mind the most lofty and sublime ideas of universal nature. To men of contemplative habits the roaming along brooks, rivers, lakes, and fields gives rise to the most refined intellectual enjoyment. Such persons move in a world of their own and experience joys and sorrows with which the world cannot meddle."—A. L. H.

**Colorado Trout Streams—** Colorado has 6,000 miles of trout streams.

**Angling Saves Words—** "Contemplation and quietness! Will these words soon be labeled in our dictionaries 'obsolete'? It would seem so; yet there will be some use for them, among old-fashioned folk, as long as the word 'angling' holds its place."—Willis Boyd Allen.

**Large-Trout Angling—**Frank Brigg, of London. England, fishing in New River, caught an 18-pound trout, the heaviest specimen of trout ever taken in a London water.

**Speculation in Angling—**"I often wonder if the basis of fishing is not founded upon the element of chance, and whether fishing does not fascinate because it is a species of gambling. To a degree it is a hazard. You take your best tackle, select your choicest bait, and you do more, for you pray to the goddess of success." —"Ancient Mariner."

**Economy in Angling—**"Don't take more fish than you can use; if you do, you take that which belongs to someone else." —"Tops'l."

**An Angling Classic—**"Angling is the only sport that boasts the honor of having given a classic [Izaak Walton's *The Compleat Angler*, 1653] to literature."— Henry van Dyke.

**How to Approach a Trout—** ". . . sense of hearing in all species of fish is a matter of concussion on the surface of the water. Sit motionless in a boat, and you may sing, "I Won't Go Home 'Til Morning," or any other gala song, to the extreme high limit of your voices, and the trout or any other fish will remain undisturbed, but, scratch your toe upon the bottom of the boat, and presto! the pool is as dead and barren as a burned prairie. Approach a pool from over the bank with a careless tread, and when you reach it the trout are gone, none know where. Crawl to the pool noiselessly on all fours and you will find your trout reposing without fear of danger. The avoidance of concussion is the great factor on a trout pool or stream in getting a satisfactory creel. Slide, rather than step, in wading, and your success will be greater."—Wm. C. Harris.

**Strike from the Reel or Hand?**— "The strike must be made with sufficient force and no more. If insufficient, the hook will not penetrate far enough to hold the fish in its subsequent struggles, and if the force is excessive the gut will break at its weakest point, and leave the fly and possibly one or more strands of gut in the trout's jaws. The angler should acquire the habit of striking from the reel, i.e., without holding the line in the hand. Many old fishermen prefer holding the line when striking, but it is at best a risky proceeding, and too likely to result in a breakage of the gut."—F. M. Halford, *The Dry-Fly Man's Handbook.* "Personally I never 'strike from the reel' . . . because less control is had over the line, likewise the fish."—Charles Zibeon Southard, *Trout Fly-Fishing in America.* I favor Mr. Halford's method—"strike from the reel"—in fly-fishing and in weakfish fishing with light tackle. In heavy bait fishing, Mr. Southard's strike with the "hand-held line" suits me.

**The Silver Hook**—"There is a good deal of fun in thinking you are going to have it."—New York *Press.*

True; Walton says the angler's anticipation of fishing is as great a joy as the realization of it.

**Angling Ailment**—"We never get over the fishing fever; it is a delightful disease, and, thank the

Lord, there is no cure."—Ira W. Moore.

**Angling and Nature—**
"Association with men of the world narrows the heart; communion with nature expands it."—Jean Paul Richter.

**Angling and Mathematics—**
"Angling may be said to be so much like the Mathematics, that it can ne'er be fully learnt; at least not so fully, but that there will still be more new experiments left for the tryal of other men that succeed us."—Izaak Walton, *The Compleat Angler*, 1653.

**Tendency of Angling—**"I am now over 76 [years in age] and owe my life to fishing, and I find the tendency of fishing is to make one careful, artful, patient, and practical." —"Watcher."

**Angling a Science—**"Angling is a science, not merely a pastime. It will broaden you and start your boy in a manly sport that will draw him to the country instead

of to the dance hall, to the fields and streams instead of to the pool room." —"Greenhorn."

**Fly vs. Worm—**"That fly-fishing is clean, and free from the muscular efforts of mountain-climbing; that it is usually rewarded with larger fish than those taken with a worm; that it has a freedom, a jollity, a certain broad, wide-spaced exhilaration, I willingly admit. But, the humbler, old-fashioned method has a charm of its own which I am not ready to forego."—Willis Boyd Allen.

**"Ye Gods and Little Fishes."—**
"When we have become familiar with the great cities with their bewildering sights and distracting sounds, the finest things remain to be discovered, and these discoveries must be made as we stand open-eyed in the presence of God's workmanship. Hills and streams, woods and flowers, bees and birds and butterflies, the flora and fauna of this earth where we have our home for a little time, should, somehow, be brought

into the life of the child. The boy who grows up into manhood without being privileged to know the world of nature by personal contact has been robbed. He may be intelligent in many things and a useful member of society, but he has missed out of life some of its deepest satisfactions and purest joys. Indeed, such an one is not symmetrically educated, and is quite likely to be put to shame as the years pass by."—Lathan A. Crandall, *Days in the Open*.

**Angling Is Its Own Reward—** "No other sportsman brings home more from his sport than he takes to it than the fisherman. His basket is heavy with present food in the morning, and loaded with future food in the afternoon, with an appetite and a sleepetite that requires three days to satisfy."— Hy. Julius.

**Ideal Angling Time—**The last two weeks in June—what lovelier period for brook trout fishing in the rich flower-lined mountain streams? When does the wild shrub smell sweeter than now, the wind blow more balmily, the songbirds trill sweeter, and the spotted trout bite better?

**Landing the Trout—**The proper time to spend in landing a fish all depends upon the condition of your fishing ground. Lead your prize away from obstructions, keep the line taut, and do not nervously hurry the play. Take your time.

**Fishes' Feeding-Time—**Fishes are said to bite better between the new moon and the first quarter; or between the last quarter and the change.

**Calmness in Angling—**Don't hurry a large fish. Subdue him as far from you as possible.

**Shadowless Angling—**Never let your shadow fall upon the angling water. Keep the sun in front of you.

**Striking and Hooking—**Nothing is more difficult to learn about fly-fishing than the art of striking or hooking the game.

**The Fishless Fisherman**—"You took a day off from your work and went fishing? Have any luck?" "Certainly. A day off is luck enough."—New York *American*.

**Angling Spirit**—"It is the way we do things and the spirit in which we prosecute our endeavors that counts. The man who takes the day to go fishing on the great ocean or in the forest and can commune with Nature can be as good a Christian as the best man that ever entered the portals of a church, cathedral, or synagogue."—"Nature Factor."

**All Sports in Angling**—"The sport that sums up dancing, song and picture, athletics and all games of chance is angling. The waves make you dance, all pictures roll before you, any chance can win the pool, and every fishing boat is a *sängerfest*."—B. M. Briggs.

**Early Trout Angling**—"Don't let anyone tell you of the folly of trout fishing in early April. It's great sport, and if you're skillful enough to get a few of the gamest and wisest fish that swims at this time of the year your success will be complete in May and June, when the ideal weather comes."—H. T. Walden.

**Skill vs. Kill**—"To qualify as a sportsman in the taking of any kind of game, a man must show much more enthusiasm in skill rather than in the kill, always remembering to give or inflict the least pain possible on the game taken by his skill."—Wes Wood.

**Rainbow Trout Angling**—"I get harder play with a three-pound rainbow trout than with a maskinonge of twenty-five pounds. I have caught only a few rainbow trout. The first one I ever caught was three years ago in the Esopus Creek in the Catskills. I felt somewhat relieved when I had him in the net. He was the gamest fish for his size I ever hooked, and I have killed ten- and twelve-pound salmon on a trout rod. The rainbow trout is first cousin to the lordly salmon."—M. J. Doyle.

**Secret of Angling**—"Fishing is more than catching. Its pleasures are the whole outdoors. Appreciation is the secret of the lure."—Theodore Macklin.

**Limit in Angling**—"It is very foolish for anglers, when they get more fishes than they want, to even give them away; far better it would be for them to stop fishing when they have caught enough for themselves, and give the fish a chance."—George Hartley.

**Age of Angling**—"The allurement of fishing is as old as the granite mountains of the Andes. Down through the ages of the past, even from the day of the anthropophagi, comes to us the fact that all the world rejoices in the gentle art of fishing. Fishing— the one word that opens up to our understanding the philosophy of nature—is the fundamental basis of our civilization."—David Jones.

**Gentility in Angling**—"Sportsmanship abhors greed and all vulgarity."—H. W. Wack.

**Angling Clears the Brain**—"When we are confused and harried by the turmoil of modern life, our heads and our hearts aching with its complex problems, its exigent demands, its rebuffs, and its bitter disappointments, let us turn once more to the forest and meadow, the peaceful stream, with the fleecy clouds or overhanging boughs kindly tempering the rays of the summer sun; let us drop our pens, abandon for the nonce our manuscript, our ledgers, or the stock reports of the day, and 'go a-fishing.'"—Willis Boyd Allen.

**Up and Down Stream**—"I fish up stream (and I think this best) and down stream and across stream— according to wind and time and weather, etc., and the sun. I have found I can get the larger fish in upstream fishing; but there are pools one can't get the flies to—the likely places—from below, nor yet from either side. When I come to such a pool I get above and cover it well by casting across stream from me—the sun being opposite—and let my flies float down, drawing them the while across current with a twitching motion, as an insect struggling to swim across. It is a deadly method if well done and gets the big ones too. I hold the line of course in my left hand, and as I gently raise the rod with my right, I take in line with my left, thus at all times having full control and ready for a strike."—Ernest L. Eubank.

**Fly-Fishing First**—"Fly-fishing comes first, then comes bait casting with the fly rod; third, still fishing; fourth, casting of live bait with the short rod from the reel, and last, if not entirely without the pale of true sportsmanship, the use of the plug."—Rayx.

**Fly Rod and Bait Rod**—"It takes some skill to keep sixty feet of line in the air when fly casting, and requires free space for the back cast. It is fascinating work and requires more delicacy in handling a fly rod than a bait rod. The fly rod, especially in Southern Missouri waters, lands more fish during the day than the bait rod, but the latter lands larger fish. The bait caster makes fewer casts on account of reeling in the line after each cast, but the water is more effectively covered. One has to be a judge of the water and determine which method should be used. In the northern lakes bait casting is far superior in results to fly casting."—M. J. Brennan.

**Land and Water**—"You're natural when fishing, and unnatural on shore. Fishing rubs the barnacles off your natural self, and makes your bodyship sail more easily."—B. M. Briggs.

**First Record of Angling**—"The first authentic record of angling appears in the Old Testament of the Bible, computed to be about 1500 years before Christ, where the Lord asked Job: 'Canst thou take out a fish with the hook?'"—John Ryan.

**Roman Angling**—The walls of Pompeii are adorned with angling scenes.

# Farming

By definition, retreats are supposed to be largely self sufficient. So, like it or not, a real retreater is going to have to be a farmer as well. Unfortunately, farming is not something that can be learned on the spot. You can't have seeds hanging around in storage for years and then suddenly expect them to grow for you if you've never done any farming before. There are a lot of good websites with helpful suggestions. Start with this one and see what else you can find: http://containergardening.about.com/od/floweringcontainer garden/u/DIYProjects.htm?p=1

There are many good books on the subject. One of the best is Coyne and Knutzen's *The Urban Homestead*. Much of what follows are influenced by that manual, and the author highly recommends it as part of the urban or suburban retreater's library. Most readers, after all, are urban and suburban dwellers with limited soil sources and very limited farming experience. Aside from teaching you how to grow your own food and raise your own animals for meat and dairy, Coyne and Knutzen's book contains information on urban foraging, and over seventy pages are dedicated to methods of preserving the harvest. Another thirty pages describe in-depth water harvesting techniques. Below are some basic concepts of farming for food supplementation. Although these apply specifically to limited-soil scenarios, the same basics apply to farming on a larger scale.

1. Basic principles:
   a. Grow only what you can use. It will save you money and farming space.
   b. Develop a clean soil resource.
   c. Use more water, but do it less frequently.

d. Do not expect any miracles. (Remember, Rome wasn't built in a day.)

e. Keep constant notes as you never know when they'll come in handy.

2. If you have no access to ground soil, grow food in containers on patios, roofs, balconies, or indoors where they will get enough sunlight. You can also look into hydroponics and vertical farming. Maximize the growing space in all directions (string or wire trellises, etc.). Food crops need six hours of sun, direct or reflected, each day. If only inside space is available, place containers next to windows and supplement with artificial light.

3. Give priority to fruit-bearing plants (beans, peas, tomatoes, melons, cucumbers, squash, etc.).

4. Build soil in these ways:

a.Compost all yard and kitchen waste and use as soil. Composting occurs when organic waste is broken down by microbial processes. When the process occurs on the forest floor, it's called mulching and the product is mulch. When the process is carried out by humans using pits or bins, it's called composting and the product is called compost. The resulting material can be used as fertilizer. Efficient composting requires careful sorting and mixing of proper ingredients. Compost needs a good supply of nitrogen-rich vegetable waste (called greens), which includes scraps from the kitchen, grass and weed clippings, fresh leaves, and even coffee grounds. It needs a nearly equal supply of carbon-rich materials (called browns), which include straw, bark, wood chips, sawdust, dry leaves, and shredded newspaper. Don't add any bones, meat, fish, oils, dog waste, or dairy products. Compost radiates heat if the nitrogen–carbon ratio is good. The warmth indicates that the aerobic bacteria, worms, and fungi are all doing their job.

When the process is nearly complete and it's ready to be used as fertilizer, the compost will be cool. Keep an eye on air and moisture levels. The microorganisms need air to work their magic, so be sure to mix it up and include some wood chips or straw to prevent vegetable products from clumping together and to keep the ventilation process going. The mixture should be damp but not wet enough to drip from the bottom. The end result is a light, soil-like material called humus—a highly nutritious topsoil that can be spread over vegetable gardens, lawns, fields, and around trees.

b.  Use mulch (leaves, etc.) to protect and build soil. Mulch holds in moisture, slows weeds down, and stabilizes soil temperature. Fall leaves, wood shavings, or small chips, straw, pine needles, corn husks, and lawn clippings can all be used as mulch. Lay down a healthy cover around plants, about 5

inches deep. The mulch will break down and thin and can be replenished annually with fall leaves. Be creative in finding or building places to grow your crops, preferably where they can get good sun exposure.

Tub Science at work. On the left is a composter made from a 33-gallon garbage can. There are many ¼-inch holes drilled into the can on the sides and on the bottom. The larger holes are screened and provide additional assurance that the mixture is getting enough air. To mix the contents, the container can be tipped and rolled every couple of days or weeks. Don't wait for the end of the world to start composting. These bins take three to four months for a family of two to fill and another six months or so to become humus, so a second or third bin will be

A raised bed built from old boards for an urban garden.

needed. In urban areas "browns" may be scarce until the fall leaves are distributed by the wind. In your storage, you'll want to start keeping old newspapers and save your sawdust.

On the right is a 34-gallon wheeled garbage can fitted with a cheap hose valve fixture to allow the hose to be turned on and off. When full, this contraption will run 50 feet of downslope soaker hose or a simple ring sprinkler at a drizzle for a couple of hours. Fill the can by using rain gutters or collector tubs. Otherwise, keep the lid on to prevent mosquito breeding. Filtered or treated gray water can also be used to help fill the can.

A self-watering 5-gallon bucket planter is big enough for herbs or a medium-sized plant. This is made from two stacked 5-gallon buckets. The inner bucket is modified as shown in the photo. A similar contraption made from large plastic storage tubs will hold a couple of tomato or half a dozen mature lettuce plants.

i. If you have some exposed soil, build it up with a raised bed, simple rock, or lumber walls a foot or two high to hold the soil.

ii. Containers can include commercial planting pots, stacked tires, kiddie pools, buckets, etc.

a. Avoid tilling the soil.

b. Rotate crops to prevent nutrient depletion and disease.

c. Don't use pesticides or herbicides.

5. Coyne and Knutzen recommend watering deeply and less frequently. Use drip systems or soaker hose. Keep the soil spongy, not dripping wet, and let plants dry out slightly between watering.

6. Watch for infestations and diseases. Clip diseased foliage off and pick or wash off aphids or other damaging bugs.

7. Not all bugs and animal visitors are bad. Ladybugs, birds, spiders, and bees are good for a garden.

8. Consider concentrating on edible perennials (plants that come back year after year without replanting), such as fruit and nut trees. Dwarf varieties can be grown in large pots or buckets and will deliver plenty of fruit.

9. The key is to get started early. The garden needs to be already planted or at least ready to be planted if you expect to produce food when you need it. Just use our process and store the food you produce and keep the garden going. You can buy seedlings at any nursery in season and transplant them wherever you want, or you can store them and start your own seeds. Some seeds start growing when planted per package directions directly in the ground. Others require special handling. Generally, here are the rules of thumb for starting seeds indoors:

1. Start a month before planting season.

2. Store seeds properly in a cool and dark location. (A refrigerator works well.)

3. Wide, flat containers prevent overcrowding. Plastic pots with good drainage are always the best to start with. Get some plant trays from the nursery, or drill some drainage holes in those old yogurt containers. Then all you have to do is add some potting soil.

4. Place seeds as directed on the soil and tamp the seeds with the bottom of a glass or bottle to ensure they make direct contact with the soil. Sprinkle some sphagnum moss or chicken grit to help keep the surface dry (helps prevent plant infections).

5. You can prevent plant infections by providing ventilation (consider a small fan on the lowest setting) and good drainage.

6. Make sure that you never overwater. Maintain the moisture level by covering the pots with plastic wrap. Check for dryness daily, and if more moisture is needed, spritz the surface soil with a spray bottle or place the pot in another container of water just deep enough to allow water to wick into the pot. Remove the plastic wrap when the seeds germinate.

7. Keeping the plant at a normal room temperature (65–75°F) encourages germination.

8. Expose (indoors) to sunlight or artificial light twelve to sixteen hours each day. Rotate the pot a quarter turn daily in relation to the available light source.

9. A weak fertilizer solution can be used once to encourage growth when the true leaves have appeared. The earliest leaves will probably be rounded food storage cells. True leaves resemble their adult versions.

10. Acclimate seedlings to direct sunlight temperature changes by exposing them outside for increasing periods over several days to prepare them for transplantation. Some seeds require even more preparation, and there will usually be instructions to that effect on the seed package. Many urban gardening manuals recommend

growing only foods that are normally scarce or expensive. But the goal of a retreat, in contrast to convenience or savings, is sustainability. You're not only going to want the small scarce or expensive stuff like berries and herbs, instead you'll want to be able to produce the inexpensive staples like potatoes, onions, corn, squash, peppers, lettuce, carrots, tomatoes, beets, garlic, etc. The following websites are excellent sources of information on how to grow and stores these types of foods: http://www.gardeners.com/Storing-Potatoes-Onions-Garlic- Squash/5021,default,pg.html http://www.gardenguides.com/114522-make-own-seedpotatoes. html http://www.garden.org/foodguide/browse/veggie/tomatoes_getting_started/372 http://www.ehow.com/how_2100121_grow-corn-container. html http://containergardening.about.com/od/vegetablesand herbs/u/VegetableContainerGardeningUP.htm

# Cooking for Hikes and Overnight Camps

The following tested receipts are given for those who go on hikes and overnight camps:

## Griddle-cakes

Beat one egg, tablespoonful of sugar, one cup diluted condensed milk or new milk. Mix enough self-raising flour to make a thick cream batter. Grease the griddle with rind or slices of bacon for each batch of cakes. Be sure to have the griddle hot.

## Bacon

Slice bacon quite thin; remove the rind, which makes slices curl up. Fry on griddle or put on a sharp end of a stick and hold over the hot coals, or better yet remove the griddle, and put on a clean, flat rock in its place. When hot lay the slices of bacon on the rock and broil. Keep turning so as to brown on both sides.

## Canned Salmon on Toast

Dip slices of stale bread into smoking hot lard. They will brown at once. Drain them. Heat a pint of salmon, picked into flakes, season with salt and pepper, and turn in a tablespoonful of melted butter. Heat in a pan. Stir in one egg, beaten light, with three tablespoonfuls evaporated milk not thinned. Pour the mixture on the fried bread.

## Roast Potatoes

Wash and dry potatoes thoroughly, bury them deep in a good bed of coals, cover them with hot coals until well done. It will take about forty minutes for them to bake. Then pass a sharpened hard-wood sliver through them from end to end, and let the steam escape and use immediately as a roast potato soon becomes soggy and bitter.

## Baked Fresh Fish

Clean well. Small fish should be fried whole with the back bone severed to prevent curling up; large fish should be cut into pieces, and ribs loosened from back bone so as to lie flat in pan. Rub the pieces in corn meal or powdered crumbs, thinly and evenly (that browns them), fry in plenty of hot fat to a golden brown, sprinkling lightly with salt just as the color turns. If fish has not been wiped dry it will absorb too much grease. If the frying fat is not very hot when fish are put in, they will be soggy with it.

## Frogs' Legs

First, after skinning, soak them an hour in cold water to which vinegar has been added, or put them for two minutes into scalding water that has vinegar in it. Drain, wipe dry, and cook. To fry: Roll in flour, season with salt and pepper, and fry not too rapidly, preferably in butter or oil. Watercress is a good relish with them. To griddle: Prepare three tablespoonsful melted butter, one half tablespoonful salt, and a pinch or two of pepper, into which dip the frogs' legs, then roll in fresh bread crumbs and broil for three minutes on each side.

## Eggs

**Boiled:** Have water to boiling point. Place eggs in carefully. Boil steadily for three minutes if you wish them soft. If wanted hard boiled, put them in cold water, bring to a boil, and keep it up for twenty minutes. The yolk will then be mealy and wholesome.

**Fried:** Melt some butter or fat in frying-pan; when it hisses drop in eggs carefully. Fry them three minutes.

**Scrambled:** First stir the eggs up and after putting some butter in the frying-pan, stir the eggs in it after adding a little condensed milk.

**Poached:** First put in the frying-pan sufficient diluted condensed milk which has been thinned with enough water to float the eggs in, and let them simmer three or four minutes. Serve the eggs on slices of buttered toast, pouring on enough of the milk to moisten the toast.

## Coffee

For every cup of water allow a tablespoonful of ground coffee, then add one extra. Have water come to boiling point first, add coffee, hold it just below boiling point for five minutes, and settle with one fourth of a cup of cold water. Serve. Some prefer to put the coffee in a small muslin bag loosely tied.

## Cocoa

Allow a teaspoonful of cocoa for every cup of boiling water. Mix the powdered cocoa with water or boiled milk, with sugar to taste. Boil two or three minutes.

These recipes have been tried out. Biscuit and bread making have been purposely omitted. Take bread and crackers with you from camp. "Amateur" biscuits are not conducive to good digestion or happiness. Pack butter in small jar: cocoa, sugar, and coffee in small cans or heavy paper; also salt and pepper. Wrap bread in a moist cloth to prevent drying up; bacon and dried or chipped beef in wax paper. Pickles can be purchased put up in small bottles. Use the empty bottle as candle-stick.

## Sample Menu for an Overnight Camp and a Day Hike or Tramp

### Breakfast

Griddle-Cakes, Fried Bacon and Potatoes, Bread, Coffee, Preserves

### Dinner

Creamed Salmon on Toast, Baked Potatoes, Bread, Pickles, Fruit

### Supper

Fried Eggs, Creamed or Chipped Beef, Cheese, Bread, Cocoa

## Ration List for Six Boys, Three Meals

2 pounds bacon (sliced thin)

1 pound butter

1 dozen eggs

1/2 pound cocoa

1/2 pound coffee

1 pound sugar

3 cans salmon

24 potatoes

2 cans condensed milk

1 small package of self-raising flour

Salt and pepper

### Utensils

Small griddle

Small stew pan

Small coffee-pot

Large spoon

Plate and cup

Matches and candle

## Dish Washing

First fill the frying-pan with water, place over the fire, and let it boil. Pour out water and you will find the pan has practically cleaned itself. Clean the griddle with sand and water. Greasy knives and forks may be cleaned by jabbing them into the ground. After all grease is gotten rid of, wash in hot water and dry with cloth. Don't use the cloth first and get it greasy.

# Canning

## Introduction to Canning

On the next few pages, you will find descriptions of proper canning methods, with details on how canning works and why it is both safe and economical. Much of the information here is from the USDA, which has done extensive research on home canning and preserving. If you are new to home canning, read this section carefully as it will help to ensure success with the recipes that follow. Whether you are a seasoned home canner or this is your first foray into food preservation, it is important to follow directions carefully. With some recipes it is okay to experiment with varied proportions or added ingredients, and with others it is important to stick to what's written. In many instances it is noted whether creative liberty is a good idea for a particular recipe, but if you are not sure, play it safe—otherwise you may end up with a jam that is too runny, a vegetable that is mushy, or a product that is spoiled. Take time to read the directions and prepare your foods and equipment adequately, and you will find that home canning is safe, economical, tremendously satisfying, and a great deal of fun!

## Why Can Foods?

Canning is fun and a good way to preserve your precious produce. As more and more farmers' markets make their way into urban centers, city dwellers are also discovering how rewarding it is to make seasonal treats last all year round. Besides the value of your labor, canning home-grown or locally grown food may save you half the cost of buying commercially canned food. And what makes a nicer, more thoughtful gift than a jar of homemade jam, tailored to match the recipient's favorite fruits and flavors?

The nutritional value of home canning is an added benefit. Many vegetables begin to lose their vitamins as soon as they are harvested. Nearly half the vitamins may be lost within a few days unless the fresh produce is kept cool or preserved. Within one to two weeks, even refrigerated produce loses half or more of certain vitamins. The heating process during canning destroys from one-third to one-half of vitamins A and C, thiamin, and riboflavin. Once canned, foods may lose from 5 percent to 20 percent of these sensitive

Canned jams and nut butters.

vitamins each year. The amounts of other vitamins, however, are only slightly lower in canned compared with fresh food.

If vegetables are handled properly and canned promptly after harvest, they can be more nutritious than fresh produce sold in local stores. The advantages of home canning are lost when you start with poor quality foods; when jars fail to seal properly; when food spoils; and when flavors, texture, color, and nutrients deteriorate during prolonged storage. The tips that follow explain many of these problems and recommend ways to minimize them.

## How Canning Preserves Foods

The high percentage of water in most fresh foods makes them very perishable. They spoil or lose their quality for several reasons:

- Growth of undesirable microorganisms—bacteria, molds, and yeasts

- Activity of food enzymes
- Reactions with oxygen
- Moisture loss

Microorganisms live and multiply quickly on the surfaces of fresh food and on the inside of bruised, insectdamaged, and diseased food. Oxygen and enzymes are present throughout fresh food tissues.

Proper canning practices include:

- Carefully selecting and washing fresh food
- Peeling some fresh foods
- Hot packing many foods
- Adding acids (lemon juice, citric acid, or vinegar) to some foods
- Using acceptable jars and self-sealing lids
- Processing jars in a boiling-water or pressure canner for the correct amount of time

Collectively, these practices remove oxygen; destroy enzymes; prevent the growth of undesirable bacteria, yeasts, and molds; and help form a high vacuum in jars. High vacuums form tight seals, which keep liquid in and air and microorganisms out.

Canning began in France, at the turn of the nineteenth century, when Napoleon Bonaparte was desperate for a way to keep his troops well-fed while on the march. In 1800, he decided to hold a contest, offering 12,000 francs to anyone who could devise a suitable method of food preservation. Nicolas Francois Appert, a French confectioner, rose to the challenge, considering that if wine could be preserved in bottles, perhaps food could be as well. He experimented until he was able to prove that heating food to boiling after it had been sealed in airtight glass bottles prevented the food from deteriorating. Interestingly, this all took place about one hundred years before Louis Pasteur found that heat could destroy bacteria. Nearly ten years after the contest began, Napoleon personally presented Nicolas with the cash reward.

Canned applesauce and peaches line this pantry's shelves.

## Canning Glossary

**Acid foods**—Foods that contain enough acid to result in a pH of 4.6 or lower. Includes most tomatoes; fermented and pickled vegetables; relishes; jams, jellies, and marmalades; and all fruits except figs. Acid foods may be processed in boiling water.

**Ascorbic acid**—The chemical name for vitamin C. Commonly used to prevent browning of peeled, lightcolored fruits and vegetables.

**Blancher**—A 6- to 8-quart lidded pot designed with a fitted, perforated basket to hold food in boiling water or with a fitted rack to steam foods. Useful for loosening skins on fruits to be peeled or for heating foods to be hot packed.

**Boiling-water canner**—A large, standard-sized, lidded kettle with jar rack designed for heat-processing seven quarts or eight to nine pints in boiling water.

**Botulism**—An illness caused by eating a toxin produced by growth of Clostridium botulinum bacteria in moist, low-acid food containing less than 2 percent oxygen and stored between 40°F and 120°F. Proper heat processing destroys this bacterium in canned food. Freezer temperatures inhibit its growth in frozen food. Low moisture controls its growth in dried food. High oxygen controls its growth in fresh foods.

**Canning**—A method of preserving food that employs heat processing in airtight, vacuum-sealed containers so that food can be safely stored at normal home temperatures.

**Canning salt**—Also called pickling salt. It is regular table salt without the anti-caking or iodine additives.

**Citric acid**—A form of acid that can be added to canned foods. It increases the acidity of low-acid foods and may improve their flavor.

**Cold pack**—Canning procedure in which jars are filled with raw food. "Raw pack" is the preferred term for describing this practice. "Cold pack" is often used incorrectly to refer to foods that are open-kettle canned or jars that are heat-processed in boiling water.

**Enzymes**—Proteins in food that accelerate many flavor, color, texture, and nutritional changes, especially when food is cut, sliced, crushed, bruised, or exposed to air. Proper blanching or hot-packing practices destroy enzymes and improve food quality.

**Exhausting**—Removing air from within and around food and from jars and canners. Exhausting or venting of pressure canners is necessary to prevent botulism in low-acid canned foods.

**Headspace**—The unfilled space above food or liquid in jars that allows for food expansion as jars are heated and for forming vacuums as jars cool.

**Heat-processing**—Treatment of jars with sufficient heat to enable storing food at normal home temperatures.

**Hermetic seal**—An absolutely airtight container seal that prevents reentry of air or microorganisms into packaged foods.

**Hot pack**—Heating of raw food in boiling water or steam and filling it hot into jars.

**Low-acid foods**—Foods that contain very little acid and have a pH above 4.6. The acidity in these foods is insufficient to prevent the growth of botulism bacteria. Vegetables, some varieties of tomatoes, figs, all meats, fish,

Green beans should be chopped into small pieces before canning.

seafood, and some dairy products are low-acid foods. To control all risks of botulism, jars of these foods must be either heat processed in a pressure canner or acidified to a pH of 4.6 or lower before being processed in boiling water.

**Microorganisms**—Independent organisms of microscopic size, including bacteria, yeast, and mold. In a suitable environment, they grow rapidly and may divide or reproduce every 10 to 30 minutes. Therefore, they reach high populations very quickly. Microorganisms are sometimes intentionally added to ferment foods, make antibiotics, and for other reasons. Undesirable microorganisms cause disease and food spoilage.

**Mold**—A fungus-type microorganism whose growth on food is usually visible and colorful. Molds may grow on many foods, including acid foods like jams and jellies and canned fruits. Recommended heat processing and sealing practices prevent their growth on these foods.

A large stockpot with a lid can be used in place of a boiling water canner for high-acid foods like tomatoes, pickles, apples, peaches, and jams. Simply place a rack inside the pot so that the jars do not rest directly on the bottom of the pot.

**Mycotoxins**—Toxins produced by the growth of some molds on foods.

**Open-kettle canning**—A non-recommended canning method. Food is heat-processed in a covered kettle, filled while hot into sterile jars, and then sealed. Foods canned this way have low vacuums or too much air, which permits rapid loss of quality in foods. Also, these foods often spoil because they become recontaminated while the jars are being filled.

**Pasteurization**—Heating food to temperatures high enough to destroy disease-causing microorganisms.

pH—A measure of acidity or alkalinity. Values range from 0 to 14. A food is neutral when its pH is 7.0. Lower values are increasingly more acidic; higher values are increasingly more alkaline.

PSIG—Pounds per square inch of pressure as measured by a gauge.

Pressure canner—A specifically designed metal kettle with a lockable lid used for heat-processing low-acid food. These canners have jar racks, one or more safety devices, systems for exhausting air, and a way to measure or control pressure. Canners with 20- to 21-quart capacity are common. The minimum size of canner that should be used has a 16-quart capacity and can hold seven one-quart jars. Use of pressure saucepans with a capacity of less than 16 quarts is not recommended.

Raw pack—The practice of filling jars with raw, unheated food. Acceptable for canning low-acid foods, but allows more rapid quality losses in acid foods that are heat-processed in boiling water. Also called "cold pack."

Style of pack—Form of canned food, such as whole, sliced, piece, juice, or sauce. The term may also be used to specify whether food is filled raw or hot into jars.

Vacuum—A state of negative pressure that reflects how thoroughly air is removed from within a jar of processed food; the higher the vacuum, the less air left in the jar.

# Proper Canning Practices

Growth of the bacterium Clostridium botulinum in canned food may cause botulism—a deadly form of food poisoning. These bacteria exist either as spores or as vegetative cells. The spores, which are comparable to plant seeds, can survive harmlessly in soil and water for many years. When ideal conditions exist for growth, the spores produce vegetative cells, which multiply rapidly and may produce a deadly toxin within three to four days in an environment consisting of:

- A moist, low-acid food
- A temperature between 40°F and 120°F, and
- Less than 2 percent oxygen.

Botulinum spores are on most fresh food surfaces. Because they grow only in the absence of air, they are harmless on fresh foods. Most bacteria, yeasts, and molds are difficult to remove from food surfaces. Washing fresh food reduces their numbers only slightly. Peeling root crops, underground stem crops, and tomatoes reduces their numbers greatly. Blanching also helps, but the vital controls are the method of canning and use of the recommended research-based processing times. These processing times ensure destruction of the largest expected number of heat-resistant microorganisms in homecanned foods.

Properly sterilized canned food will be free of spoilage if lids seal and jars are stored below 95°F. Storing jars at 50 to 70°F enhances retention of quality.

## Food Acidity and Processing Methods

Whether food should be processed in a pressure canner or boiling-water canner to control botulism bacteria depends on the acidity in the food. Acidity may be natural, as in most fruits, or added, as in pickled food. Low-acid canned foods contain too little acidity to prevent the growth of these bacteria. Other foods may contain enough acidity to block their growth or to destroy them rapidly when heated. The term "pH" is a measure of acidity: The lower its value, the more acidic the food. The acidity level in foods can be increased by adding lemon juice, citric acid, or vinegar.

Low-acid foods have pH values higher than 4.6. They include red meats, seafood, poultry, milk, and all fresh vegetables except for most tomatoes. Most products that are mixtures of low-acid and acid foods also have pH values above 4.6 unless their ingredients include enough lemon juice, citric acid, or vinegar to make them acid foods. Acid foods have a pH of 4.6 or lower. They include fruits, pickles, sauerkraut, jams, jellies, marmalade, and fruit butters.

Although tomatoes usually are considered an acid food, some are now known to have pH values slightly above 4.6. Figs also have pH values slightly above 4.6. Therefore, if they are to be canned as acid foods, these products must be acidified to a pH of 4.6 or lower with lemon juice or citric acid. Properly acidified tomatoes and figs are acid foods and can be safely processed in a boiling-water canner. Botulinum spores are very hard to destroy at boiling water temperatures; the higher the canner temperature, the more easily they are destroyed. Therefore, all low-acid foods should be sterilized at temperatures of 240 to 250°F, attainable with pressure canners operated at 10 to 15 PSIG. (PSIG means pounds per square inch of pressure as measured by a gauge.) At these temperatures, the time needed to destroy bacteria in low-acid canned foods ranges from 20 to 100 minutes. The exact time depends on the kind of food being canned, the way it is packed into jars, and the size of jars. The time needed to safely process low-acid foods in boiling water ranges from 7 to 11 hours; the time needed to process acid foods in boiling water varies from 5 to 85 minutes.

Label your jars after processing with the contents and the date.

## Know Your Altitude

It is important to know your approximate elevation or altitude above sea level in order to determine a safe processing time for canned foods. Since the boiling temperature of liquid is lower at higher elevations, it is critical that additional time be given for the safe processing of foods at altitudes above sea level.

## What Not to Do

Open-kettle canning and the processing of freshly filled jars in conventional ovens, microwave ovens, and dishwashers are not recommended because these practices do not prevent all risks of spoilage. Steam canners are not recommended because processing times for use with current models have not been adequately researched. Because steam canners may not heat foods in the same manner as boiling-water canners, their use with boiling water processing times may result in spoilage.

So-called canning powders are useless as preservatives and do not replace the need for proper heat processing. It is not recommended that pressures in excess of 15 PSIG be applied when using new pressure canning equipment.

## Ensuring High-Quality Canned Foods

Examine food carefully for freshness and wholesomeness. Discard diseased and moldy food. Trim small diseased lesions or spots from food. Can fruits and vegetables picked from your garden or purchased from nearby producers when the products are at their peak of quality—within 6 to 12 hours after harvest for most vegetables. However, apricots, nectarines, peaches, pears, and plums should be ripened one or more days between harvest and canning. If you must delay the canning of other fresh produce, keep it in a shady, cool place. Fresh, home-slaughtered red meats and poultry should be chilled and canned without delay. Do not can meat from sickly or diseased animals. Put fish and seafood on ice after harvest, eviscerate immediately, and can them within two days.

## Maintaining Color and Flavor in Canned Food

To maintain good natural color and flavor in stored canned food, you must:

- Remove oxygen from food tissues and jars,
- Quickly destroy the food enzymes, and
- Obtain high jar vacuums and airtight jar seals. Follow these guidelines to ensure that your canned foods retain optimal colors and flavors during processing and storage:
- Use only high-quality foods that are at the proper maturity and are free of diseases and bruises.
- Use the hot-pack method, especially with acid foods to be processed in boiling water.

- Don't unnecessarily expose prepared foods to air; can them as soon as possible.
- While preparing a canner load of jars, keep peeled, halved, quartered, sliced or diced apples, apricots, nectarines, peaches, and pears in a solution of 3 grams (3,000 milligrams) ascorbic acid to 1 gallon of cold water. This procedure is also useful in maintaining the natural color of mushrooms and potatoes and for preventing stem-end discoloration in cherries and grapes.

You can get ascorbic acid in several forms:

*Pure powdered form*—Seasonally available among canning supplies in supermarkets. One level teaspoon of pure powder weighs about 3 grams. Use 1 teaspoon per gallon of water as a treatment solution.

*Vitamin C tablets*—Economical and available yearround in many stores. Buy 500-milligram tablets; crush and dissolve six tablets per gallon of water as a treatment solution.

*Commercially prepared mixes of ascorbic and citric acid*— Seasonally available among canning supplies in supermarkets. Sometimes citric acid powder is sold in supermarkets, but it is less effective in controlling discoloration. If you choose to use these products, follow the manufacturer's directions.

- Fill hot foods into jars and adjust headspace as specified in recipes.
- Tighten screw bands securely, but if you are especially strong, not as tightly as possible.
- Process and cool jars.
- Store the jars in a relatively cool, dark place, preferably between 50 and 70°F.
- Can no more food than you will use within a year.

## Advantages of Hot Packing

Many fresh foods contain from 10 percent to more than 30 percent air. The length of time that food will last at premium quality depends on how much air is removed from the food before jars are sealed. The more air that is removed, the higher the quality of the canned product.

Raw packing is the practice of filling jars tightly with freshly prepared but unheated food. Such foods, especially fruit, will float in the jars. The entrapped air in and around the food may cause discoloration within two to three months of storage. Raw packing is more suitable for vegetables processed in a pressure canner. Hot packing is the practice of heating freshly prepared food to boiling, simmering it three to five minutes, and promptly filling jars loosely with the boiled food. Hot packing is the best way to remove air and is the preferred pack style for foods processed in a boiling-water canner. At first, the color of hot-packed foods may appear no better than that of raw-packed foods, but within a short storage period, both color and flavor of hot-packed foods will be superior. Whether food has been hot packed or raw packed, the juice, syrup, or water to be added to the foods should be heated to boiling before it is added to the jars. This practice helps to remove air from food tissues, shrinks food, helps keep the food from floating in the jars, increases vacuum in sealed jars, and improves shelf life. Preshrinking food allows you to add more food to each jar. Controlling Headspace The unfilled space above the food in a jar and below its lid is termed headspace. It is best to leave a ¼-inch headspace for jams and jellies, ½-inch for fruits and tomatoes to be processed in boiling water, and from 1 to 1½ inches in low-acid foods to be processed in a pressure canner. This space is needed for expansion of food as jars are processed and for forming vacuums in cooled jars.

The extent of expansion is determined by the air content in the food and by the processing temperature. Air expands greatly when heated to high temperatures—the higher the temperature, the greater the expansion. Foods expand less than air when heated.

## Jars and Lids

Food may be canned in glass jars or metal containers. Metal containers can be used only once. They require special sealing equipment and are much more costly than jars. Mason-type jars designed for home canning are ideal for preserving food by pressure or boilingwater canning.

Regular and wide-mouthed threaded mason jars with self-sealing lids are the best choices. They are available in half-pint, pint, 1.-pint, and quart sizes. The standard jar mouth opening is about 2 3/8 inches. Wide-mouthed jars have openings of about 3 inches, making them more easily filled and emptied. Regular-mouthed decorative jelly jars are available in 8-ounce and 12-ounce sizes. With careful use and handling, mason jars may be reused many times, requiring only new lids each time. When lids are used properly, jar seals and vacuums are excellent.

## Jar Cleaning

Before reuse, wash empty jars in hot water with detergent and rinse well by hand, or wash in a dishwasher. Rinse thoroughly, as detergent residue may cause unnatural flavors and colors. Scale or hard-water films on jars are easily removed by soaking jars for several hours in a solution containing 1 cup of vinegar (5 percent acid) per gallon of water.

## Sterilization of Empty Jars

Use sterile jars for all jams, jellies, and pickled products processed less than 10 minutes. To sterilize empty jars, put them right side up on the rack in a boiling-water canner. Fill the canner and jars with hot (not boiling) water to 1 inch above the tops of the jars. Boil for 10 minutes. Remove and drain hot, sterilized jars one at a time. Save the hot water for processing filled jars. Fill jars with food, add lids, and tighten screw bands. Empty jars used for vegetables, meats, and fruits to be processed in a pressure canner need not be sterilized beforehand. It is also unnecessary to sterilize jars for fruits, tomatoes, and pickled or fermented foods that will be processed 10 minutes or longer in a boiling-water canner.

## Lid Selection, Preparation, and Use

The common self-sealing lid consists of a flat metal lid held in place by a metal screw band during processing. The flat lid is crimped around its bottom edge to form a trough, which is filled with a colored gasket material.

When jars are processed, the lid gasket softens and flows slightly to cover the jar-sealing surface, yet allows air to escape from the jar. The gasket then forms an airtight seal as the jar cools. Gaskets in unused lids work well for at least five years from date of manufacture. The gasket material in older, unused lids may fail to seal on jars. It is best to buy only the quantity of lids you will use in a year. To ensure a good seal, carefully follow the manufacturer's directions in preparing lids for use. Examine all metal lids carefully. Do not use old, dented, or deformed lids or lids with gaps or other defects in the sealing gasket.

After filling jars with food, release air bubbles by inserting a flat, plastic (not metal) spatula between the food and the jar. Slowly turn the jar and move the spatula up and down to allow air bubbles to escape. Adjust the headspace and then clean the jar rim (sealing surface) with a dampened paper towel. Place the lid, gasket down, onto the cleaned jar-sealing surface. Uncleaned jar-sealing surfaces may cause seal failures. Then fit the metal screw band over the flat lid. Follow the manufacturer's guidelines enclosed with or on the box for tightening the jar lids properly.

- If screw bands are too tight, air cannot vent during processing, and food will discolor during storage. Overtightening also may cause lids to buckle and jars to break, especially with rawpacked, pressure-processed food.

- If screw bands are too loose, liquid may escape from jars during processing, seals may fail, and the food will need to be reprocessed. Do not retighten lids after processing jars. As jars cool, the contents in the jar contract, pulling the self-sealing lid firmly against the jar to form a high vacuum. Screw bands are not needed on stored jars. They can be removed easily after jars are cooled. When removed, washed, dried, and stored in a dry area, screw bands may be used many times. If left on stored jars, they become difficult to remove, often rust, and may not work properly again.

## Selecting the Correct Processing Time

When food is canned in boiling water, more processing time is needed for most raw-packed foods and for quart jars than is needed for hot-packed foods and pint jars. To destroy microorganisms in acid foods processed in a boiling-water canner, you must:

- Process jars for the correct number of minutes in boiling water.
- Cool the jars at room temperature. To destroy microorganisms in low-acid foods processed with a pressure canner, you must:
- Process the jars for the correct number of minutes at 240°F (10 PSIG) or 250°F (15 PSIG).

- Allow canner to cool at room temperature until it is completely depressurized. The food may spoil if you fail to use the proper processing times, fail to vent steam from canners properly, process at lower pressure than specified, process for fewer minutes than specified, or cool the canner with water. Processing times for haft-pint and pint jars are the same, as are times for 1–2 pint and quart jars. For some products, you have a choice of processing at 5, 10, or 15 PSIG. In these cases, choose the canner pressure (PSIG) you wish to use and match it with your pack style (raw or hot) and jar size to find the correct processing time.

## Recommended Canners

There are two main types of canners for heat-processing home-canned food: boiling-water canners and pressure canners. Most are designed to hold seven one-quart jars or eight to nine one-pint jars. Small pressure canners hold four one-quart jars; some large pressure canners hold eighteen one-pint jars in two layers but hold only seven quart jars. Pressure saucepans with smaller volume capacities are not recommended for use in canning. Treat small pressure canners the same as standard larger canners; they should be vented using the typical venting procedures. Low-acid foods must be processed in a pressure canner to be free of botulism risks. Although pressure canners also may be used for processing acid foods, boiling-water canners are recommended because they are faster. A pressure canner would require from 55 to 100 minutes to can a load of jars; the total time for canning most acid foods in boiling water varies from 25 to 60 minutes. A boiling-water canner loaded with filled jars requires about 20 to 30 minutes of heating before its water begins to boil. A loaded pressure canner requires about 12 to 15 minutes of heating before it begins to vent, another 10 minutes to vent the canner, another 5 minutes to pressurize the canner, another 8 to 10 minutes to process the acid food, and, finally, another 20 to 60 minutes to cool the canner before removing jars.

## Boiling-Water Canners

These canners are made of aluminum or porcelain-covered steel. They have removable perforated racks and fitted lids. The canner must be deep enough so that at least 1 inch of briskly boiling water will cover the tops of jars during processing. Some boiling-water canners do not have flat bottoms. A flat bottom must be used on an electric range. Either a flat or ridged bottom can be used on a gas burner. To ensure uniform processing of all jars with an electric range, the canner should be no more than 4 inches wider in diameter than the element on which it is heated.

### Using a Boiling-Water Canner

Follow these steps for successful boiling-water canning:

1. Fill the canner halfway with water.

2. Preheat water to 140°F for raw-packed foods and to 180°F for hot-packed foods.

3. Load filled jars, fitted with lids, into the canner rack and use the handles to lower the rack into the water; or fill the canner, one jar at a time, with a jar lifter.

4. Add more boiling water, if needed, so the water level is at least 1 inch above jar tops.

5. Turn heat to its highest position until water boils vigorously.

6. Set a timer for the minutes required for processing the food.

7. Cover with the canner lid and lower the heat setting to maintain a gentle boil throughout the processing time.

8. Add more boiling water, if needed, to keep the water level above the jars.

9. When jars have been boiled for the recommended time, turn off the heat and remove the canner lid.

10. Using a jar lifter, remove the jars and place them on a towel, leaving at least 1 inch of space between the jars during cooling.

## Pressure Canners

Pressure canners for use in the home have been extensively redesigned in recent years. Models made before the 1970s were heavy-walled kettles with clamp-on lids.

They were fitted with a dial gauge, a vent port in the form of a petcock or counterweight, and a safety fuse.

Modern pressure canners are lightweight, thinwalled kettles; most have turn-on lids. They have a jar rack, gasket, dial or weighted gauge, an automatic vent or cover lock, a vent port (steam vent) that is closed with a counterweight or weighted gauge, and a safety fuse.

Pressure does not destroy microorganisms, but high temperatures applied for a certain period of time do.

The success of destroying all microorganisms capable of growing in canned food is based on the temperature obtained in pure steam, free of air, at sea level. At sea level, a canner operated at a gauge pressure of 10 pounds provides an internal temperature of 240°F.

Air trapped in a canner lowers the inside temperature and results in under-processing. The highest volume of air trapped in a canner occurs in processing raw-packed foods in dial-gauge canners. These canners do not vent air during processing. To be safe, all types of pressure canners must be vented 10 minutes before they are pressurized.

To vent a canner, leave the vent port uncovered on newer models or manually open petcocks on some older models. Heating the filled canner with its lid locked into place boils water and generates steam that escapes through the petcock or vent port. When steam first escapes, set a timer for 10 minutes. After venting 10 minutes,

close the petcock or place the counterweight or weighted gauge over the vent port to pressurize the canner.

Weighted-gauge models exhaust tiny amounts of air and steam each time their gauge rocks or jiggles during processing. The sound of the weight rocking or jiggling indicates that the canner is maintaining the recommended pressure and needs no further attention until the load has been processed for the set time. Weighted-gauge canners cannot correct precisely for higher altitudes, and at altitudes above 1,000 feet must be operated at a pressure of 15. Check dial gauges for accuracy before use each year and replace if they read high by more than 1 pound at 5, 10, or 15 pounds of pressure. Low readings cause overprocessing and may indicate that the accuracy of the gauge is unpredictable. If a gauge is consistently low, you may adjust the processing pressure. For example, if the directions call for 12 pounds of pressure and your dial gauge has tested 1 pound low, you can safely process at 11 pounds of pressure. If the gauge is more than 2 pounds low, it is unpredictable, and it is best to replace it. Gauges may be checked at most USDA county extension offices, which are located in every state across the country. To find one near you, visit www.csrees.usda.gov. Handle gaskets of canner lids carefully and clean them according to the manufacturer's directions. Nicked or dried gaskets will allow steam leaks during pressurization of canners. Gaskets of older canners may need to be lightly coated with vegetable oil once per year, but newer models are pre-lubricated. Check your canner's instructions. Lid safety fuses are thin, metal inserts or rubber plugs designed to relieve excessive pressure from the canner. Do not pick at or scratch fuses while cleaning lids. Use only canners that have Underwriter's Laboratory (UL) approval to ensure their safety.

Replacement gauges and other parts for canners are often available at stores offering canner equipment or from canner manufacturers. To order parts, list canner model number and describe the parts needed.

**Using a Pressure Canner**
Follow these steps for successful pressure canning:

1. Put 2 to 3 inches of hot water in the canner. Place filled jars on the rack, using a jar lifter. Fasten canner lid securely.
2. Open petcock or leave weight off vent port. Heat at the highest setting until steam flows from the petcock or vent port.
3. Maintain high heat setting, exhaust steam 10 minutes, and then place weight on vent port or close petcock. The canner will pressurize during the next three to five minutes.
4. Start timing the process when the pressure reading on the dial gauge indicates that the recommended pressure has been reached or when the weighted gauge begins to jiggle or rock.

Using a pressure canner.

5. Regulate heat under the canner to maintain a steady pressure at or slightly above the correct gauge pressure. Quick and large pressure variations during processing may cause unnecessary liquid losses from jars. Weighted gauges on Mirro canners should jiggle about two or three times per minute. On Presto canners, they should rock slowly throughout the process. When processing time is completed, turn off the heat, remove the canner from heat if possible, and let the canner depressurize. Do not force-cool the canner. If you cool it with cold running water in a sink or open the vent port before the canner depressurizes by itself, liquid will spurt from the jars, causing low liquid levels and jar seal failures. Forcecooling also may warp the canner lid of older model canners, causing steam leaks.

Depressurization of older models should be timed. Standard size heavy-walled canners require about 30 minutes when loaded with pints and 45 minutes with quarts. Newer thin-walled canners cool more rapidly and are equipped with vent locks. These canners are depressurized when their vent lock piston drops to a normal position.

1. After the vent port or petcock has been open for two minutes, unfasten the lid and carefully remove it. Lift the lid away from you so that the steam does not burn your face.

2. Remove jars with a lifter, and place on towel or cooling rack, if desired.

## Cooling Jars

Cool the jars at room temperature for 12 to 24 hours. Jars may be cooled on racks or towels to minimize heat damage to counters. The food level and liquid volume of raw-packed jars will be noticeably lower after cooling because air is exhausted during processing, and food shrinks. If a jar loses excessive liquid during processing, do not open it to add more liquid. As long as the seal is good, the product is still usable.

### Testing Jar Seals

After cooling jars for 12 to 24 hours, remove the screw bands and test seals with one of the following methods:

**Method 1**: Press the middle of the lid with a finger or thumb. If the lid springs up when you release your finger, the lid is unsealed and reprocessing will be necessary.

**Method 2**: Tap the lid with the bottom of a teaspoon. If it makes a dull sound, the lid is not sealed. If food is in contact with the underside of the lid, it will also cause a dull sound. If the jar lid is sealed correctly, it will make a ringing, high-pitched sound.

**Method 3**: Hold the jar at eye level and look across the lid. The lid should be concave (curved down slightly in the center). If center of the lid is either flat or bulging, it may not be sealed.

## Reprocessing Unsealed Jars

**Using a pressure canner.** If a jar fails to seal, remove the lid and check the jar-sealing surface for tiny nicks. If necessary, change the jar, add a new, properly prepared lid, and reprocess within 24 hours using the same processing time. Another option is to adjust headspace in

Testing jar seals.

unsealed jars to 1½ inches and freeze jars and contents instead of reprocessing. However, make sure jars have straight sides. Freezing may crack jars with "shoulders." Foods in single, unsealed jars could be stored in the refrigerator and consumed within several days.

## Storing Canned Foods

If lids are tightly vacuum-sealed on cooled jars, remove screw bands, wash the lid and jar to remove food residue, then rinse and dry jars. Label and date the jars and store them in a clean, cool, dark, dry place. Do not store jars at temperatures above 95°F or near hot pipes, a range, a furnace, in an uninsulated attic, or in direct sunlight. Under these conditions, food will lose quality in a few weeks or months and may spoil. Dampness may corrode metal lids, break seals, and allow recontamination and spoilage. Accidental freezing of canned foods will not cause spoilage unless jars become unsealed and re-contaminated.

However, freezing and thawing may soften food. If jars must be stored where they may freeze, wrap them in newspapers, place them in heavy cartons, and cover them with more newspapers and blankets.

## Identifying and Handling Spoiled Canned Food

Growth of spoilage bacteria and yeast produces gas, which pressurizes the food, swells lids, and breaks jar seals. As each stored jar is selected for use, examine its lid for tightness and vacuum. Lids with concave centers have good seals. Next, while holding the jar upright at eye level, rotate the jar and examine its outside surface for streaks of dried food originating at the top of the jar. Look at the contents for rising air bubbles and unnatural color. While opening the jar, smell for unnatural odors and look for spurting liquid and cotton-like mold growth (white, blue, black, or green) on the top food surface and underside of lid. Do not taste food from a stored jar you discover to have an unsealed lid or that otherwise shows signs of spoilage. All suspect containers of spoiled, low-acid foods should be treated as having produced botulinum toxin and should be handled carefully as follows:

- If the suspect glass jars are unsealed, open, or leaking, they should be detoxified before disposal.
- If the suspect glass jars are sealed, remove lids and detoxify the entire jar, contents, and lids.

## Detoxification Process

Carefully place the suspect containers and lids on their sides in an 8-quart-volume or larger stockpot, pan, or boiling-water canner. Wash your hands thoroughly.

Carefully add water to the pot. The water should completely cover the containers with a minimum of 1 inch of water above the containers. Avoid splashing the water.

Place a lid on the pot and heat the water to boiling. Boil 30 minutes to ensure detoxifying the food and all container components.

## Testing jar seals.

Cool and discard lids and food in the trash or bury in soil. Thoroughly clean all counters, containers, and equipment including can opener, clothing, and hands that may have come in contact with the food or the containers. Discard any sponges or washcloths that were used in the cleanup. Place them in a plastic bag and discard in the trash.

## Canned Foods for Special Diets

The cost of commercially canned, special diet food often prompts interest in preparing these products at home. Some low-sugar and low-salt foods may be easily and safely canned at home. However, it may take some experimentation to create a product with the desired color, flavor, and texture. Start with a small batch and then make appropriate adjustments before producing large quantities.

## Canning without Sugar

In canning regular fruits without sugar, it is very important to select fully ripe but firm fruits of the best quality.

It is generally best to can fruit in its own juice, but blends of unsweetened apple, pineapple, and white grape juice are also good for pouring over solid fruit pieces. Adjust headspaces and lids and use the processing recommendations for regular fruits. Add sugar substitutes, if desired, when serving.

# Old-Time Jerky Making

No matter what the main ingredient was or is—mastodon, elk, deer, African or Australian game, beef, fish, you name it—the old-fashioned method of making jerky has been around for a long time. Old-time jerky is still easy to make and still provides a great food source. In the old days, jerky making was very simple. The Native Americans simply cut thin strips of meat from game they had killed, then hung the strips over racks made of thin branches. In the dry Southwest and the Plains, meat dried quickly and easily with the use of this method. In the North, a small, smoky fire was often used to speed the drying process. Not only did this help the drying process, but it also kept away the blowflies. In the Northwest, smoke houses were constructed to protect the meat and aid in the drying process. If the Native Americans had access to salt, it was applied as well. The Native Americans also dried salmon, placing them on long racks as they removed fish from the fish wheels in the rivers. One of my favorite outdoor writers from earlier days was Colonel Townsend Whelen. This is his description of jerky making: Jerky is lean meat cut in strips and dried over a fire or in the sun. Cut the lean, fresh red meat in long, wide strips about half an inch thick. Hang these on a framework about 4 to 6 feet off the ground. Under the rack, build a small, slow, smoky fire of any nonresinous wood. Let the meat dry in the sun and wind. Cover it at night or in rain. It should dry in several days. The fire should not be hot enough to cook the meat since its chief use is to keep flies away. When jerked, the meat will be hard, more or less black outside, and will keep almost indefinitely away from damp and flies. It is best

The traditional Native American method of drying meat for jerky consisted of hanging meat strips over racks made of thin branches. A small smoky fire under the meat not only kept away insects but also added flavor and aided in the drying process.

eaten just as it is; just bite off a chunk and chew. Eaten thus, it is quite tasty. It may also be cooked in stews and is very concentrated and nourishing. A little goes a long way as an emergency ration, but alone it is not good food for long, continued consumption, as it lacks the necessary fat. Following is a campsite jerky technique I learned from an old-time Wyoming big-game guide. He described his method of making jerky to me as we chewed on some while glassing for elk: Cut the meat into strips, lay on a flat surface, and sprinkle both sides with black pepper. Lightly sprinkle with salt. Rub the salt and pepper well into all sides of the strips. Cut holes in the ends of the strips and thread white cotton or butchers cord through each hole, tying off into loops. Bring a pot of water to boil and immerse the strips into the boiling water for 15 to 20 seconds, remove, then re-dip. Hang the strips to dry. If the strips are hung outside in the sunshine, cover them with a cheesecloth tent to keep off insects and make sure they're high enough so dogs and other critters can't get to them. The strips can also be hung on clothesline in a

The old-time method of jerky making using only the sun has been a tradition in many cultures, including those of the American West.

cold, dry room. The strips should be dry in 4 to 5 days.

Another traditional method involves the use of curing salt, an old-time product. It's easy to make your own curing salt. Take 1 pound of canning salt, 6 ounces of Prague powder, 3 ounces of sugar, and 2 ounces of white pepper.

You can substitute brown sugar and black pepper. If you like hot jerky, add ground red pepper or cayenne pepper to suit. Mix all together and rub the mix

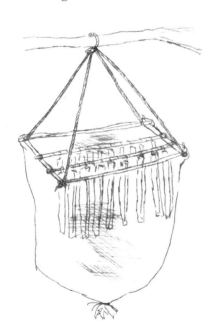

A bag or "tent" of cheesecloth was often used to help keep off insects while the jerky dried.

over all the meat slices. Leave in a cool place overnight, then dry. In damp weather, the slices can be dried in an oven or meat smoker. An old-time oven method is to lay strips in a glass dish, place a drop of Liquid Smoke over each strip, and use a pastry brush to evenly coat each strip. Sprinkle seasoning salt and seasoned pepper over the layer. Add a light sprinkling of sugar and garlic powder if you like garlic. Add another layer of strips, brush with Liquid Smoke, sprinkle with salt and pepper, then add another layer of strips. Continue adding and seasoning until the dish is full or you run out of strips. Cover the dish and set in a refrigerator or cool area (below 40°F) overnight. Dry in an oven set to 200°F or in a dehydrator.

## Pemmican

Made from jerky, pemmican was also a staple food of the Native Americans. Another of my favorite old-time writers, George Leonard Herter, in his *Professional Guides' Manual*, published in 1966,

One old-time method of preheating jerky strips was to place loops of string through holes cut in the ends of the strips. These were threaded onto a stick and dipped in a pot of boiling water.

stated: "Pemmican properly made is one of the finest foods that you can take into the wilderness or for a survival food in case of atomic bombing. Pemmican keeps indefinitely. Today, in our wonderful atomic age, pemmican is part of the survival ration of the newest United States Air Corps jet bombers." According to Col. Townsend Whelen, "To make pemmican you start with jerky and shred it by pounding. Then, take a lot of raw animal fat, cut it into small pieces about the size of walnuts, and fry these out in a pan over a slow fire, not letting the grease boil up. When the grease is all out of the lumps, discard these and pour the hot fat over the shredded jerky, mixing the two together until you have about the consistency of ordinary sausage. Then, pack the pemmican in waterproof bags. The Indians used skin bags."

The proportions should be about half lean meat and half rendered fat. The Native Americans also added fruits such as wild grapes, dried berries and beans, corn, herbs, and other items. These added vitamin C, which prevents scurvy as well as other nutrients and gave the pemmican different tastes. To use, place the dried block of pemmican in water and bring to a boil. Herter suggests dropping in some chili powder, soaking some beans overnight, adding them, and then "You will have an excellent chili con carne."

If you want to try making pemmican, the following is a recipe to make approximately 10 pounds.

5 lb. jerky
½ lb. brown sugar
½ lb. raisins or dried currents
4 lb. melted fat

Pound the jerky until it crumbles, and mix all ingredients together.

If you want to make a more modern version, first run the jerky through a food processor. Then, add ½ cup of raisins, ½ cup of salted peanuts, and ½ cup brown sugar for each pound of jerky. Other dried fruits such as cranberries can also be used. Sugar is optional, a matter of taste. The sugar can also be replaced with chocolate or any other flavor of chips (butterscotch, semi-sweet, milk chocolate, and so on). Press the mixture into a pan, packing tightly. Pour melted suet or other fat over the mixture, using only enough fat to hold the ingredients together. It's easy to get too much fat. A modern alternative to

Add raisins or other dried fruits and nuts to the pulverized jerky, then stir in the warm, melted fat, adding only enough fat to hold the mixture together. A butter-flavored shortening is a good alternative to bacon grease or rendered suet.

melted suet or bacon grease is a butter-flavored shortening. Allow the mixture to cool and then cut into squares for storage and use. To make a chili version, leave out the sugar and dried fruit and stir in chili seasoning with the ground jerky and fat. To use, add a chunk of the chili flavored pemmican to a pot of cooking beans. This makes a very hardy camp meal. For long-term storage, it's best to keep your jerky supply in the freezer and make pemmican just before consuming. Except for short periods of time, keep pemmican in the refrigerator, especially in warm weather.

# Outdoor Games and Fun

## Active Sports and Games. Evenings in Camp. Around the Campfire. Quiet Games, Songs, and Stories. Lighting Fires Without a Match.

Camp fun should have a place, and an important one, in your plans for the trail. For the time being the camp is your home and it should never be allowed to become dull for want of a little gayety and wholesome amusement. In a permanent camp there will be days when the entire party will be loafing and then is the time to start a frolic of some kind.

## Obstacle Races

Competitive sports are always entertaining, and races, of one kind or another, are the most exciting. The Boy Scouts have a race in which the competitors drop first their staffs, then their hats, their neckties, leggins, and, finally struggling out of the blouse of their uniform, they drop that

also. All this must be done while on the way and before they cross a given line. At the line they turn to go back over the course and, while running, take up their various belongings and put them on before they reach the home goal.

A race planned on these lines will be most amusing. A smooth course is not necessary, you probably won't have it at camp, and to get over the uneven ground, with the detentions of first dropping, then picking up the articles dropped, will add to the excitement of the sport. An entertaining variation of this will be to have those taking part in the race appear in impromptu costumes (worn over the ordinary dress) which they must remove piece by piece as they run and put the things all on again while returning over the course. Such hastily adjusted costumes cannot help but be funny.

## Medals

The winner of the race should be given a medal as a prize. The medal can be made of any handy material. A tin circular disk cut from the top of a tin can will do. Drive a nail through this tin medal near the edge and pass a string through the hole so that it may be hung around the neck of the winner. Or instead of giving a medal, the victor may be crowned, like the ancient Greeks, with a wreath of leaves.

## Blindfold Obstacle Walk

Another amusing camp sport is the blindfold obstacle walk. Place six or eight good-sized stones on the ground in a row, about 2 feet apart. The stones should be flat on top so that you can stand a tin cup filled with water on each stone. Let one member of the party make a trial trip over the cups, stepping between them as she passes down the row; then blindfold her, place two people as a guard, one on each side of her, to hold her hands and prevent a fall, and let them lead her to the end of the line of cups and tell her to go over it again.

The guard will steady her in case she stumbles but must in no way guide her course aright. The stepper will step high and be absurdly careful not to kick over one of the cups, for wet feet would probably be the result. Sometimes the stepper will leave the line of her own accord; sometimes her guard will purposely, and without her knowing it, lead her off the course and then her careful, high steps over nothing add to the fun of the onlookers.

Any number may take part in the sport, and in turn act as stepper. At the end a prize should be given by vote to the one who afforded the greatest amusement.

## Hunting the Quail

This is something like the old game of hide-and-seek, with which all girls are familiar, and it will not be difficult to learn. The players are divided into "hunter" and "quails." The hunter is "It," and any counting-out rhyme will decide who is to take that part. When the hunter, with closed eyes, has counted her hundred, and the quails have scurried away to their hiding-places behind trees, bushes, or rocks, the hunt begins, and at the same time begins the cry of the quails: "Bob-White! Bob-White! Bob-White!" These calls, coming from every direction, are very bewildering, and the hunter must be alert to detect the direction of one particular sound and quick to see the flight of a quail and catch her before she can reach the home goal and find shelter there. The first quail caught becomes hunter in her turn, and the noisy, rollicking game continues as long as the players wish.

## Trotting-Horse

Another romping game is called trooting-horse. It is warranted to put in circulation even the most sluggish blood and to warm the coldest feet, and it is fine for the almost frosty weather we sometimes have in the mountains.

The players form a circle in marching order; that is, each girl faces the back of another, with a space between every two players. Trotting-horse, the "It" of the game, stands in the center of the circle. When she gives the signal, the players forming the circle begin to run round and round, keeping the circle intact, while trotting-horse, always trotting, tries to slip between the ranks, which close up to prevent her escape. Trotting-horse must trot, not run. If she runs when making her escape she must go back into the ring and try once more to break away. When she succeeds fairly in getting through the ranks the player in front of whom she slips becomes "It" and takes the place of trotting-horse.

## Wood Tennis

Wood tennis is of the woods, woodsy. Green pine-cones take the place of balls; hands, of rackets; and branches, of tennis-net. Lay out a regular tennis-court by scraping the lines in the earth, or outlining the boundaries with sticks or other convenient

When Darkness Closes In

materials. Build a net of branches by sticking the ends in the ground, and collect a number of smooth, green cones for balls.

Wood tennis must, of necessity, differ somewhat from the regulation game. Since pine-cones will not bounce and there are no rackets for striking them, they must be tossed across the net, caught in the hands, and quickly tossed back. In other respects the rules of the established game may be used entire or simplified if desired.

## Around the Campfire

When darkness creeps through the woods, closing in closer and closer; when it blots out, one by one, the familiar landmarks and isolates the little camp in a sea of night, with the mutual wish for nearer companionship, we gather around the campfire, the one light in all the great darkness. We are grateful for its warmth, as the evenings are chill, and its cheery blaze and crackle bring a feeling of hominess and comfort welcome to everyone. If there are men in the party they light their pipes and then begin the stories of past experiences on the trail, which are of the keenest interest to all campers. These stories, told while one gazes dreamily into the glowing coals of the fire or looks beyond the light into the mysterious blackness of the forest, have a charm that is wanting under different surroundings. The stories are not confined to the men, for in these days when girls and women are also on the trail, they too can relate things worth the telling.

## Songs

Then come the songs. If there is someone in the party who can lead in singing, she can use a familiar air with a rousing chorus as a frame upon which to hang impromptu verses, made up of personalities and local hits. This is always fun and you are surprised how quickly doggerel rhymes suggest themselves when your turn comes to furnish a verse to the song.

The leader begins something like this, using, perhaps, the air and refrain of an old chantey or college song.

*Leader*
"I spotted a beaver,
But he wasn't very nye."

*Chorus*
"Don't you rock so hard!"

*Second Soloist*
"His fur was all ragged
And he had but one eye."

*Chorus*
"Don't you rock so hard.
Oh! You rock and I rock, and
Don't you rock so hard!
Everybody rocks when I rock, and
Don't you rock so hard."

*Third Soloist*
"You may laugh at the beaver,
But he's always up to time."

*Chorus*
"Don't you rock so hard!"
*Fourth Soloist*
"Oh, do drop the beaver,
And start a new rhyme."

*Chorus as before*
A song like this may go on indefinitely or until the rhyming powers of the party are exhausted.

## Bird-Call Match

In a camp where the members are all familiar with the calls of the various wild birds, a bird-call match makes a charming game when the party is gathered around the campfire. The leader begins by whistling or singing the call of a wild bird; if it can be put into words so much the better. For instance, we will take the first few notes of the wood-thrush, which F. Schuyler Mathews has put into notes and words as follows:

Wood-thrush.

Or the yellow-throated vireo, which he gives in this way:

Yellow vireo.

If the leader is correct the next player gives the call of another bird. When a player gives a bird call which is known to be incorrect—that is, absolutely wrong—and some one else can supply the proper rendering, the first player is dropped from the game just as a person is dropped out of a spelling-match when she misspells a word. If there is no one who can give the call correctly, she retains her place. This is excellent training in woodcraft as well as a fascinating game. Your ears will be quickened to hear and to identify the bird calls by playing it; and storing bird notes in your memory for use in the next bird-call match will become a habit.

## Vary the Game

You can vary this game by giving the calls of wild animals and the characteristic noises they make when frightened or angry.

Living even for a short time in the wild will develop unsuspected faculties and qualities in your make-up, and to perfect yourself in knowledge of the woods and its inhabitants will seem of the utmost importance. While learning the cries of birds and animals in sport, you will wish to retain them in earnest, and to enter the wilderness equipped with some knowledge of its languages, will open vistas to you that the more ignorant cannot penetrate

## A Happy and Sane Sunday in Camp

It is a good idea to carefully plan for your Sundays in camp, have every hour mapped out and never allow the time to drag. Make special effort and determine that the day shall be the very happiest day of each week, a day in which every one of the campers will be especially interested and will look forward to with genuine pleasure.

Sit down quietly and think it all out. You will want the day to differ from weekdays; you will want it filled with the real life, not half-life, the life only of the physical and mental, but the true, entire life for each camper; you will want to emphasize this higher, inner life, which is the spiritual.

To this end, when you arise in the morning, form the resolution that the day shall be a peaceful, enjoyable one for all the girls. When you take your morning plunge resolve that not only will you be physically clean, but you will also be both mentally and spiritually clean; then all through the day keep in mind that you *can* rule your thoughts and that you *will*, for power to do this will be given to you from the source of all power. Allow not one thought to remain which is not kind, friendly, cheerful, and peaceful. Should other thoughts intrude be firm and severe with them, have no mercy on them, talk to those thoughts as you would to robbers and thieves, tell them to go, *go*,GO, BEGONE, that you have nothing in common with them and you *command* them to *go*; then immediately busy yourself with active work, building the fire, cooking, tidying up the camp, etc.

Have your Sunday breakfast especially nice, with a few flowers, vines, leaves, or grasses on the table for a Sunday centerpiece, and keep the conversation on wholesome, happy topics.

After breakfast is over and the camp in order, with all the campers go for a short walk to some attractive spot either by the water or inland, and when the place is reached, having previously selected certain songs containing cheerful, religious elements, ask the entire camp to join in the singing. If one of the girls can sing a solo, let her do so, or it may be that two can sing a duet; then sit quietly while one of the group reads something helpful, interesting, and beautiful, which will be verses from the Bible probably, but may be one of Emerson's essays, or extracts from other thoughtful and helpful writers.

Close the simple exercises with another hymn and return to camp.

In addition to the camp dinner prepare some one dish as a pleasant surprise for the other girls. When dinner is over, the dishes washed, and camp again in order, the girls should have one hour of quiet, to read, write letters, sketch, or lie down and rest. Each camper should respect the demands of the hour for quiet and rest and *not talk*, but leave her companions to their own thoughts and occupations. If you should see your special friend seated off by herself, do not disturb her during the rest hour; it is each girl's right to remain unmolested at that time.

When the hour is up, the campers can each pack her portion of the evening meal, and in a moment's time be ready to hit the trail, or take the canoe for a paddle to the place previously selected where supper is to be enjoyed, and if the trip be on land, all may play the observation game while on the way.

## Observation Game

The leader counts 3 to the credit of the girl who first sees a squirrel, 2 for the girl who sees the second one, and 1 for every succeeding squirrel discovered by any member of the party. A bird counts 6, if identified 12. A wood-mouse counts 4, when identified 8. A deer 20, beaver 12, muskrat 8, chipmunk 10, porcupine 14, eagle 30, mink 16, rabbit 1. The player holding the highest record when reaching the supper grounds is victor. Keep your records tacked up in your shelter to compare with those you will make on the following Sunday.

In this game every time a player stumbles on the trail 5 is taken from her credit; if she falls, she loses 10.

It is a rule of the game that the winner be congratulated by each camper in turn, that she be crowned with a wreath of leaves, grasses, or vines and sit at the head of the table. Keep this game for your Sunday afternoons and play others during the week.

In the evening, as the campers sit quietly around the campfire, if the camp director will talk to the girls gently and seriously for a little while on some phase of their real life, the talk will be welcome and appreciated; then just before retiring all should stand while singing the good-night song.

It is hardly possible to present Sunday plans for each variety of camp and campers. The suggestions given are for helping girl campers to look upon Sunday in its true light, and to aid them in working out plans in accordance with the purpose of the day, that they may enjoy happy, sane Sundays in camp.

### All-Around Athletic Championship

This contest was instituted in America in 1884 to give athletes an opportunity to demonstrate their ability in all-around work. The contest is rapidly becoming the blue ribbon championship event in America for track athletes. The following ten events are contested for:

- 100-yard dash
- High jump
- Long jump
- Vault
- Throwing 16-pound hammer
- Putting a 16-pound shot
- Throwing 56-pound weight
- 120-yard hurdle race
- Half-mile walk
- One-mile run

The system of scoring in the All-around Championship is complicated. Each contestant has his score made up independently. The world's best amateur record is taken as a basis and 1,000 points are allowed for it. For example, the best record (amateur) for the 100-yard dash is 9⅗ seconds and for each ⅕ of a second more than this that the runner in the All-around Championship contest makes in his trial 42 points are deducted from this score. The same method is used in all the events. In the ten events the maximum score where the contestant equalled every world's record would be 10,000 points. The contest was won in 1909 by the remarkable score of 7,385 points.

## Archery

Archery is the art of shooting with a bow and arrow. It is especially adapted as a lawn game for ladies and gentlemen, but boys and girls can practice archery and become proficient with bows and arrows just as the Indians were or the boys in England in the days of Robin Hood. Of course the invention of gunpowder has practically done away with the bow and arrow either as a means of warfare or as a weapon to be used in the chase, but it is still used by savages.

The modern bow used in archery is made of lancewood or yew and for men's use is usually 6 feet long and for women and children 6 inches shorter. The strength or pull necessary to bend the bow, given in pounds, determines its classification. The arrows for men's use should be 28 inches long and for women 24 to 25 inches. The target is a straw-filled canvas disk painted in bright colors. There are usually five circles and the object in archery, as in shooting with firearms, is to hit either the centre ring or "bull's-eye" or as near to it as possible. In scoring, a shot in the inner gold center counts nine; red ring, seven; inner white ring, five; black ring, three, and outer white ring, one. Targets are of various sizes from 18 inches in diameter to 4 feet, depending on the distance of the range. A common distance will be from 50 to 100 yards.

Each archer should have some distinguishing mark or color on his arrows. Standard lancewood bows will cost two or three dollars, arrows from one to two dollars a dozen, and targets from two to five dollars each, with three dollars extra for the target stand.

In championship matches in archery the customary range for men is 60 yards with 96 arrows, and the same number of arrows at 50 yards for women. A recent match championship was decided for men with 90 hits and a total score of 458, and for women with 85 hits and a total score of 441.

## Association Football or Soccer

A game similar to rugby football except that it more closely resembles what its name implies and kicking predominates. A round, leather-covered ball is used and the game is considered to be much safer than our college football. Efforts consequently have been made to introduce the game into American colleges because of its less dangerous character. As there is practically no tackling or falling, the "soccer" uniform does not require the same amount of padding as a rugby player's uniform. The game is ordinarily played in running trousers with a full sleeved shirt and special shoes with leather pegs or cleats. The stockings are rolled down just below the knee. The association football goal net into which the ball is kicked is fastened to the ground and is made of tarred rope. Thus far, the game has not been very popular in America, although a number of exhibition match games have recently been played by visiting English teams which attracted considerable attention. As a game, soccer is fast and exciting, and splendid opportunities are given for team work; but for some reason it has not succeeded in displacing our American game of rugby, although possibly it is more interesting for the spectator.

## Badminton

An English outdoor game similar to lawn tennis but played with shuttlecocks. The net is 5 feet above the ground. The shuttlecock is a cork in which feathers have been inserted. The shuttlecock is served and returned as in tennis and either two or four may play. A badminton court is 30 feet wide and 44 feet long.

## Bandy

A game very similar to hockey, except that it is played out of doors instead of in a covered rink and a ball is used in place of a puck or rubber disk.

The name "bandy" is sometimes applied also to shinney or shinty and in England it is also applied to our American game of ice hockey.

## Baseball

The national game of America. The game is played by eighteen persons, nine on a side, called "nines." The positions are pitcher, catcher, first base, second base, third base, shortstop, right-field, left-field, center-field. The first six positions are called the in-field, and the last three, the out-field. The diamond or field where the game is played is a square plot of ground with sides 90 feet long. At each corner of the square are bases called first, second, third, and home plate. A game consists of nine innings, in each of which both teams have an opportunity to bat the ball and to score runs. The players bat in turn and attempt to reach the various bases without being put out by their opponents. Each year the rules are changed in some slight particulars, consequently a beginner in baseball must be thoroughly familiar with the rules of the game before attempting to play. The pitcher attempts to pitch the ball over the home plate to the catcher and the batsman endeavors to hit it. If the ball after being hit is caught by one of the opposing players, or if it is thrown to the base to which the batsman is running before he reaches the base, he is "out." Otherwise he is "safe" and will try to make the next base. If he completes the circuit of the four bases without being put out, he scores a run for his team or nine. When a player makes the entire circuit without being forced to stop for safety he makes a "home run." A hit which gains him a single base only is called a "base hit." Similarly if he reaches second base it is a "two-bagger," and third base, a "three-bagger."

After three players are put out, the other side has its "innings," and at the completion of nine full innings the side having scored the greatest number of runs is the winner. The game of baseball has become very scientific and the salaries of professional players are almost as high as those of the highest salaried men in business life.

The ball used in the game is made of the best all wool yarn with a horsehide cover and a rubber center. Baseball bats are usually made of ash.

## Basketball

A game of ball which may be played either indoors or out, but which is especially adapted to indoor play when weather conditions make out-door sports impossible. Two baskets suspended on wire rings are placed at the two opposite ends of a room or gymnasium and the players strive to knock or pass the ball from one to another on their own side and to throw it so that it will fall into the basket. It is not permissible to run with the ball as in rugby football. The ball used is round, but in other respects resembles the ball used in football. It is made in four sections of grained English leather and is inflated by means of a rubber bladder. The players use rubber-soled shoes with peculiar knobs, ridges, or depressions to prevent slipping. The conventional uniform is simply a gymnasium shirt, running trousers, and stockings which are rolled down just below the knees.

The game of basketball is especially adapted to women and girls and consequently it is played very largely in girls' schools and colleges.

Any level space may be used for basket ball. A convenient size is 40 by 60 feet. The baskets used for goals are 18 inches in diameter and are fixed 10 feet above the ground or floor. The official ball weighs about 18 ounces and is 31 inches in circumference. Five players constitute a team. The halves are usually twenty minutes, with a ten-minute intermission for rest.

It is not permissible to kick, carry, or hold the ball. Violation of a rule constitutes a foul and gives the opponents a free throw for the basket from a point 15 feet away. A goal made in play counts two points and a goal from a foul one point.

## Bean Bags

This game is known to everyone by name and yet its simple rules are often forgotten. A couple of dozen bean bags are made in two colors of muslin. The players stand in two lines opposite each other and evenly divided. At the end of the line is a clothes basket. The bags are placed on two chairs at the opposite end of the line and next to the two captains. At a signal the captains select a bag and pass it to the next player, who passes it along until finally it is dropped into the basket. When all the bags are passed they are then taken out and passed rapidly back to the starting point. The side whose bags have gone up and down the line first scores a point. If a bag is dropped in transit it must be passed back to the captain, who starts it again. Five points usually constitute a game.

***Best College Athletic Records***

These records have been made in the Intercollegiate contests which are held annually under the Intercollegiate Amateur Athletic Association of America.

| | | |
|---|---|---|
| 100-yard dash | 9⅘ seconds | made in 1896 |
| 220-yard dash | 21⅕ seconds | made in 1896 |
| 440-yard dash | 48⅘ seconds | made in 1907 |
| Half-mile run | 1 min. 56 seconds | made in 1905 |
| One-mile run | 4 min. 17⅘ seconds | made in 1909 |
| Two-mile run | 9 min. 27⅗ seconds | made in 1909 |
| Running broad jump | 24 feet 4½ in. | made in 1899 |
| Running high jump | 6 feet 3¼ in. | made in 1907 |
| Putting 16-pound shot | 46 feet 5½ in. | made in 1907 |
| Throwing the hammer | 164 feet 10 in. | made in 1902 |
| Pole vault | 12 feet 3¼ in. | made in 1909 |
| 120-yard high hurdle | 15⅕ seconds | made in 1908 |
| 220-yard hurdle | 23⅗ seconds | made in 1898 |
| One-mile walk | 6 min. 45⅖ seconds | made in 1898 |

## Blind Man's Buff

This game is played in two ways. In each case one player is blindfolded and attempts to catch one of the others and to identify him by feeling. In regular blind man's buff, the players are allowed to run about at will and sometimes the game is dangerous to the one blindfolded, but in the game of "Still Pon" the one who is "it" is turned several times and then announces, "Still Pon no more moving," and awards a certain number of steps, which may be taken when in danger of capture. After this number is exhausted the player must stand perfectly still even though he is caught.

## Bull In the Ring

In this game the players form a circle with clasped hands. To be "bull" is the position of honor. The bull is supposed to be locked in by various locks of brass, iron, lead, steel, and so on. He endeavors to break through the ring by catching some of the players off their guard. He will then run until captured, and the one who catches him has the position of bull for the next game. In playing, it is customary for the bull to engage one pair of players in conversation by asking some question such as, "What is your lock made of?" At the answer, brass, lead, etc., he will then make a sudden rush at some other part of the ring and try to break through.

## Call Ball

In this game a rubber ball is used. One of the players throws it against a wall and as it strikes calls out the name of another player, who must catch it on its first bounce. If he does so he in turn then throws the ball against the wall, but if he misses he recovers it as quickly as possible while the rest scatter, and calls "stand," at which signal all the players must stop. He then throws it at whoever he pleases. If he misses he must place himself against the wall and each of the others in turn has a free shot at him with the ball.

## Cane Rush

This contest is usually held in colleges between the rival freshman and sophomore classes. A cane is held by some non-contestant and the two classes endeavor by pulling and pushing and hauling to reach the cane and to hold their hands on it. At the end of a stated time, the class or side having the most hands on the cane is declared the winner. It is a very rough and sometimes dangerous game and in many colleges has been abolished on account of serious injuries resulting to some of the contestants.

## Canoe Tilting

This is a revival of the ancient game of tilting as described in "Ivanhoe," except that the tilters use canoes instead of horses and blunt sticks in place of spears and lances. The object is for the tilter to shove his opponent out of his canoe, meanwhile seeing to it that the same undesirable fate does not fall to his own lot. In singles each contestant paddles his own canoe with one end of his pike pole, but the sport is much greater if each canoe has two occupants, one to paddle and the other to do the "tilting."

## Cat

A small block of wood pointed at both ends is used in this game. The batter strikes it with a light stick and as it flies into the air attempts to bat it with the stick. If the cat is caught the batter is out. Otherwise he is entitled to a score equal to the number of jumps it will take him to reach the place where the cat has fallen. He then returns to bat again and continues until he is caught out.

## Counting-Out Rhymes

Almost every section has some favorite counting-out rhyme of its own. Probably the two most generally used are:

"My mother told me to take this one,"

and that old classic—

*"Ena, mena, mona, mite. Pasca, laura, bona, bite. Eggs, butter, cheese, bread. Stick, stock, stone dead."*

The object of a counting-out rhyme is to determine who is to be "it" for a game. As each word is pronounced by the counter someone is pointed at, and at the end of the verse the one last pointed at is "it."

### Court Tennis

This game, though very similar to rackets and squash, is more scientific than either. The court is enclosed by four walls. A net midway down the court divides the "service" side from the "hazard" side. The rackets used in court tennis have long handles and a large face. The balls used are the same size as tennis balls, but are heavier and stronger. In play, the ball rebounds over the court and many shots are made against the roof. While somewhat similar to lawn tennis, the rules of court tennis are extremely complicated. The game is scored just as in lawn tennis, except

that instead of calling the server's score first the marker always announces the score of the winner of the last stroke.

### Cricket

A game of ball which is generally played in England and the British provinces, but which is not very popular in the United States. There are two opposite sides or sets of players of eleven men each. At two points 22 yards apart are placed two wickets 27 inches high and consisting of three sticks called stumps. As in baseball, one side takes the field and the other side is at the bat. Two men are at bat at a time and it is their object to prevent the balls from being bowled so that they will strike the wickets. To do this a broad bat is used made of willow with a cane handle, through which are inserted strips of rubber to give greater spring and driving power. The batsman will either merely stop the ball with his bat or will attempt to drive it. When the ball is being fielded the two batsmen exchange wickets, and each exchange is counted as a run, and is marked to the credit of the batsman or striker. The batsman is allowed to bat until he is out. This occurs when the ball strikes the wicket and carries away either a bail, the top piece, or a stump, one of the three sticks. He is also out if he knocks down any part of his own wicket or allows the ball to do it while he is running, or if he interferes with the ball by any part of his person as it is being thrown, or if one of the opposing players catches a batted ball before it touches the ground, as in baseball.

When ten of the eleven men on a side have been put out it constitutes an inning, and the side in the field takes its turn at the bat. The game usually consists of two innings, and at its completion the side having scored the greater number of runs is the winner. The eleven positions on a cricket team are called bowler, wicket-keeper, long stop, slip, point cover-slip, cover-point, mid-off, long-leg, square-leg,

mid-on. The one at bat is, as in baseball, called the batsman. The two lines between which the batsmen stand while batting are called "popping creases" and "bowling creases."

## Croquet

A game played with wooden balls and mallets, on a flat piece of ground. The game consists in driving the ball around a circuitous course through various wire rings called "wickets" and, after striking a wooden peg or post, returning to the starting place. Any number may play croquet either independently or on sides. Each player may continue making shots as long as he either goes through a wicket, hits the peg or post, or hits the ball of an opponent. In this latter case he may place his ball against that of his opponent and, holding the former with his foot, drive his opponent's ball as far as possible from the croquet ground. He then also has another shot at his wicket.

A croquet set consists of mallets, balls, wickets, and stakes and may be bought for two or three dollars. Experts use mallets with much shorter handles than those in common sets. They are made of either maple, dogwood, or persimmon. In place of wooden balls, championship and expert games are often played with balls made of a patented composition. All croquet implements are usually painted in bright colors. The game of "roque" is very similar to croquet.

Croquet can be made more difficult by using narrow arches or wickets. Hard rubber balls are more satisfactory than wood and also much more expensive.

As a rule the colors played in order are red, white, blue, and black. According to the rules any kind of a mallet may be used, depending upon the individual preference of the player.

## Curling

An ancient Scotch game played on the ice, in which the contestants slide large flat stones, called curling stones, from one point to another. These points or marks are called "tees." In playing, an opportunity for skill is shown in knocking an opponent out of the way, and also in using a broom ahead of the stone as it slides along to influence its rate of speed.

At the present time the greatest curling country is Canada. Curling is one of the few outdoor games that are played without a ball of some kind.

## Dixie's Land

This game is also called "Tommy Tiddler's Land." It is a game of tag in which a certain portion of the playground is marked off as the "land." The one who is "it" endeavors to catch the others as they invade his land. When a player is tagged he also becomes "it," and so on until the game ends because all the invaders are captured. The game is especially interesting because of the variety of verses and rhymes used in various parts of the country to taunt the one who is "it" as they come on his land.

## Duck on a Rock

This game is also called "Boulder Up." It is not customary to "count out" to decide it. For this game usually some one suggests, "Let's play Duck on a Rock," and then every one scurries around to find an appropriate stone, or "duck." As fast as they are found the fact is announced by the cry, "My one duck," "My two duck," etc. The last boy to find a stone is "drake," or "it."

The drake is larger than the ducks and is placed on an elevated position such as a boulder. Then from a specified distance ducks attempt to hit the drake and to knock him from his position. If they miss they are in danger of being tagged by the drake, as it is his privilege to tag any player who is not in possession of his duck. If, however, the drake is knocked from his perch, the ducks have the privilege of rushing in and recovering their stones, but unless they do so before the drake replaces his stone on the rock they may be tagged. The first one tagged becomes "it" and the drake becomes a duck.

## Fat

This is the universal game of marbles. It is sometimes called "Yank," or "Knuckle There." A ring is scratched in the ground a foot or two in diameter. It is then divided into four parts by two lines drawn through the diameter. The first step is for each player to "lay a duck," which in simple language means to enter a marble to be played for. This is his entrance fee and may be either a "dub," an "alley," a "crystal," or sometimes a "real," although this is very rare as well as extravagant. About 10 feet from this ring a line is made called a "taw line." The first player, usually determined as soon as school is out by his having shouted, "First shot, fat!" stands behind the taw line and shoots to knock out a marble. If he is successful he continues shooting; if not he loses his turn and Number 2 shoots. Number 1 after his first shot from the taw line must then shoot from wherever his marble lies. If Number 2 can hit Number 1 he has a right to claim all the marbles that Number

1 has knocked out of the ring. In this way it is very much to the advantage of each player to leave himself as far from the taw line as possible.

### Feather Race

The contestants endeavor to blow a feather over a certain course in the shortest time. The rule is that the feather must not be touched with the hands. Out of doors this game is only possible on a very still day.

### Foot and a Half

This is a game of "Leap Frog" also called "Par" or "Paw." One of the boys is chosen "down," who leans over and gives a "back" to the rest, who follow leader, usually the boy who suggests the game. He will start making an easy jump at first and over "down's" back, then gradually increase the distance of the point at which he lands, and each of those following must clear this line or become "it" themselves. The leader must also surpass his previous jumps each time or he becomes "down"

himself. In this way the smaller or less agile boys have a more equal chance with the stronger ones.

### Football

The present game of football as played in American schools and colleges is a development of the English game of rugby. There are twenty-two players, eleven on a side or team. The game is played on a level field, at each end of which are goal posts through which the team having the ball in its possession attempts to force or "rush" it, while their opponents by various means, such as tackling, shoving, or blocking, strive to prevent the ball from being successfully forced behind the goal line or from being kicked over the crossbar between the goal-posts. A football field is 330 feet long by 160 feet wide. It is usually marked out with white lines 5 yards apart, which gives the field the name of "gridiron." The various positions on a football team are center rush, right and left guards, right and left tackles, right and left ends, quarter-back, right and left half-back, and full-back. As in baseball, the rules of football are constantly being changed and the game as played ten or fifteen years ago is very different from the modern game. The various changes in rules have been made with a view to making the game less dangerous to the players and more interesting to the spectator.

The principal scores in football are the "touchdown" and the "field goal." In a touchdown the ball is carried by one of the players and touched on the ground behind the opponents' goal line. In a field goal, or, as it is often called, "a goal from the field," the ball is kicked over the crossbar between the goal posts. In a field goal the player executing it must not kick the ball until after it has touched the ground. Such a kick is called a "drop kick" as distinguished from a "punt" where the ball is released from the hands and immediately kicked before touching the ground. A team in possession of the ball is allowed a certain number of attempts to advance it the required distance.

Each of these attempts is called a "down." If they fail to gain the necessary distance, the ball goes to their opponents. It is customary on the last attempt, or down, to kick the ball so that when the opposing team obtains possession of it it will be as far as possible from the goal line toward which they are rushing. In this play a "punt" is allowed. There are also other scores. A safety is made when a team is forced to touch the ball down behind its own goal line.

The ball used in American football is a long oval case made of leather and inflated by means of a rubber bag or envelope. The football player's uniform consists of a heavily padded pair of trousers made of canvas, moleskin, khaki, or other material, a jacket made of the same material, a tight-fitting jersey with elbow and shoulder pads, heavy stockings, and cleated shoes. Players will often use other pads, braces, and guards to protect them from injury. Football is usually played in the fall months after baseball has been discontinued on account of the cold weather. A full game consists of four fifteen-minute periods.

### Garden Hockey

This game is played between two parallel straight lines, 3 feet 6 inches apart and marked on the lawn with two strips of tape. At the opposite two ends of the tape are two goal posts 14 inches apart with a crossbar. The length of the tapes should be 36 feet when two or four players engage in the game, and may be extended for a greater number. The game is played with balls and hockey sticks. The game is started by placing the ball in the center of the field. The two captains then face each other and at a signal strike off. If the ball is driven outside the tape boundaries it must be returned to the center of the field opposite the place where it crossed the line. The object of the game is to score a goal through your opponents' goal posts as in ice hockey. If a player steps over the tape into the playing space he commits a foul. The penalty for a foul is a free hit for his opponents.

### Golf

A game played over an extensive piece of ground which is divided into certain arbitrary divisions called holes. A golf course is usually undulating with the holes laid out to afford the greatest possible variety of play. The ordinary course consists of either nine or eighteen holes from 100 to 500 yards apart. An ideal course is about 6,000 yards long. The holes which mark the termination of a playing section consist of tin cans 4 inches in diameter sunk into and flush with the level of the surrounding turf, which is called "the putting green." The game is played with a gutta-percha ball weighing about 1¾ ounces and with a set of "clubs" of various odd shapes and for making shots under various conditions. Usually a boy accompanies each player to carry his clubs. Such boys are called "caddies." The clubs are peculiarly named and it is optional with each player to have as many clubs as he desires. Some of the more common ones are called "driver," "brassie," "cleek," "iron," "mashie," "niblick," "putter," and "lofting iron."

The game, which may be played by either two or four players, consists in endeavoring to drive the ball over the entire course from hole to hole in the fewest possible number of strokes. At the start a player takes his position on what is called the "teeing ground" and drives the ball in the direction of the first hole, the position of which is shown in the distance by a flag or tin sign with a number. Before driving he is privileged to place the ball on a tiny mound of earth or sand which is called a "tee." The players drive in order and then continue making shots toward the hole until finally they have all "holed out" by "putting" their balls into the hole, and the lowest score wins the hole.

Golf is a game in which form is more essential than physical strength and which is adapted for elderly people as well as the young. The wooden clubs are usually made with either dogwood or persimmon heads and with split hickory handles or shafts. The handles are usually wound with a leather grip. Golf clubs of good quality will cost from two to three dollars apiece and a set for most purposes will consist of four to six clubs. The caddy bag to carry the clubs is made of canvas or leather and will cost from two dollars up. Standard quality golf balls will cost about nine dollars a dozen. Almost any loose-fitting outdoor costume is suitable for playing golf and the tendency in recent years is to wear long trousers in preference to what are known as "golf trousers."

A golf course—sometimes called a "links," from a Scotch word meaning a flat stretch of ground near the seashore—should be kept in good condition in order to enjoy the game properly. The leading golf clubs maintain a large force of men who are constantly cutting the grass, repairing damages to the turf, and rolling the greens. For this reason it is a game only adapted to club control unless one is very wealthy and can afford to maintain private links.

## Golf-Croquet

This game may be played either by two or four persons. Wickets are placed at irregular distances, and the object of the game is to drive a wooden ball 2¾ inches in diameter through these wickets. It may be played either as "all strokes," in which the total number of strokes to get through all the wickets is the final score, or as in golf, "all wickets," in which the score for each wicket is taken separately, as each hole in golf is played. The mallet used is somewhat different from a croquet mallet. The handle is longer and a bevel is made on one end to raise or "loft" the ball as in golf.

The size of a golf-croquet course will depend upon the field available. A field 200 yards long will make a good six-wicket course.

## Hab-Enihan

This game is played with smooth stones about the size of a butter dish. A target is marked on the sand or on any smooth piece of ground, or if played on the grass the target must be marked with lime similar to marks on a tennis court. The outside circle of the target should be 6 feet in diameter, and every 6 inches another circle described with a piece of string and two pegs for a compass.

The object of the game is to stand at a stated distance from the "enihan," or target, and to toss the "habs" as in the game of quoits. The player getting the best score counting from the inside ring or bull's-eye wins the game.

## Haley Over

The players, equally divided, take positions on opposite sides of a building such as a barn, so that they can not be seen by their opponents. A player on one side then throws the ball over the roof and one of his opponents attempts to catch it and to rush around the corner of the building and throw it at one of the opposing side. If he succeeds, the one hit is a prisoner of war and must go over to the other side. The game continues until all of one side are captured.

## Hand Ball

A game of ancient Irish origin which is much played by baseball players and other athletes to keep in good condition during the winter when most outdoor sports are impossible.

A regulation hand ball court has a back wall 30 feet high and 50 feet wide. Each game consists of twenty-one "aces." The ball is 1⅞ inches in diameter and weighs 1⅝ ounces. The ball is served and returned against the playing wall just as in many of the other indoor games and is similar in principle to squash and rackets.

## Hand Polo

A game played with a tennis ball in which two opposing sides of six players each endeavor to score goals by striking the ball with the hands. The ball must be struck with the open hand. In play, the contestants oppose each other by shouldering and bucking and in this way the game can be made a dangerous one.

The goal is made into a cage form 3 feet 6 inches square. At the beginning of the game the ball is placed in the center of the playing surface and the players rush for it. The umpire in hand polo is a very important official and calls all fouls, such as tripping, catching, holding, kicking, pushing, or throwing an opponent. Three fouls will count as a goal for the opponents.

## Hand Tennis

A game of lawn tennis in which the hand is used in place of a racket. A hand tennis court is smaller than a regulation tennis court. Its dimensions are 40 feet long and 16 feet wide. The net is 2 feet high. The server is called the "hand in" and his opponent the "hand out." A player first scoring twenty-five points wins the game. A player can only score when he is the server.

A foul line is drawn 3 feet on each side of the net, inside of which play is not allowed. In all essential particulars of the rules the game is similar to lawn tennis.

## Hat Ball

This game is very similar to Roley Boley except that hats are used instead of hollows in the ground. The ball is tossed to the hats and the first boy to get five stones, or "babies," in his hat has to crawl through the legs of his opponents and submit to the punishment of being paddled.

## High Kick

A tin pan or wooden disk is suspended from a frame by means of a string and the contestants in turn kick it as it is drawn higher and higher until finally, as in high jumping, it reaches a point where the survivor alone succeeds in touching it with his toe.

## Hockey

Hockey is usually played on the ice by players on skates, although, like the old game of shinney, it may be played on any level piece of ground. The hockey stick is a curved piece of Canadian rock elm with a flat blade. Instead of a ball the modern game of ice hockey is played with a rubber disk called a "puck." In hockey, as in many other games, the whole object is to drive the puck into your opponents' goal and to prevent them from driving it into yours. Almost any number of boys can play hockey, but a modern team consists of five players. Hockey skates are of special construction with long flat blades attached to the shoes. The standard length of blade is from 14½ to 15½ inches. They cost from three to six dollars. The hockey player's uniform is a jersey, either padded trousers or tights, depending upon his position, and padded shin guards for the goal tenders.

## Hop Over

All but one of the players, form a ring standing about 2 feet apart. Then by some "counting out" rhyme someone is made "it." He then takes his place in the center of the circle, holding a piece of stout string on the end of which is tied a small weight or a book. He whirls the string about and tries to strike the feet or ankles of some one in the circle, who must hop quickly as the string comes near him. If he fails to "hop over" he becomes "it."

### Hop Scotch

Hop scotch is a game that is played by children all over the world. A court about 20 feet long and 4 or 5 feet wide is drawn with chalk, coal, or a piece of soft brick on the sidewalk or scratched with a pointed stick on a piece of level ground. A line called the "taw line" is drawn a short distance from the court. The court is divided into various rectangles, usually eleven divisions, although this varies in different sections. At the end of the court a half circle is drawn, variously called the "cat's cradle," "pot," or "plum pudding." The players decide who is to be first, second, etc., and a flat stone or piece of broken crockery or sometimes a folded piece of tin is placed in division No. 1. The stone is called "potsherd." The object of the game is to hop on one foot and to shoot the potsherd in and out of the court through the various divisions until they are all played. He then hops and straddles through the court. Whenever he fails to do the required thing the next player takes his turn.

### Hunt the Sheep

Two captains are chosen and the players divided into equal sides. One side stays in the home goal and the other side finds a hiding place. The captain of the side that is hidden or "out" then goes back to the other side and they march in a straight line to find the hidden sheep. When they approach the hiding place their own captain shouts, "Apple!" which is a warning that danger is near. When he is sure of their capture or discovery he shouts, "Run, sheep, run!" and all the party make a dash for the goal.

*Intercollegiate Amateur Athletic Association of America*

This association controls the field athletic contests between the colleges known as the "Intercollegiates."

It is generally known as the I.C.A.A.A.A. To win a point for one's college in this contest is the highest honour that a track athlete may obtain. In these games, which take place annually, the following thirteen events are contested for:

- Mile run
- Shotput
- 440-yard run
- 120-yard hurdles
- 100-yard dash
- Running high jump
- Two-mile run
- 880-yard run
- 220-yard low hurdles
- Pole vault
- Broad jump
- 220-yard dash
- Hammer throw

*Ispy*

This game is sometimes called "Hide and Seek," One of the players is made "it" by any of the familiar counting-out rhymes. The rest then secure a hiding place while he counts fifty or one hundred. A certain tree or fence corner is considered "home." "It" then attempts to spy his hidden playmates in their hiding places and to run "home" shouting, "I spy" and their names. If the one discovered can get home before "it," he does so, shouting, "In free!" with all the breath that is left in him. The game is especially interesting just at dusk, when the uncertain light makes the "outs" brave in approaching home without detection. If "it" succeeds in capturing all the players the first one caught is "it" for the next game.

*Japanese Fan Ball*

This game is especially adapted for a lawn party for girls. Either Japanese fans or the ordinary palm-leaf fans will do for rackets. The balls are made of paper and should be 6 or 8 inches in diameter and in various colors. At opposite ends of a space about the size of a tennis court are erected goal-posts similar to those used in football, but only 6 feet above ground. These may be made of light strips of wood. There is also a similar pair of posts and a crossbar midway between the goals.

The game is played by two contestants at a time. Each takes an opposite end of the court and tosses the ball into the air. Then by vigorous fanning she endeavors to keep it aloft and to drive it over the opponent's goal-post. At the middle posts the ball must be "fanned" under the crossbar. If the ball falls to the ground it may be picked up on the fan and tossed aloft again, but it must not be touched by the hands. The winner is the one who first drives the ball the length of the court and over the crossbar.

### Kick the Stick

One player is chosen to be "it" and the rest are given a count of twenty-five or fifty to hide. A stick is leaned against a tree or wall and this is the home goal. As soon as the goal keeper can spy one of the players he runs in and touches the stick and makes a prisoner, who must come in and stand behind the stick. If one of the free players can run in and kick the stick before the goal tender touches it, he frees all the rest and they scurry to a place of hiding before the stick can again be set up and the count of twenty-five made. As the object of the game is to free your fellow-prisoners, the free players will attempt all sorts of ruses to approach the stick without being seen or to make a dash for it in hope of kicking it ahead of the goal keeper. The game is over when all the players are captured, and the first prisoner is "it" for the next game.

### King of the Castle

This can be made a very rough game, as it simply consists in a player taking a position on a mound or hillock and defying any one to dislodge him from his position by the taunting words:

*"I'm the King of the Castle, Get down you cowardly rascal."*

The rest try to shove him from his position and to hold it successfully against all comers themselves. The game, if played fairly, simply consists in fair pulls and pushes without grasping clothing, but if played roughly it is almost a "free-for-all" fight.

## Lacrosse

A game of ball played by two opposing teams of twelve players each. The lacrosse field is a level piece of ground with net or wire goals at each end. The players strive to hurl the ball into their opponents' goal by means of a lacrosse stick or "crosse." This is a peculiar bent stick with a shallow gut net at one end. It somewhat resembles a tennis racket, but is more like a snowshoe with a handle. The game originated with the Indians and is much played in Canada.

In playing, the ball must not be touched with the hands, but is hurled from one player to another by the "lacrosses" until it

is possible to attempt for a goal. It is also passed when a player is in danger of losing the ball.

Lacrosse sticks cost from two to five dollars each and are made of hickory with rawhide strings. The players wear specially padded gloves to protect the knuckles. The usual uniform for lacrosse is a tight-fitting jersey and running trousers.

## Lawn Bowls

This is a very old game and of great historic importance. The famous Bowling Green in New York City was named from a small park where the game was played by New Yorkers before the Revolution. The game is played with wooden balls 5 inches in diameter and painted in various gay colors. Usually lignum vitae is the material used. They are not perfectly round but either slightly flattened at the poles into an "oblate spheroid" or made into an oval something like a modern football. Each player uses two balls, which are numbered. A white ball, called a "jack ball," is then thrown or placed at the end of the bowling green or lawn and the players in turn deliver their balls or "bowl" toward the jack. The whole game consists in placing your ball as near to the jack as possible and of knocking away the balls of your opponents. It is also possible to strike the jack and to drive it nearer to where the balls of your side are lying. When all the players have bowled, the two balls nearest the jack each count a point for the side owning it. The game if played by sides is somewhat different from a two-handed contest. The main point first is to deliver the ball as near to the jack as possible and then to form a barrier or "guard" behind it with succeeding balls to block those of your adversaries. Sometimes the Jack is placed in the middle of the green and the teams face each other and bowl from opposite ends. A green is about 70 feet square with closely cropped grass. Four players form a "rink" and are named "leader," "second," "third," and "skip" or captain.

The position from which the balls are delivered is called the "footer." It is usually a piece of cloth or canvas 3 feet square.

### Lawn Bowling

This game is similar in every respect to indoor bowling except that no regular alley is used. A net for a backstop is necessary. The pins are set upon a flat surface on a lawn and the players endeavor to knock down as many pins as possible in three attempts. The scoring is the same as in indoor bowling. To knock down all ten pins with one ball is called a "strike," in two attempts it is a "spare." In the score, the strike counts ten for the player and in addition also whatever he gets on the next two balls. Likewise he will count ten for a spare, but only what he gets on one ball for a bonus. As a consequence the maximum or perfect score in bowling is 300, which is a series of ten strikes and two more attempts in which he knocks down all the pins. In lawn bowling the scores are very low as compared with the indoor game, where good players will often average close to 200 on alleys where they are accustomed to bowl. Lawn bowling is a different game from lawn bowls, which is described in a preceding paragraph.

### Lawn Hockey

This game is played on a field a little smaller than a football field, being 110 yards long and from 50 to 60 yards wide. The ball used is an ordinary cricket ball. The goals are two upright posts 12 feet apart and with a crossbar 7 feet from the ground. Eleven men on a side constitute a full team, but the game may be played with a fewer number. The positions are known as three forwards, five rushes, two backs or guards, and the goal tender.

The object of the game is very simple, being to drive the ball between your opponents' goals. The ordinary ice hockey stick will be satisfactory to play with. The principal thing to remember in lawn hockey is not to commit a "foul," the penalty for which is a "free hit" at the ball by your opponents. It is a foul to raise the stick above the shoulders in making a stroke, to kick the ball (except for the goal tender), to play with the back of the stick, to hit the ball other than from right to left, and any form of rough play such as tripping, pushing, kicking, or striking.

Lawn hockey is an excellent game and is really the old game of "shinney" or "shinty" played scientifically and with definite rules.

### Lawn Skittles

From a stout pole which is firmly fixed in the ground a heavy ball is suspended by means of a rope fastened to the top of the pole. Two flat pieces of stone or concrete are placed on opposite sides of the pole. The game is played with nine-pins, which are set up on one stone, the player standing on the other and endeavoring by hurling the ball to strike down a maximum number of pins. Usually he has three chances and the number of pins knocked down constitutes his score.

### Lawn Tennis

A game of ball played on a level piece of ground, called a court, by two, three, or four persons. When two play the game is called "singles," and when four play it is called "doubles." The game is played with a rubber ball, and rackets made by stringing gut on a wooden frame. The dimensions of a tennis court are 36 by 78 feet. In addition to this, space must be allowed for the players to run back, and it is customary to lay out a court at least 50 by 100 feet to give plenty of playing space. The court is divided into various lines, either by means of lime applied with a brush or by tapes. Midway between the two rear lines and in the center of the court a net is stretched, supported by posts.

In playing one of the players has the serve—that is, he attempts to strike the ball so that it will go over the net and into a specified space on the opposite side of the net. His opponent then attempts to return the serve—that is, to strike the ball either on the fly or the first bound and knock it back over the net somewhere within the playing space as determined by the lines. In this way the ball is volleyed or knocked back and forth until one of the players fails either to return it over the net or into the required space. To fail in this counts his opponents a point. Four points constitute a game except where both sides have obtained three points, in which case one side to win must secure two points in succession.

The score is not counted as 1, 2, 3, and 4, but 15, 30, 40, game. When both sides are at 40 it is called "deuce." At this point a lead of two is necessary to win. The side winning one of the two points at this stage is said to have the "advantage," or, as it is expressed, "vantage in" or "vantage out," depending upon whether it is the side of the server or his opponents, the server's score always being called first.

A set of tennis consists of enough games to permit one side to win six, or if both are at five games won, to win two games over their opponents.

## Last Tag

There are a great many games of "tag" that are familiar to boys and girls. One of the common games is "last tag," which simply means that a boy tags another and makes him "it" before leaving the party on his way home. It is the common boys' method of saying "good-bye" when leaving school for home. The principal rule of last tag is that there is "no tagging back." The boy who is "it" must not attempt to tag the one who tagged him, but must run after some one else. It is a point of honour with a boy not to be left with "last tag" against him, but he must try to run some one else down, when he is then immune and can watch the game in safety, or can leave for home with no blot on his escutcheon.

## LUGE-ING

A form of coasting very much practiced in Switzerland at the winter resorts where the sled used is similar to our American child's sled with open framework instead of a toboggan or the more modern flexible flyer which is generally used by boys in America.

## Marathon Race

A long-distance race, held in connection with the Olympic Games and named from a famous event in Greek history. The accepted Marathon distance is 26 miles, 385 yards. The race was won at the Olympic Games held in England in 1908 by John Hayes, an American, in 2 hours 44 minutes.

## Olympic Games

The Olympic Games are open to the athletes of the world. The following events are contested for:

- 60-meter run
- 100-meter run

- 200-meter run
- 400-meter run
- 800-meter run
- 1500-meter run
- 110-meter hurdles
- 200-meter hurdles
- 400-meter hurdles
- 3,200-meter steeplechase
- 2,500-meter steeplechase
- 4,000-meter steeplechase
- Running long jump
- Running high jump
- Running triple jump
- Standing broad jump
- Standing high jump
- Standing triple jump
- Pole vault
- Shot put
- Discus throwing
- Throwing 16-pound hammer
- Throwing 56-pound weight
- Marathon race
- Weight lifting, one hand
- Weight lifting, two hands
- Dumb-bell competition
- Tug-of-war
- Team race
- Team race 3 miles
- Five-mile run
- Throwing stone
- Throwing javelin
- Throwing javelin held in middle
- Penthathlon
- 1,500-meter walk
- 3,500-meter walk
- 10-mile walk
- Throwing discus Greek style

### Marbles

There is a large variety of games with marbles and the expressions used are universal. Boys usually have one shooter made from agate which they call a "real." To change the position of the shooter is called "roundings," and to object to this or to any other play is expressed by the word "fen." The common game of marbles is to make a rectangular ring and to shoot from a line and endeavor to knock the marbles or "mibs" of one's opponents out of the square. A similar game is to place all the mibs in a line in an oval and to roll the shooter from a distance. The one coming nearest to the oval has "first shot" and continues to shoot as long as he drives out a marble and "sticks" in the oval himself.

Reals are often supposed to have superior sticking qualities. Playing marbles "for keeps" is really gambling and should be discouraged. The knuckle dabster is a small piece of cloth or leather that boys use to rest the hand on when in the act of shooting. The best kind of a "dabster" is made from a mole's skin.

### Names of Marbles

The common marbles used by boys everywhere are called mibs, fivers, commies, migs, megs, alleys, and dubs. A very large marble is a bumbo and a very small one a peawee. Glass marbles are called crystals and those made of agate are called reals. The choicest real is supposed to be green and is called a "mossic" or "moss real."

### Mumblety Peg

This game is played with a penknife. A piece of turf is usually the best place to play. Various positions for throwing the knife are tried by each player, following a regular order of procedure, until he misses, when the knife is surrendered to the next in turn. When he receives the knife each player tries the feat at which he failed before. The last player to accomplish all the feats has the pleasure of "pulling the peg." The peg consists of a wedge-shaped piece of wood the length of the knife blade which is driven into the ground by the back of the knife and must be pulled by the teeth of the unfortunate one who was last to complete the necessary feats. The winner has the honor of driving the peg, usually three blows with his eyes open and three with them closed. If he succeeds in driving it out of sight the feat is considered especially creditable and the loser is greeted with the cry, "Root! Root!" which means that he must remove the sod and earth with his teeth before he can get a grip on the peg top. There are about twenty-four feats or "figures" to be gone through in a game of mumblety peg, throwing the knife from various positions both right and left handed. In each feat the successful result is measured by having the knife stick into the ground at such an angle so that there is room for two fingers to be inserted under the end of the handle without disturbing the knife.

## One Old Cat

This is a modified game of baseball that may be played by three or four. Generally there is only one base to run to, and besides the batter, pitcher, and catcher the rest of the players are fielders. Any one catching a fly ball puts the batter out and takes his turn at bat, or in another modification of the game, when one is put out each player advances a step nearer to batsman's position, the pitcher going in to bat, the catcher becoming pitcher, first fielder becoming catcher, and so on, the batsman becoming "last fielder."

## Pass It

This game may be played on a lawn. Four clothes baskets are required as well as a variety of objects of various sizes and kinds, such as spools of thread, pillows, books, matches, balls, pencils, umbrellas, pins, and so on. Two captains are chosen and each selects a team, which stands in line facing each other. Two of the baskets are filled with the various articles and these two baskets are placed at the right hand of the two captains. The empty baskets are on the opposite ends of the line. At a signal the captains select an object and pass it to the next in line. He in turn passes it to his left and finally it is dropped into the empty basket. If the object should be dropped in transit it must go back to the captain and be passed down the line again. Two umpires are desirable, who can report the progress of the game to their own side as well as keep an eye on their opponents.

## Pelota

A game similar to racquets, sometimes called "Jai-a-li," that is much played in Spain and in Mexico. The game is played with a narrow scoop-like wicker basket or racket which is fastened to the wrist. The players catch the ball in this device and hurl it with terrific force against the wall of the court. Pelota is a hard, fast game, and sometimes serious injuries result from playing it.

## Plug in the Ring

This is the universal game that boys play with tops. A ring 6 feet in diameter is described on the ground and each player puts a top called a "bait" in the center. The baits are usually tops of little value. The "plugger," however, is the top used to shoot with and as a rule is the boy's choicest one. As soon as the players can wind their tops they stand with their toes on the line and endeavor to strike one of the baits in such a way as to knock it out of the circle and still leave their own tops within the circle and spinning. If they miss, the top must be left spinning until it "dies." If it fails to roll out of the ring, the owner must place another bait top in the ring, but if it leaves the circle he may continue shooting. It is possible to play tops for "keeps," but, like marbles for "keeps," it should be discouraged, as it is gambling.

## Polo or Equestrian Polo

A game played on horseback, which originated in Eastern countries and was first played by the English in India. It has been introduced both into England and America. Polo is a rich man's game and requires a great deal of skill in horsemanship as well as nerve. A polo team consists of four men, each of whom must have a stable of several horses. These horses, or "polo ponies," are trained carefully, and a well-trained pony is as essential to good playing as a skilful rider.

The game is played with a mallet, the head of which is usually ash, dogwood, or persimmon, and has a handle about 50 inches long. The ball is either willow or basswood. The principle of the game is similar to nearly all of the outdoor games played with a ball: that of driving it into the opponents' goal, meanwhile preventing them from making a score on one's own goal.

*Potato Race*

In this game as many rows of potatoes are laid as there are players. They should be placed about 5 feet apart. The race consists in picking up all of the potatoes, one at a time, and carrying them to the starting point, making a separate trip for each potato. At the end of the line there should be a basket or butter tub to drop them into. The game is sometimes made more difficult by forcing the contestants to carry the potatoes on a teaspoon.

*Prisoner's Base*

Two captains select sides. They then mark out on the ground two bases, or homes. They also mark out two "prisons" near each home base. Then each side stands in its own home and a player runs out and advances toward the enemy's home. One of the enemy will then run out and endeavor to tag him before he can run back to his own base, and one of his side will try to tag the enemy, the rule being that each in turn must have left his home after his opponent. If a player is tagged, he becomes a prisoner of the other side and is put into the prison. The successful tagger may then return to Ids home without danger of being tagged. A prisoner may be rescued at any time if one of his side can elude the opponents and tag him free from prison. The game ends when all of one side are made prisoners.

*Push Ball*

A game usually played on foot but sometimes on horseback, in which the object is to push or force a huge ball over the opponents' goal line. A regulation "push ball" is 6 feet in diameter and costs three hundred dollars.

In push ball almost any number may play, but as weight counts, the sides should be divided as evenly as possible.

*Quoits*

A game played with flattish malleable iron or rubber rings about 9 inches in diameter and convex on the upper side, which the players endeavor to loss or pitch so that they will encircle a pin or peg driven into the ground, or to come nearer to this peg than their opponents. The peg is called a "hob." A certain form of quoits is played with horseshoes throughout the country districts of America. A quoit player endeavors to give the quoit such a position in mid-air that it will not roll but will cut into the ground at the point where it lands. The game is remotely similar to the ancient Greek game of throwing the discus. Iron quoits may be purchased for a dollar a set.

The average weight of the quoits used by experts is from seven to nine pounds each. Sixty-one points constitute a game. The distance from the peg shall be either 10, 15, or 18 yards. For a space 3 feet around the pin or peg the ground should be clay. In match games, all quoits that fall outside a radius of 18 inches from the center of the pin are "foul," and do not count in the score.

### Racquets or Rackets

One of the numerous court games similar to lawn tennis that is now finding public favor, but played in a semi-indoor court. A racquet court is 31 feet 6 inches wide and about 63 feet long. The front wall, against which the ball is served, has a line 8 or 10 feet from the floor, above which the ball must strike. The server, as in tennis, takes his position in a service box with a racket similar to a lawn tennis racket except that it has a smaller head and a longer handle.

Either two or four players may play racquets. A game consists of fifteen "aces," or points.

### Red Line

In this game, also called Red Lion, the goal must be a straight line, such as the crack in a sidewalk or the edge of a road. The one who is "it" runs after the rest as in tag, and when he has captured a prisoner he brings him into the "red line," and the two start out again hand in hand and another is captured, then three together, and two pair, and so on until all are prisoners. The first prisoner is "it" for the next game.

### Roley Boley

This game is also called Roll Ball, and is played by children all over the civilized world. A number of depressions are hollowed in the ground corresponding to the number of players and a hole is chosen by each one. A rubber ball is then rolled toward the holes, and if it lodges in one of them the boy who has claimed that hole must run in and pick up the ball while the rest scatter. He then attempts to hit one of the other players with the ball. If he succeeds a small stone called a "baby" is placed in the hole belonging to the boy struck. Otherwise the thrower is penalized with a "baby." When any boy has five babies he must stand against the wall and be a free target for the rest to throw the ball at.

### Roque

This game may be called scientific croquet. A roque mallet has a dogwood head 9½ inches long, with heavy nickel ferrules. Roque balls are made of a special composition that is both resilient and practically unbreakable.

A skillful roque player is able to make shots similar to billiard shots. The standard roque court is 60 feet long, 30 feet wide, with corner pieces 6 feet long. The playing ground is of clay and should be as smooth as it is possible to make it. A very light top dressing of sand is used on the clay. The wickets, or "arches," are driven into blocks of wood to secure firmness and buried into the ground with the top of the arch 8 inches above the surface.

The roque balls are 3¼ inches in diameter and the arches only 3½ wide, which gives an idea of the difficulty of playing this game. To be an expert requires an accurate eye and a great deal of practice.

There is a National Roque Association, and an annual

championship tournament is held to determine the champion. The home of roque is in the New England States.

### Rowing Record

The best amateur intercollegiate record for the eight-oared race of 4 miles is 18 minutes 53⅕ seconds, made by Cornell, July 2, 1901.

### Rubicon

This game may be played with any number of players, and is especially adapted for a school or lawn game. Two players are chosen as pursuers and the rest are divided equally and stand two by two facing each other in two columns. The two pursuers stand at the head of each column and face each other. When ready they say, "Cross the Rubicon," and at this signal the rear couple from each line must run forward and try to reach the rear of the other line. The pursuers must not look back, but as soon as the runners are abreast of them must try to tag them before they reach the place of safety. The captured runners become pursuers, and the one who was "it" takes his or her place at the rear of the other line.

### Sack Racing

A form of sport where the contestants are fastened in sacks with the hands and feet confined and where they race for a goal by jumping or hopping along at the greatest possible speed under this handicap. A sack race should not be considered one of the scientific branches of sport, but is rather to afford amusement for the spectators.

### Scotland's Burning

This game is based upon the song of the same name. The players form a ring, with three judges in the center. Each player with appropriate gestures in turn begins the song,

"Scotland's burning. Scotland's burning, Look out! Look out! Fire! Fire! Fire! Pour on water! Pour on water!"

The whole party are soon singing, but each four are singing

different words. The object of the judges is to detect someone in the circle either making gestures that are not appropriate to the words or to be singing out of order. The penalty is to turn around and sing with the back to the circle. The three who are facing in last then become judges.

### Skiing

This sport has recently received wide popularity in sections of the country where the winters make it possible. Skis—or, as they are sometimes spelled, skee—are a pair of flat runners from 5 to 10 feet long which are attached to the feet in such a way as to be easily cast off in case of accident. By means of skis a ski-runner may either make rapid progress over level snow or may coast down sharp declivities and make jumps of great extent.

Skis are usually made of ash and the standard lengths are from 6 to 8 feet. They cost from five to seven dollars a pair. In skiing it is customary to use a pair of steel-shod poles with leather wrist straps, but in ski-running or coasting the use of poles is very dangerous.

### Spanish Fly

In this game of leap frog various tricks are attempted by the leader, as in the game of "stump master." Each of the boys following is expected to do as the leader or to drop out and become "down" himself. "Torchlight" is to jump with one hand only, using the other to wave his cap as if it were a torch. In "hats on deck" each jumper in turn is supposed to leave his cap on "down's" back. Naturally the last one over may have a large pile of hats to clear. If he disturbs any of them or knocks them off, he is "it." "Hats off" means for each jumper in turn to take his own hat without knocking off any of the others. In all games of leap frog it is considered proper for the jumper to direct "down" to give him the kind of a "back" he desires. Consequently he will say high or low back, depending upon whether he wishes "down" to stand almost upright or to bend close to the ground.

## Squash

This game is similar to racquets, but is less violent or severe on a player. It is played in a court 31 feet 6 inches wide. The front wall must be 16 feet high. The service line above which the ball must strike on the serve is 6 feet from the floor. Below this line and 2 feet from the floor is the "tell tale," above which the ball must strike in play. A squash racket is similar to a tennis racket, but slightly smaller.

In squash, a game is "fifteen up." At the score of 13 a player may "set the score" back to 3 or 5, after which the player first winning either 3 or 5 points, or aces, as they are called, is the winner. The object of this is to endeavor to overcome the advantage that the server may have.

In a regulation squash court the spectators' gallery is above the walls of the court, and the game is played in the pit below the gallery.

## Stump Master

In this game one of the players is chosen master. It is usually the one who first suggests the game by saying. "Let's play stump master." He then leads the line of players, going through various "stumps," or, as we should call them now, "stunts," such as climbing fences and trees, turning somersaults, crawling through narrow places, or whatever will be difficult for the rest to copy. The game is capable of all sorts of variations.

## Suckers

This can scarcely be called a game, but the use of the sucker is so familiar to most boys that a description of it is surely not out of place in this chapter. A piece of sole leather is used, 3 or 4 inches square. It is cut into a circle and the edges carefully pared thin. A hole is made in the center and a piece of string or top twine is knotted and run through the hole. The sucker is then soaked in water until it is soft and pliable. The object of the sucker is to lift stones or bricks with it. This, too, is of special interest in New England towns, where there are brick sidewalks. The sucker is pressed firmly on a brick by means of the foot, and it will be found to adhere to it with sufficient force to lift it clear of the ground.

### Tether Tennis

This game has been developed out of lawn tennis. A wooden pole extending 10 feet above the surface is placed in a vertical position and firmly imbedded in the ground. The pole must be 7½ inches in circumference at the ground and may taper to the top. Six feet above the ground a black band 2 inches wide is painted around the pole. The court is a smooth piece of sod or clay similar to a tennis court, but a piece of ground 20 feet square is sufficient.

At the base of the pole a circle is described with a 3-foot radius. A line 20 feet long bisects this circle, and 6 feet from the pole on each side are two crosses, which are known as service crosses.

An ordinary tennis ball is used which has been fitted with a tight-fitting linen cover. The ball is fastened to the pole by means of a piece of heavy braided line. Ordinary heavy fish line will do. The ball should hang 7½ feet from the top of the pole or 2½ feet from the ground. Regulation tennis rackets are used.

The game consists in endeavoring to wind the ball and string around the pole above the black mark in a direction previously determined. The opponent meanwhile tries to prevent this and to wind the ball in the opposite direction by striking it as one would volley in tennis.

Each player must keep in his own court. The points are scored as "fouls." Eleven games constitute a set. A game is won when the string is completely wound around the pole above the black mark. The penalty for a foul, such as stepping outside of one's court, allowing the string to wind around the handle of the racket or around the pole below the black mark, provides for a free hit by one's opponent.

## Three-Legged Racing

A race in which the contestants are paired off by being strapped together at the ankles and thighs. Remarkable speed can be obtained by practice under this handicap. There are definite rules to govern three-legged races, and official harness may be bought from sporting goods outfitters. As a race, however, it is like sack racing, to be classed among the sports designed to afford amusement rather than as a display of skill.

## Tub Racing

These races are often held in shallow lakes. Each contestant sits in a wash tub, and by using his hands as paddles endeavors to paddle the course first. As a wash tub is not a particularly seaworthy craft, and spills are of frequent occurrence, it is well for the tub racers also to know how to swim.

## Volleyball

This game is extremely simple and may be played by any number of players, provided that there is space and that the sides are evenly divided. The best dimensions for a volley ball court are 25 feet wide and 50 feet long, but any square space evenly divided into two courts will do. The game consists of twenty-one points.

The ball is made of white leather and inflated with a rubber bladder. A net divides the two courts and is 7 feet high. The standard volley ball is 27 inches in circumference and weighs between 9 and 12 ounces.

The whole object of the game is to pass the ball back and forth over the net without permitting it to touch the floor or to bound. In this way it somewhat resembles both tennis and hand ball.

Volleyball is an excellent game for gymnasiums and has the decided advantage of permitting almost any number to play.

## Warning

The "warner" takes his position at a space called "home" and the rest of the players stand some distance from him. He then clasps his hands and runs out, trying to tag an opponent with his clasped hands. This would be practically impossible except that the players endeavor to make him unclasp his hands by pulling at his arms and drawing temptingly near him. As soon as he has tagged a victim he runs for home as fast as possible. If he himself is tagged before he reaches home he is out, and the tagger becomes "warner." If both the warner and the one tagged reach home safely they clasp hands, and finally the line contains all the players but one, who has the honour of being warner for the next game. The game receives its name from the call, "Warning!" which the warner gives three times before leaving home.

## Washington

In this game a player stands blindfolded and another player comes up and taps him. The one who is "it" then gives a penalty, such as "climb a tree or run to the corner and back," and then tries to guess who it was that tapped him. The one tapped must answer some question so that he may be recognized by his voice or laugh.

If "it" is correct in his guess, the player must do as directed, but if his guess is wrong he must do it himself. The result of this game is that the blindfolded player will measure the severity of his "forfeits," or "penalties," to his certainty of guessing correctly the name of the player.

## Water Polo

This game is played in a swimming pool. A white ball made of rubber fabric is used. The ball must be between 7 and 8 inches in diameter. The goals are spaces 4 feet long and 12 inches wide at each end of the tank and placed 18 inches above the water line. Six men on a side constitute a team.

It is a game in which skill in swimming is absolutely essential. It is also a very rough game. The player endeavors to score goals by swimming with the ball, and his opponents are privileged to tackle him and to force him under water or in other ways to attempt to secure the ball from him. Meanwhile the other players are blocking off opponents, and in general the game resembles a football game in its rudiments.

## Water Race
In this game the contestants run a race carrying a glass or tin cup full of water on top of the head, which must not be touched by the hands. The one finishing first with a minimum loss of water from his cup is the winner.

## Wicket Polo
A game played by two teams of four players each. The ball used is a regulation polo ball. A wicket polo surface is 44 feet square, in which sticks or wickets are set up. The object of the game is to knock down the wickets of one's opponents by a batted ball and to prevent them from displacing our own. A crooked stick 4 feet in length and a little over an inch in diameter is used. Each player has a fixed position on the field or surface.

## Wolf and Sheep
In this game "it" is the wolf. The sheep choose a shepherd to guard them. The wolf then secures a hiding place and the sheep and shepherd leave the fold and endeavor to locate him. When this is done the shepherd cries, "I spy a wolf!" and every one stands while he counts ten. Then the sheep and shepherd scatter for the fold, and if tagged before they reach it the first becomes wolf for the next game.

## Wood Tag
In this class are also "iron tag," "stone tag," and "tree tag." They are all simply the game of tag with the additional rule that when a player is in contact with iron, stone, trees, wood, and so on he is safe from being tagged by the one who is "it." The game of "squat tag" is similar, except that to be safe the one pursued must squat quickly on the ground before "it" catches him. In cross tag, "it" must select a victim and continue to run after him until someone runs ahead and crosses his path, when "it," who may be breathless by this time, must abandon his victim for a fresh one, who may soon be relieved and so on until someone is tagged, or "it" is exhausted.